YOUR
FAMILY
AND ITS
MONEY

HELEN M. THAL

with the collaboration of
MELINDA HOLCOMBE

HOUGHTON MIFFLIN COMPANY • BOSTON

Atlanta • Dallas • Geneva, Illinois • Hopewell, New Jersey • Palo Alto

YOUR
FAMILY
AND ITS
MONEY
Revised Edition

ABOUT THE AUTHORS

Helen M. Thal is the Director of the Education Division and Chairman of the Family Economics Studies Program at the Institute of Life Insurance, New York. She has been an instructor in the Department of Home and Family Life, Teachers College, Columbia University, where she received an Ed.D. degree. For over a quarter of a century, Dr. Thal has been examining, exploring, and researching the ways families live with money. She has contributed many articles to major professional publications; she has been responsible for an extensive teaching aids program sponsored by the Institute; she has served as consultant to federal government agencies, state departments of education, and to private agencies. She is a member of the American Home Economics Association, American Vocational Association, Association for Supervision and Curriculum Development, and other professional organizations.

Melinda Holcombe is Assistant Professor of Education and Family Resources in the College of Home Economics at the University of Nebraska, where she received her B.S. and M.S. degrees. Previously, she taught and supervised home economics in the Exeter Public Schools and at the University High School, Lincoln, Nebraska. She has held offices in the National Association of Vocational Home Economics Teachers and in the Teacher Educators of Home Economics section. Mrs. Holcombe has served also as a consultant in home management and consumer education workshops.

Printed in the U.S.A.

ISBN 0–395–14225–3

Library of Congress Catalog Card Number: 72–3497

FOREWORD

Most American families have more money to manage than ever before. But just because there is more money doesn't mean that people have fewer problems. Although as individuals or as families we may aspire to be wealthy, research has indicated that we actually have mixed feelings about money and what it does to us, individually and as a society.

This book is intended to help students view money in the context of family living and from that perspective. The authors believe that money can bring tremendous satisfaction to family life when we have learned to be comfortable with it. That comfort will derive from our attitudes about money and about ourselves.

At the time the first edition of this book appeared, consumer education had once again emerged as a recognized area of study in the Nation's schools. It has continued to gain acceptance and emphasis. The need for informed and educated consumers has become a national issue; leadership has been given the movement by government, business, and private agencies.

The authors of this text believe that consumer education extends beyond buying and acquiring goods. Consumer education, as we see it, has its roots in management, and should lead the student toward self-understanding and into the development of a life style reflecting personal and family attitudes and values. The ultimate objective will be the achievement of those goals that have been given priority at each stage of the life cycle. Securing goods and services and utilizing the market and its institutions will be the means, rather than the end.

Like all books intended for teaching purposes, this book has many contributors: hosts of secondary school teachers with whom the authors have worked; students who have shared their ideas and suggestions; professional colleagues who have lent support and constructive criticism. Special thanks for assisting in the preparation of this edition must be given to Miss Arlene Lilly and Mrs. Rosemarie Shomstein, both on the staff of the Division of Statistics and Research, Institute of Life Insurance.

April, 1972   *H.M.T.*

CONTENTS

PART THREE

Financial Information to Aid
in Decision-Making   131

EPILOGUE

Money Matters—People Count   258

Prologue:
You and Your Money

The economics of family life, if told as a tale of history, would be a story about people and how they have used their resources. It would relate their hopes and ambitions; it would describe the ways in which families have met adversity and opportunity; and it would record the strengths and dreams of individual families and how they have become the strengths and dreams of a people. The economic life of a family is but the reflection of all that the family stands for, all that it believes in, and all that it strives for. The ways in which families live with money, therefore, tell us much about families and how they live.

To promote an understanding of the role of money in family living is the purpose of this textbook. This text is not about budgets, it is not about how to be a wise shopper, and it is not an economics textbook. To be sure, in its pages there will be something about budgets, and about one's role as a consumer, and about economics. But this book is about families and how they live with money.

WHAT IS MONEY?

Practically everyone who lives in the United States, even children in nursery school, knows what money is. In our society money is something we cannot do without, and so we seldom bother to think about what it means. If we examine some of the definitions that have been given to money, however, we discover that money means different things to different people. Children think of money in terms of what their nickels and dimes will buy. High school students have more sophisticated ways of looking at money; they may see it as a way of measuring the value of the services they perform; or they may look at it as a symbol indicating their position or status; or they may recognize it as a means for achieving a goal, such as further education. Some people think of money as a source of power; others think of it as a vehicle for doing good. Money has different meanings for each of us.

But regardless of the meanings that have been given to it, money, consisting of coins and bills, has no meaning by itself. A dollar bill is but a slip of paper as it lies on the table or as it is tucked in your billfold. It assumes meaning only as it is put to use. When you step up to the counter and buy lipstick or a book or a ticket to a movie, the dollar bill becomes valuable. Its value is determined by the value of the goods or services you receive in exchange for it. In such a case, money is defined as *a measure of worth or value.*

Frequently money is defined as *a medium of exchange.* In our complex commercial world it would be quite impossible, if not ridiculous for each buyer in need of a product or service to approach the merchant with another product or service to offer as payment. Instead, in return for the lipstick, book, or movie ticket, you give the seller your dollar. The transaction is simple and uncomplicated; you as a buyer have secured what you want, and the seller has received your dollar with which he can replenish his lipstick stock, or buy more books, or pay his salesman. Your dollar has served as the medium of exchange.

Money, then, is a measure of value and it is a medium of exchange. There is still another way of defining money. Money, regardless of how much or how little it may amount to, is one of the *resources* people have at their disposal that enable them to secure everyday needs and to achieve individual and family goals. In this book we will recognize all of these definitions, but emphasis will be placed on money as a family and personal resource that can serve as a tool in achieving a satisfactory life.

WHAT RESOURCES DO INDIVIDUALS AND FAMILIES HAVE?

Money is not the only resource at our disposal. The dictionary tells us that a resource is "a new or a reserve source of supply or support;" that it is "something in reserve or ready if needed." "Source of supply . . . ready if needed" suggests that our resources consist of everything we possess that can be used to help us accomplish some goal. What are these possessions?

An inventory of the resources of a typical high school student might begin with his *physical health and energy.* Most young people have these resources in abundance. Their strength and bounce enable them to plunge into an activity or job and get it done. It is the energy that wins games, stages the class play, transforms the gym into an enchanting setting for the senior prom, mows the lawn, washes the dishes, irons the clothes, and tends the babies.

Time is another resource. A certain amount of time is already committed; a number of hours are spent in sleeping, in attending school and studying, in after-school jobs of one kind or another, and in eating. But there are few people whose time is so completely occupied that none remains. Time, unlike some resources, cannot be stored away for use later on, as can money, nor can it be built up and increased in the way that we can build up our energy. On the other hand, time is like all other resources in that it is limited in amount, and it can be managed in some meaningful fashion by individuals and families. In the overall functioning of personal and family life, time is a valuable and important resource.

Knowledge and skill are additional resources that can be used to help you accomplish something. Possibly you know how to make your own clothes, or how to entertain youngsters, or how to make cookies, or how to drive a car, or how to type, or how to help a fifth-grader with his arithmetic, or how to teach a child to swim, or how to paint a table or a wall. Whatever skill one possesses and whatever knowledge one has stored in his mind can be put to use and counted on as resources. The sharper the skills and the more knowledge acquired, the more useful these resources will be.

The *equipment and facilities that you own* are resources. If you have a typewriter, for example, it is a resource that enables you to perform a task or to meet a responsibility—possibly typing a theme for English, or a letter to the editor, or an order for a new coat. An electric hair dryer is a resource, just as is the family's washer or steam iron. In economics, these appliances or possessions would be called "durable consumer goods." These possessions, the washer for instance, are not wanted just for themselves but for the services they perform. We might borrow another term from the economist and call these durables "capital goods," because they are essential to the operation of the household.

The *goods and services available from family members and communities* are resources. Parents and other family members possess knowledge and skill that can be called upon. The father who can fix a bike, or mend a doll, or change a tire and the mother who soothes a hurt, or fries the picnic chicken, or explains how to remove a grease stain from a blouse or a pair of slacks are serving family members as resource persons. In the same way, the knowledge and skill you possess are resources that other family members may call on.

Within the community there are any number of resources, including, for example, the school and the public library. The park, swimming pool, tennis courts, and golf course that serve people in meeting their needs for recreation are also resources. Many people in the community can be of advisory service—the clergyman, the school counselor, the school nurse, teachers, social workers; all of these people and many others have special knowledge that can help one in making decisions about how to use resources to accomplish a goal or to meet a particular need.

Finally, *money* is a resource. Like all of these other resources money is a means to an end, something to be used in order to achieve a goal or to satisfy a need.

Resources, including money, are available in varying amounts at different times and for different people. On some days we possess more energy and time than on other days; or we have more money at one time than at another. Some people possess more skill than others, or have larger incomes than others, or live in communities where more services are provided than in other places. The availability of all these resources often influences how money is used, and is one factor that accounts for the different ways that families and individuals live with money.

If we examine this list of resources we notice that they fall into two categories. Energy, knowledge, and skill are *human* resources; they are part of people. Equipment, home and community facilities, and money are called *material* resources; they are impersonal and non-human items that have a particular utilitarian value. In examining how families use their money, this book will help you to recognize the role that all resources play in day-to-day living and to be aware of how the use of money is often influenced by the availability of other resources.

HOW IMPORTANT IS MONEY?

Even children in nursery school know that it takes a dime to buy an ice cream bar and thus that their dimes are important. By the time we reach high school we realize that *money is important, not only for what it will buy, but also for what it enables us to do.* These two ideas deserve further attention: money is important because it enables people to buy the necessities of life, which makes money important indeed; but it is equally important for the things it helps people achieve or become.

We live in what has often been described as a "money world," a world in which money makes possible the flow of goods and services between the producer and the consumer. The bread we eat, for example, had its start on a farm in the Midwest where the wheat was raised. The farmer sold it to the mill where it was made into flour, which in turn was sold to the baker who converted it into bread, which was then sold to the grocer who finally sold it to you. Very few families living in the United States today perform these processes themselves; if bread is to be served, somebody buys it. Likewise families need money in order to secure all the other items that are basic to everyday living.

Money is important to families in our kind of world for another reason. It makes possible doing things that enrich personal and family

*Children and adults alike find one community resource—
the science museum—a fascinating and rewarding place.*

life and that promote the emotional, mental, and spiritual growth of each member of the family. It makes possible doing things that take the family from one goal to another and that add a quality of individuality to the lives of family members. What these "things" are will differ in every family. It may be straightening Jane's teeth, thus helping her to be a more attractive girl; or it may be Bill's attending a remedial reading course so that he might perform better on his job; or it may be nurse's training for Sally, or a university education for Charles, or Mrs. Block's visiting her grandchildren, or Mr. Martin's weekend when deer-hunting season opens each fall. Whatever the "thing" is, it will be important to the individual, and more often than not, it will involve money in some amount.

The importance of money is only in what it enables people to be or do. It serves as a medium for solving perplexing family problems, for meeting needs, and achieving goals. How money can be used to accomplish these functions will be examined in this book.

MONEY IN YOUR LIFE

By the time you have reached your teens, money is no stranger to you, for you have already had considerable experience with it. Today's teenager belongs to a segment of the population characterized by wealth. Representing approximately 14 per cent of the total population in 1970, young people from age thirteen through nineteen were spending an estimated $19 billion. Nineteen billion dollars is big money. For example, it is more money than was earned in 1970 by the ten largest corporations in the United States combined: American Telephone and Telegraph, General Motors, Standard Oil of New Jersey, Texaco, Ford, Sears, Gulf Oil, Standard Oil of California, Mobil Oil, and IBM. It would add another $1,000 to the annual incomes of 19 million families, or approximately 36 per cent of all the families in the United States in 1970.

Wealth of this kind does not go unnoticed. Consequently, the teenage market is eyed with respect by countless manufacturers and merchandisers who seek to share in the teen dollar. Entire industries exist almost solely on what young people spend: for example, the pop record business and the soft drink or motion picture industries. Magazines whose pages are filled wih advertising directed to the teenage consumer enjoy wide circulation.

Teenage dollars are of real importance to the economy of the nation, and often the teenage dollar is essential to the economy of the family. Most of all, your dollars are important to you. In some cases, your money may give you financial independence from your family; for some of you, your money is the means to further your education; for all of you, your money is providing you with experience in learning to spend and to save; you are discovering something about financial planning; you are experiencing the problems of decision-making that are a part of using money. In short, you are a trainee in money management.

With your present money you are practicing for your role in the years ahead, when you will have responsibilities for managing, or helping to manage, your family's income. This income adds up to an astonishing sum over the years. For a man who graduates from high school, earnings to age sixty-five may amount to more than $370,000; if he graduates from college, his earnings will climb to half a million dollars, if not more. If his wife is also employed, which is more than likely to be the case, their family income will be even greater. Although the amount of one's lifetime earnings may be a matter of personal concern, what matters even more is how these earnings will be used. Toward what will these dollars be directed? Using this money with effectiveness will depend on one's skills in goal-setting and in decision-making, both of which are sharpened by practice and experience.

Learning how families live with money means learning how families make decisions, how they use their resources to meet needs, solve problems, and achieve goals. It means looking at how families are different and understanding how each family or person is related to the community of families and persons. Finally, it means examining the financial operations that engage families from time to time, and seeing why financial institutions and services are essential to family life in a money world.

These are the things this book is about.

1

The Social and Economic Setting in Which Families Live

1 Each Family is Unique

What this chapter is about

Although common sense tells us that families differ in a variety of ways, we tend to lump them together and to think of groups of families as being alike. So we refer to "farm families" or to "southern families" or to "rich families" or to "Irish families." Actually, the only way that the families in any of these groups are alike is that they either live on a farm or in the South, or they have more money than other families, or they are of Irish descent. Their differences far outnumber their similarities.

In this chapter we will review some of the differences that exist among families and observe how these differences affect family money management. Among these differences we will note in particular individual and family values and goals; source, frequency, and amount of income; and the number and types of wage earners. These are the important ideas:

1. Families differ in many ways.

2. Family values and goals affect the way money is used.

3. Family incomes vary in amount, in source, and in frequency.

4. Families may have more than one wage earner.

FAMILIES DIFFER IN MANY WAYS

In order to understand how families manage their financial lives, it will be helpful to examine some of the characteristics that make each family different. These many differences cause individuals and families to use their money in different ways. If you were to look beyond the

The arrival of the first baby causes exciting changes and creates new financial responsibilities.

picture window in the house down the street, or across the back porch, or up the stairs, or through the apartment door, you would find that each family has a different set of needs and different ways of meeting them. Some of these differences are obvious and quickly observed; other differences may not show outside the four walls of the home but are nonetheless strong influences on what the family does financially.

Families differ in size.   Everyone knows that some families are small and that others are large. The "typical" American family often is described as numbering four persons. The U.S. Bureau of the Census would accept such a description; census figures indicate that, on the average, the family consists of three to five persons.

However, the truth of the matter is that families come in many sizes. Among the families on any street or in any block, there are some that consist of only a husband and wife; there are some with one child, others with two, and there are those with three or more, or possibly even seven or eight children. There are families in which there is but one parent, or in which grandparents or other relatives are part of the immediate family, as well as parents and children. There is no fixed rule that describes the size of all families, nor who constitutes a family.

Families differ in age.   Some families are young and just becoming established, others are old, and others are in between. Age of family members is directly related to family needs and thus to the use of family money. For example, a family consisting of parents and one infant will need to spend considerably less for food than the family in which there are three teenage boys with ravenous appetites. The family that con- sists only of adults, all of whom are middle- or old-aged, will have another set of needs.

A descriptive device that is helpful in examining families of various ages and stages of development is the *family life cycle*. This device illustrates the journey through life as most families appear to live it; therefore, it is frequently used by economists and sociologists as a tool in studying families. The family begins as a newly-married couple, and moves through the years that include having babies and raising them to adulthood and independence, and finally concludes with the couple in old age.

The family life cycle is separated into specific stages, each stage characterized by different needs and different responsibilities. For the purposes of our study, the cycle is divided into seven stages in order to show the distinct uses of money that occur during the life-time of an average American family. It must be emphasized, however, that seldom does a family fit the cycle perfectly; it is a rare family that moves from one stage to the next without overlapping: the adolescent stage may oc- cur while at the same time the family may be in the expanding stage.

1. *Bride and groom.*   The family begins. At this time a couple de- velops its own scheme for money management; husband and wife dis- cover their attitudes about money and begin to recognize some of the financial responsibilities that are a part of marriage. During this forma- tive period the major needs requiring expenditures of money will center on housing and furnishings and equipment for the home. These expenditures are large, and they come at a time when income is most often low. The husband is becoming established in his job and is still several years away from his peak earning period. The wife is probably employed, and her income is frequently relied on to provide some of the household goods and equipment.

2. *Beginning parenthood.*   If the first stage was a period of adjust- ment, the second stage may be even more so. Pregnancy followed by a

baby in the house drastically alters the lives of both father and mother. Their responsibilities no longer center on themselves; their freedom, in many ways, has been curtailed. Their medical needs, housing situation, savings, and insurance needs have to be reconsidered. All of these changes occur at a time when family income may drop because the mother is no longer employed.

3. *Expanding family.* More often than not, one baby is followed by another in time. This stage of the life cycle includes the preschool and elementary school years when the days are crowded with the care of children and their unceasing needs for attention. Family income is

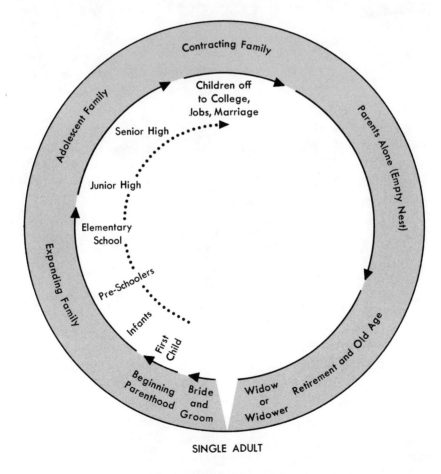

The Family Life Cycle shows the stages a family might go through, beginning with the single adult entering marriage, and ending with the single adult as widow or widower.

probably rising, but not fast enough to meet the demands on it. In-evitably there will be the dimes for the ice cream man and the dollars for new shoes, the dentist, and the baby sitter. Housing needs may change, additional insurance protection is required, and the numerous needs created by children must be met.

How many stages of the family life cycle are shown here?

4. *Adolescent family.* A look at your own family may give you a picture of what this stage is like. Strains on the family pocketbook are usually severe. The food bill will soar, particularly if there are several teenagers in the family; clothing costs will be up; school expenses are greater for high school students than for youngsters in elementary grades. If vocational training or college follows the high school years, the expenses will be even greater. Financially speaking, the ray of hope for most parents of the adolescent family is knowing that the end is in sight. In not too many years their teenagers will be independent adults. Fortunately, family income is rising; in fact, for many families income is nearing its peak. Also at this time many mothers return to jobs outside the home and thus contribute to family income.

5. *Contracting family.* Life around the house is beginning to calm down. One by one the children leave home to launch lives of their own —taking jobs, marrying, and assuming their own financial responsibilities. The pressures on family money gradually ease as each of the young persons in the family steps out on his own.

6. *The parents alone.* The period in the family life cycle that is sometimes called the "empty nest" stage consists of the years between the last child's departure from home and the parents' retirement. Income will reach its highest point, if it hasn't occurred earlier. It is not unusual for parents now to change their housing and to find smaller quarters. During this period, too, more attention is paid to providing for their retirement years and for pursuing their own special interests.

7. *Retirement and old age.* Eventually a whole new pattern of life develops. The older couple finds new ways to use their time; they may change the place where they live; they probably will have to adjust to living on a smaller income. During these years medical expenses may increase considerably, although other expenses, such as those for food, will be less.

Just as it is said that there is an exception to every rule, so there are many households that do not fit the family life cycle as it is outlined here. Among the exceptions are the households of the single adult who remains single, the one-parent family, and the no-children family. These individuals and families have different sets of needs, different patterns of living, and different supplies of resources, all of which contribute to the ways they use their money.

In spite of these exceptions, the family life cycle is a convenient way to organize ideas about families. It makes it possible to predict family needs and it helps, to some extent, to chart the rise and fall of family income. Once individual and family needs are known and the income peak is estimated, we can look at the ways families plan ahead in order to meet their anticipated needs.

Families differ because of where they live.   Rural families in the Midwest will not be like city families in the East; nor will southern families be the same as northern families. To be sure, they all may look alike, dress alike, watch the same movies and television programs, and read the same best-sellers and popular magazines. But their needs will not be the same.

The farm family may raise its own vegetables, chickens, and dairy cattle. Thus, its expenditures for food will be less than those of the city family. The family in a northern state where the winters are long and cold, Maine or Minnesota, for instance, will have to spend more for heating their homes and for warm coats, sweaters, and boots than the family that lives in Florida or Arizona. The city family may have no need for an automobile, whereas for the farm family at least one car is considered a necessity.

Families differ in cultural backgrounds.   American families share the American culture, but because the United States is a land of many peoples, all of whom have come originally from other parts of the world, there are many cultures within America. You may live in a community that is predominantly Scandinavian, for example. The people who originally settled there came from Norway, Sweden, or Denmark, and their families grew, flourished, and stayed on. The culture and traditions of those northern European countries still prevail in the area; in the homes one sees arts and crafts typical of Scandinavia, and the meals frequently include the breads, cakes, pastries, and other dishes native to the "old country." The same kind of cultural marks remain in those communities or neighborhoods settled by families from Italy, Poland, Japan, China, Mexico, or other foreign lands.

Each national or racial group has brought with it a culture that continues to shape the attitudes, feelings, and beliefs of the people, and that is reflected in the ways families live. Cultural influence may be noted in how the children are reared, in the way authority in the family is delegated, in the roles assigned to men and to women, in the things to which special importance is attached, and in the ways families use money.

Families differ in their values and goals.   The differences that have been described so far are more or less obvious. It is easy to see that

Families that have been in this country for several generations often retain elements of their original cultural background.

families are of various sizes and ages; it is usually easy to observe regional and cultural differences. But there are some important differences among people and families that are very difficult to "see" or to "look at," for they don't show. They exist inside individuals. Not even close friends or relatives may be aware of them. These invisible differences are a person's or family's *values* and *goals*. Personal and family values determine what goals exist in the life of the family, and goals, in turn, dictate how family money is used. This idea is basic to understanding family money management.

FOR DISCUSSION

1. In what way, or ways, would the size of a family affect the family pocketbook?
2. What is the average size of all the families represented by your class?
3. At what stage in the family life cycle would occur the greatest demands for money? At what stage would time, as a resource, be in abundance? How might the family life cycle be used for predicting other needs involving the use of resources or calling for family decisions or changes? Give examples.
4. What family needs are peculiar to the region in which you live? How do these needs affect the way your family uses its money and other resources?
5. How are cultural background and influences reflected in your family?

FAMILY VALUES AND GOALS AFFECT THE WAY MONEY IS USED

The importance of values in personal and family living is not easy to measure and to describe. From all that is known about them we recognize that individual and family values are subtle factors that motivate behavior. They have their roots in an individual's personal philosophy. They determine goals and direct activities; they influence the ways in which children are reared, the manner in which resources are used, and the relationships that develop among people.

What are values?   Important as values are, the word "values" remains a term that is difficult to define. We might say that it means a set of beliefs and ideas that we develop as we grow and learn and as we design our lives. These ideas or beliefs give direction to a person's life, guide his behavior, and frequently determine what he will do with his time, his money, and his many other resources.

Values are not something we can touch or feel; they are intangible. They are in our minds, and have to do with our perception of ourselves, our relationships to people, our expectations for the future, our image of who we are and what we want to become. Values give reason to what we do, how we react, how we relate, how we use our time and our resources, and how we take care of ourselves. They help us understand other people; when we are aware of another person's values we know "what makes him tick"—such an understanding helps in bringing people together.

Another way of defining values might be to say that a value is something that is desirable in itself, a quality or a condition that in and of itself is meaningful. For example, *love* might be considered a value, for it is a quality or condition that becomes central to one's relationship with other people, and is therefore desirable. Another such value might be *thrift*. Another one is *health*.

In an effort to help people understand this concept of values, scholars have found various ways to classify them. In one such classification system, devised by a group of psychologists at Harvard University, values have been grouped into six categories: aesthetic, religious, theoretical, social, economic, and political.[1] Borrowing these six categories, we can list some values appropriate to each. People who have strong *aesthetic* values place value on artistic experiences and harmony in their environment; their interests and hobbies will include, very possibly, music, poetry, painting, sculpture, and design. *Religious* values derive from one's spiritual faith and might include reverence for life, prayerfulness, and dedication to God. The set of values classified as *theoretical* will be important to people who value learning, the pursuit of knowledge, and scientific discovery. The values classified as *social* are represented by a strong sense of social justice, concern for the welfare of others, a desire to be of service, recognition of other peoples' needs, and a desire to be with people. People who adhere to a set of *economic* values are concerned with practical matters related to how resources are used; they are interested in getting things done efficiently and at the least expense in terms of time, money, energy, and material; economic values are expressed by words such as thrift, security, and conservation. *Political* values would include power, competition, prestige, and influence.

[1] Allport, Vernon, Lindzey, *Study of Values,* 3rd ed. Test Booklet and Manual (Boston: Houghton Mifflin Company, 1960.)

Aesthetic values are probably dominant in families that have a strong interest in music.

This is only one classification system. There are other ways of organizing these abstract ideas. But most of us are not so formal in our thinking; we are not concerned with cataloguing or classifying our values. We know that in our own lives there are ideals or principles that are right, desirable, and enduring for us. Friendship, love, health, and knowledge might be among one's values; or success, prestige, and security.

People interpret the same values differently.   Although there is no single set of values that has been identified as common to every person, scholars have found that there are values shared by large numbers of people. Many people value love, health, religion, family, freedom. But even though a given value may be accepted by many people, each person has his own way of interpreting it and responding to it. For example, beauty is a value held by many people. But what one person thinks is beautiful may be displeasing to another. Not only do different people interpret the same value in different ways, but the same person may express a value in one way at a particular time in his life, and at a later age he may find another mode of expression for the same value. In other words, your present concept of what is beautiful may change considerably by the time you are twenty-five or thirty years old.

We acquire our values from several sources. We learn our values from the social groups of which we are a part. These include family, friends, and school, as well as the larger community. In school, for example, the value system includes scholastic achievement, discipline, cooperation, respect, integrity. These values determine the standards by which students, and teachers too, are evaluated; thus the overall behavior pattern of the student body reflects the value system of the school. It is not unusual, however, for a student's personal values to conflict with the school's, causing him difficulty. Possibly you have observed this conflict among some of your friends at school.

What are goals? "Goals," like values, are not obvious to an observer and they are personal in nature. But goals are less abstract and easier to identify and define. Very simply, goals are the objectives toward which we work; they are the marks to be achieved, the mountains to be climbed, the dreams to be realized. They serve as targets toward which we direct our lives. Some goals are set for the near future—they are things to be accomplished this week or this month or this year. Often we call these our *short-term goals*. Then we have *long-term goals* —goals that will not be realized for many years.

Goals are often related to each other. They may serve as steps, one leading to another, until finally a major or long-term goal is achieved. Take, for example, the young person whose goal is to become a teacher. In order to reach that goal the person must first graduate from high school. With scholarship aid, or by working part-time, or by using savings, he then must get through college. Finally he will need to be certified according to the state teaching requirements. Each of these steps represents an intermediate goal leading to the long-term goal. The list of intermediate goals that leads to becoming a teacher will be long, but taken one by one they lead directly to the long-term goal.

Goals are related to values. We can see how goals are related to each other. They also have a direct relationship to values. In fact, a person's major goals are a reflection of his values. They have their roots in what he considers desirable—in his value system. Perhaps we might illustrate this idea by meeting a contemporary of yours.

Bill is a senior at Jefferson High. After school on Thursdays and Fridays, he hustles to the local supermarket where he has a job. Bill's ambition is to get out of the slum area in which he lives. He has seen enough of door-to-door salesmen, of the oppression and defeating illegalities practiced by slum landlords, and of a system that seems to operate against the poor. His aim is to become a lawyer, for he believes that he can best be of service to poor people through the practice of law. He believes further that a competent lawyer is one who learns as much as he possibly can about the law, about people, and about the society in which people live. *Service* and *knowledge* seem to be the important values that dominate Bill's life. To become a lawyer it is necessary to go to college. To be admitted to college Bill knows he must earn good grades. He knows too that he must earn some money. His imme-

A student whose goal is to attend college must have as an intermediate goal a good scholastic record in high school.

diate goals, therefore, are to graduate from high school with a good academic record and to have some money in the bank for college in the fall. His long-range goal is to become a lawyer in order to be of service to people. His goals and values have a direct relationship to each other.

FOR DISCUSSION

1. How would you define "values" in your own words? Can you give an example of a value and how it operates in your life?
2. It is possible that a person's values may conflict with his parents' values. Can you give some examples?
3. Can you relate to your values some goals you plan to accomplish over the next few weeks? Can you relate your vocational goals to your values? How might the goal of marriage and family reflect a person's values? What values might these be?

FAMILY INCOMES VARY IN AMOUNT, IN SOURCE, AND IN FREQUENCY

Incomes in the United States vary. In March, 1971, there were over 52 million families in the United States. Their 1970 incomes ranged from under $1,000 to several hundreds of thousands of dollars. Most of the families, 69 per cent, received incomes amounting to $7,000 or more; 31 per cent earned less than $5,000 and 49 per cent received more than $10,000. With such a large proportion of families with incomes of $7,000 or more, we can see why the United States is often described as a country of middle-income families. In 1970, the median family income was $9,900. This means that half of all the families had incomes less than $9,900, and the other half had incomes greater than $9,900. The graph on page 24 shows that some families have considerably more money to work with than other families. Since differences exist in the amount of money available to families, it is logical to assume that families will have very different ways of using their money.

Size of income affects family life. The amount of income a family receives affects the way in which that family is able to live. Of course, factors other than income, such as family size and location, also affect a family's financial situation. For instance, an income that is adequate for a family of three may be totally inadequate for a family of six. A city family with an income of $6,000 may be severely limited in housing, food, clothing, and other needs, whereas the same income may be sufficient for a family of the same size to live comfortably in a small town. However, although size of income is not the only factor that determines whether a family lives in poverty or by middle-income standards, it is the important one in most cases.

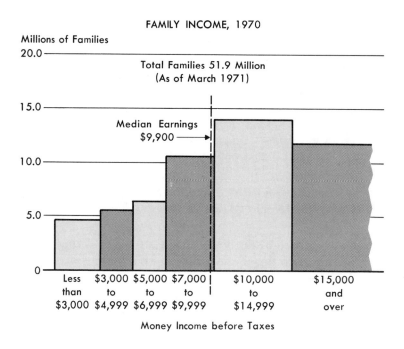

FAMILY INCOME, 1970

Money Income before Taxes

The conditions under which many families are forced to live because of severely limited incomes have been brought to public attention and concern as a result of what once was popularly called the "war on poverty." The Economic Opportunity Act of 1964 was aimed specifically at relieving the conditions of the poor in order to enable low-income families to increase their annual earnings. Provisions in the legislation touch on education, health, housing, job training, and other areas of living that by improvement will ultimately improve the earning potential and quality of life for families in poverty.

Since 1964 there have been additional proposals for bringing about an improvement in the economic well-being of families: both at the state and federal levels, attempts have been made at welfare reform; economists in and out of government have devised new programs and tax reforms aimed at equalizing the economic conditions of families. Currently being studied are various plans that will result in a "guaranteed annual income." This concept assures all families that, through the mechanism of the federal government, every family (or single individual) will receive an annual income set at a minimum level. (President Nixon's proposed Family Assistance Plan sets the minimum at $2,400 for a family of four.)

The limitations imposed by inadequate income extend beyond food, shelter, and clothing. Many low-income families are discouraged; they see little in the future that will improve their lot. The available money is inadequate to permit freedom from worry and anxiety, or to allow for developing the relationships within the family that promote a satisfying home life.

The amount of income a family receives depends on several factors. The factors most significant in determining family income are: the level of education reached by the family wage earner; his occupation; and the geographical location of the family.

Education. Over half of the families living in poverty, as defined by the federal government, are headed by persons who have no education beyond elementary school. On the average, the more years of schooling, the higher the income. It is as simple as that. A person who has graduated from high school will earn more than one who stopped attending school after the eighth grade. A person who acquires a vocational or technical education after high school will receive a larger income than the person who does not go beyond high school. The college graduate and the professionally trained man or woman will earn even more. These facts suggest *one* reason for a person to continue his education: it pays in terms of dollars and cents.

Occupation. Some occupations pay more than others. Although most people do not choose their lifetime occupations on the basis of earnings alone but consider more important the personal satisfactions their careers will provide, it is generally true that the vocations requiring the greatest amount of education and training usually bring high incomes and personal rewards.

Location. The annual income of the average family in metropolitan areas such as New York, Chicago, Los Angeles, or Detroit generally is greater than that of the average family living in small towns or rural areas. But it is also true that the cost of living in the large cities may be substantially higher, making it necessary that incomes be greater.

Besides the influence of education, occupation, and family location, there are other factors that determine income: the skills, talents, and abilities possessed by family members, their capacity to be productive, the amount of responsibility they are willing to assume, and their initiative and drive. Factors that further determine income are the physical and mental health and the ages of family members.

The source and frequency of income vary. Family income may be derived from more than one source; it may be payable on a regular fixed schedule; it may be payable in lump sums once or twice a year; it may rise or fall with the seasons or fluctuate as business conditions go up or down.

Salaries and wages. For most families in the United States—the large middle-income group—income is derived primarily from salaries or wages, payable on a regular schedule. These families know in advance approximately what their income will total over the year and can plan ahead of time how it will be used. They are secure in the knowledge that a paycheck will come along regularly.

Fees and commissions. Professional people—doctors and lawyers, for example—charge a fee for their services to patients or clients. Many sales persons or agents earn a commission on each sale they complete; that is, a percentage of the sale is paid to the person responsible for the transaction. Commissions and fees will vary from one month to another, depending on the numbers of customers or clients.

Farm income. There are farm families that receive the largest portion of their income in a lump sum following the sale of the major crop. The amount of income thus earned will depend on the current market price for the commodity, as well as on the quality and amount of the product. Take the wheat farmer, for example. He will sell his grain after the fall harvest. If the season has been good, his yield per acre will be high and he will have much grain to take to market. If the growing season was poor, too dry or too wet possibly, his yield will be less. He may supplement his income during the year by the sale of other produce, by raising other crops, or by working part-time off the farm; but the income from the wheat is the primary income and bears the burden of maintaining the farm and family over the year ahead.

Rents, profits, dividends, and interest. Income derived from such sources as rents, profits, dividends, and interest may constitute the total income for a family, or it may serve as an important supplement. *Rents* are earned on property that is used by someone other than the owner. Landlords who own apartment houses collect monthly rental fees from each tenant. *Profits* and *dividends* are the return on one's investment in a business enterprise and represent the stockholder's

*A good yield from the fall crop means more income for a
farmer and his family.*

or owner's share in the earnings of the company in which he has invested money. *Interest* is the fee paid for the use of money. Any money
a family or individual may lend to another should earn interest; money
on deposit in a bank or savings and loan association will earn interest
—the bank or association pays interest for being able to use money to
lend or invest.

Transfer payments.   Payments transferred from public treasuries to
individuals or families, for which no service of any kind is required at
the time payments are being made, are termed transfer payments.
Money paid to families under Social Security are transfer payments, as
are disability payments to veterans, unemployment benefits, pensions
to retired military personnel, and all public welfare payments.

Gifts, inheritances, bonuses, and benefit payments.   There are other
sources of income that do not fit into any of the categories mentioned

so far. It is not known how many families live on an income derived exclusively from *gifts*, but for many families gifts constitute an important income supplement. For instance, many young families gain a portion of their income from parents. Young couples in college may depend on the generosity of parents or other relatives. Old people, too, will often receive a portion of their total income as gifts from their children.

An *inheritance* is money a family receives as a bequest from a deceased relative or close family friend. These bequests are not usually large enough to be considered a source of total income, but the "windfall" may be helpful in achieving a particular goal.

At the end of the year some business organizations give their employees *bonuses* based on the annual earnings of the employee. The employee is paid a percentage of his annual salary in a single lump sum. Since bonuses are paid at the discretion of the management, however, a family cannot be certain to receive this money each year. Thus, it would be unwise to count on a bonus and make plans in advance for using it.

Individuals or families may receive *benefit payments* from life or health insurance policies, from retirement and pension plans, and from Social Security. Such payments may constitute a major portion, if not all, of the total income for families or retired persons.

FOR DISCUSSION

1. Is size of income the only factor that determines poverty? What other factor or factors might be considered?
2. Can you give examples of famous people whose income is exceptional because they possess a particular skill or ability?
3. From what source do most families in the United States derive their income? Is this true of the families represented in your class at school?
4. How does regularity of income affect the way a person manages his money?

SOME FAMILIES HAVE MORE THAN ONE WAGE EARNER

Historically, the father has been the breadwinner of the family. He has assumed the leadership role in the family, and it is he who has gone into the world to labor and toil in order to supply his family with the goods necessary to life. It is the men in society who have been trained for employment; the men have become the farmers, the merchants, the doctors, the lawyers, the engineers, the builders, the craftsmen, the preachers, and the scientists. Women have been the keepers of the household, the mothers, the nurses, the teachers—the "caring" persons in society.

Wives and mothers participate in the labor force.   Traditions change, however, and by the mid-twentieth century more and more wives and mothers were leaving the home and entering the world of work. In 1970 about 40 per cent of all employed workers in the United States were women (29.7 million); of this group, three-fifths were married and living with their husbands. One study of 205 families in Florida showed that the income earned by the wife raised the median family income from $5,700 to $8,500 annually.[2] These earnings put almost $3,000 more in the family pocketbook. According to the Women's Bureau of the U.S. Department of Labor, working wives supply about 35 to 40 per cent of the family's total income when they work full-time and more than 20 per cent when they work part-time.

Many families (5.6 million in 1969) are headed by women without the presence of a husband or father in the home. Most of these families fall into the low-income group. The median income of families headed by women in 1971 was $5,100. Often without adequate education, these women are frequently forced to take whatever jobs they can secure, or rely on welfare payments.

The phenomenon of the working wife and mother appears to be a fact of life. There is no indication that women will cease to seek paid employment; rather, the predictions are that the numbers of employed women will increase. Although in her romantic dreams the school girl seldom pictures herself as working outside the home after she is married, the facts indicate there is more than a possibility that she will. Not only will she work immediately following her marriage, but it is very likely that she will return to a job by the time she is forty years of age. It is now estimated that women can expect to spend approximately twenty-five years at least in paid employment. From the U.S. Department of Labor, we learn that the average girl now in high school will spend at least twenty-five years in paid employment whether she marries or not. Does this fact suggest that young women should think carefully about preparation for occupational roles?

[2] Ann Hussey Caudle, "Financial Management Practices of Employed and Unemployed Wives," *Journal of Home Economics* (March, 1963).

More wives and mothers than ever before are among the rush-hour crowds hurrying to and from work.

Women are working in paid employment for various reasons, but primarily they work in order to earn money. Some are the chief wage earners for their families; they work because they have to. Others are working to add to family income, either for the purpose of raising the family's level of living, or in order to accomplish a particular goal for the family. Typical of such purposes is to send a youngster to college, to buy a house, or to build funds for retirement.

Teenagers and other family members are also wage earners. Other family members may contribute, either directly or indirectly, to the total family income. For a number of families, the total income includes pensions or old-age retirement benefits paid to a grandparent who may be a member of the household. Teenage sons and daughters often add their earnings to the family. Young people who buy their own clothes out of their earnings are indirectly adding to the family income, since they are not drawing on it for their personal needs. Some teenagers contribute dollars to the family by paying "board and room," which they may do out of a sense of responsibility as well as recognition of a family need.

FOR DISCUSSION

1. What is the chief reason that wives and mothers work in paid employment? Can you suggest other reasons why many women return to work after their children start to school?
2. How may family members contribute indirectly to income?

Summary for Chapter 1

Many differences exist among families; these make each family unique; that is, no one family is like any other family. Each family and each individual has particular needs, goals, and values, and each has its own way of meeting these needs, achieving goals, and expressing values. Families differ, too, in the amount of money they have to work with and in the sources from which their money is derived. All of these factors that cause families to differ also cause them to use money differently.

CAN YOU EXPLAIN?

1. family life cycle
2. short-term goal
3. long-term goal
4. salaries and wages
5. bonuses
6. wage earner
7. values
8. income

HOW WOULD YOU ANSWER?

1. What are some of the ways that sizes of families and ages of family members may cause differences in how families use money?
2. How does an understanding of the family life cycle help a family to predict its needs?
3. In what ways do some of your family's traditions reflect your cultural background? Do you see any relationship between your traditions and the ways you use money?
4. Would the presence of a physically handicapped person in the family cause a family to use money in a particular way? Explain.
5. From what you know about your own family, what are the factors that seem to influence how your family uses its money?

OTHER THINGS TO DO

1. Review your expenditures for the past five days. Does your recent use of money reflect a particular value or set of values? How can one's use of money indicate one's values?

2. Imagine you were given $25 to spend in any way you desired. Write a short paper explaining how you would use the money and what your choices show about your values. Compare papers within the class to see what values the class as a whole expresses. Are they similar?

3. Make a list of five or ten of your personal values. Rank them in order of importance to you. Then ask each of your parents to list their values in order of importance to them. Is there a difference between your list and that of your parents? Try to analyze the sources of your values. Do you think society expects individuals and families to have certain values? Why or why not? What are some general values that society has accepted for individuals and families? Did you list your values or those that society expects?

4. Interview someone in your community who has firsthand knowledge of family life in another country to discuss the family customs, values, and goals of that country. Are the values of the foreign family similar to your values? In what ways?

5. Observe several families that you know who are at various stages in the family life cycle. Can you identify their income needs? How and why are these needs likely to shift at various stages?

6. Think about the following words: hard up, pinched for money, poor, needy, impoverished, and destitute. Each of these words, all implying financial inadequacy, has a different meaning, although they all seem to say about the same thing. Try to define each one exactly. Explain how each situation affects the life style and values of the individual.

7. Read a book such as MR. AND MRS. BO JO JONES, by Ann Head (New American Library) and identify all of the values that you can. Show evidence to support each of the values. Identify three values that you think are not important to the characters in the book. List the goals that you consider to be important to them. In making these judgments, did you consider the life cycle of this particular family and the values that fit that life cycle, did you measure their values against those that are generally accepted by society, or did you impose your *own* set of values? Think very carefully about this.

8. Using the kit entitled "An Introduction to Value Clarification" (J. C. Penney Company), try to determine your own values and describe your efforts to support and/or achieve them.

9. Find a comic strip, a cartoon, or the lyrics from a currently popular song that expresses certain values. What are they? Can you support those values?

10. Think through carefully what you want to do with your life. List the goals you will need to attain. Which are short term? Long term? Is there a relationship between your values and goals? Which goals have you achieved? How long will it take to achieve all of your goals?

11. Draw a circle graph showing the approximate time a person spends in the various phases of the family life cycle: draw another graph of the stages that a single person goes through. Make a list of characteristics and adjustments a person must make at the various stages. Then compare the individual life cycle to the family life cycle.

12. Interview individuals or couples at the various stages of the life cycle to learn about the problems and needs they have encountered at the various stages. For example, when does a person or family seem to have the most money? least money? most energy? least energy?

13. Find some articles in current periodicals on the American family today. From these articles identify the differences in life styles of individuals and families.

14. Form buzz groups and discuss the following questions: Where do we secure our values? Why do we need to recognize our values? Can values be changed? How do age, education, and experience affect personal values? What are the values that seem to be expressed in the home economics room or environment? Should people impose their values on others? What are the values that seem to be important to most families?

2 A Family is People

What this chapter is about

To understand how families use money we have to recognize the family as people. Family finance begins, not with dimes and dollars, but with the warm, needful human beings who make up the family, each with his own interests, needs, abilities, and aspirations. In spite of individual differences among families and family members, however, there are certain basic needs that all people have in common. In this chapter we will look first at what these basic needs are. Then we will examine the ways in which our values and attitudes determine how we use our money and other resources to meet our needs.

1. All people have the same basic needs.

2. People meet needs in terms of their values and resources.

3. Money management begins with self-understanding.

ALL PEOPLE HAVE THE SAME BASIC NEEDS

All people everywhere share certain basic physical and emotional needs. These are equally important to the rich and to the poor, to Europeans and to Asians, to men and women, to the aged and to children. Meeting these needs consumes much of a family's time, effort, skill, and money. What are these needs that people share in common?

Every person needs food, shelter, and clothing.   Since the beginning of time, man has spent his days in providing for himself and his family the physical needs essential to life. These needs have motivated men and women throughout history to improve their lands and houses in order that their children would eat better and be sheltered more adequately. Food is necessary for growth and strength and is the first defense against disease. Shelter is necessary for privacy and for protection from the elements and the ravages of animals and strangers; it is a place to keep possessions and to return to for warmth, comfort, and rest. Clothing, like shelter, is protection against the weather and a safeguard against insects; it is one way in which we express our individuality; and in our society it is a requirement. Today, families in the United States are better fed, more adequately clothed, and better housed than are families in many parts of the world. This is not to say there are no families in want—there are. But for the majority of American families these physical needs are being met.

Essential as these needs are, not all families require them in the same degree. The amount of food, clothing, and sheltered space needed by each family will vary, depending on several factors. The environment in which a family lives is one determining factor. In tropical areas of the world, for instance, family shelter takes a form different from that in Arctic areas; the same is true of clothing. People require different kinds of food if they live in hot, humid climates than if they live where it is cold. The number of persons in the family also influences the requirements for food, clothing, and housing. The extent to which these needs are required is determined, too, by the age of each individual in the family. An adolescent youth needs more food per day than does his grandfather; a growing child will require more clothing over a year's time than his father; and an infant requires less space than his ten-year-old brother. In other words, the need for food, shelter, and clothing changes, as the individual grows, matures, and ages.

The fact remains, however, that regardless of a person's age or whether he lives in tropical Tahiti or in wintry Alaska, he needs food to eat, a place to sleep, and clothes to wear. At no time can he do without them.

Every person needs to love and be loved. Children need love in order to feel secure; their parents' love gives them a sense of being cared for, protected, and desired. Adolescents need love in order to know that they are accepted and respected persons. Adults need love to support and encourage them in coping with their responsibilities. Old people need love in order to feel needed and for comfort and security in their late years.

It isn't enough, however, to be loved; there is also a need to love. Inherent in each human being is the need to identify with other persons

Life on the subtropical desert creates different clothing and shelter needs than life in the snow country.

in a warm, intimate way, to give of one's self to others, to respond to the needs of others in the same way that others respond to him. We smile when we see a little child pat his mother's cheek, or hug his big brother, or cuddle a puppy. He is gratifying his need to love, just as is the parent who brings his children a surprise or who finds thoughtful ways of showing that he cares.

There is no set pattern by which people express love and show affection. Some people can be openly affectionate, and others are shy and aloof. Regardless of how one expresses love, it is a strong motivating force in the lives of individuals. For its sake, parents have sacrificed even their own lives for their children.

Every person needs protection and security.   Since earliest times man has struggled to protect himself, his family, and his goods from *physical* harm and danger. To be secure from the severities of weather, the marauding of wild animals, and the threats of strange tribes was a goal that consumed much of his time and energy. As civilization progressed, man developed greater understanding of his environment and of his own nature, and although his need for security did not diminish, he learned new ways to achieve it. In our time, he has found ways of joining with his fellows to protect his family and property from destruction and harm. We rely on policemen, firemen, public health doctors and nurses, and other specialists to make our communities safe; we expect our federal government to maintain our national safety; and we look to the United Nations to find ways to increase the security of all people everywhere. Because of these protective agencies, families in the United States have been relatively safe from physical harm, disease, and destruction.

Now man seeks security of another kind. For the past several generations, families in the United States have sought ways of building *economic* security so that no family member would experience want or privation. Economic security is seen as another dimension of the total stability and security of the family.

Security, of course, is not only a matter of being rid of harm and of economic loss, important as these are. We have learned that as individuals we must be secure in other ways. Psychologists have explained this kind of security in terms of *emotional* need. Charlie Brown describes it as being "one of the gang" or as "knowing all your lines."[1] In other words, one needs to be accepted by the group and to be confident about what he is doing. Security has many dimensions.

[1] Charles M. Schultz, *Security is a Thumb and a Blanket* (San Francisco: Determined Productions, Inc., 1963).

*The ocean is overwhelming the first time you see it, and
a small boy needs the reassurance of Dad's strong arms.*

People have a need for self-realization. Every person needs to become the most effective person he is capable of becoming. Psychologists call this the need for "self-realization" or "self-actualization." (We might use a simpler phrase: self-fulfillment.) In order to meet this need, one must learn to know and understand himself as a person and to be comfortable and at home with himself. He needs to achieve some of his goals and ambitions; he needs to develop and to use his abilities, whatever they may be. This need is not met at one time; becoming an effective person is a process that goes on for as long as one lives.

Psychologists have pointed out that unless the need for self-realization is being met, people are frustrated and restless. They feel that they are wasting themselves, that they aren't "getting anywhere," that they

don't amount to much. The image they have of themselves is negative
—they see little in themselves that is good or worthwhile.

To counteract these feelings it is necessary for people to experience
growth—to know within themselves that they are achieving, contributing, and succeeding individuals. A first-grade child senses his *self*
when he reads his first story without help. As he grows older he will
realize himself even more when his contribution to a group activity
is given credit by the others—the score he makes in the basketball
game, or his baritone voice in the male chorus. When the young adult
masters a new task or an especially complicated assignment, he cap-
tures a sense of his self and is able to appreciate himself and what he
can do. These are people who like themselves.

*Playing basketball
provides a feeling of
accomplishment, as
well as a chance to
form new relation-
ships.*

Self-realization calls for an investment in one's self; for time given to learning, to developing skills, to thinking and experimenting with ideas, to acquiring an understanding of one's environment and one's place in it, and to forming stimulating relationships with a variety of other people. This kind of investment will be made again and again; the process of becoming is on-going. Personal growth and development does not stop with graduation; indeed, commencement speakers frequently emphasize the fact that with commencement comes a new beginning, not an end to intellectual development and activities.

To invest in one's self calls for time, energy, skill, knowledge, ability, and money. Many resources will be used, for the process of becoming depends on all that one brings to his life that can add growth, wisdom, and understanding.

FOR DISCUSSION

1. What are the basic physical needs common to all people? What are some basic emotional needs?
2. What is the meaning of self-realization?

PEOPLE MEET NEEDS IN TERMS OF THEIR VALUES AND RESOURCES

Although people have in common the same basic needs for food, shelter, clothing, love, security, and self-realization, each person interprets these needs according to his own culture, tastes, and values. In the previous chapter you learned that values are the personal, intimate factors that determine how a person lives and uses resources to meet his goals. Family members do not always share the same values, and as a result, conflict may occur. When it does, it frequently erupts over the use of family money. A recognition of individual differences in values and an understanding of them, therefore, can be an aid in living satisfactorily with money and with other people. With that idea in mind, let us now examine how values determine the way we use our money to meet our needs.

People measure tangible needs differently. Resources will be allocated for food, shelter, and clothing according to the meaning a family gives to these needs. If in one family food and meal time are important for family togetherness and family relations, then probably greater time will be spent in meal preparation and more money will happily be spent for food. But the more money spent for food, the less there is available for other things. This comparison can be drawn also for any of the physical needs. People will allocate resources in proportion to the importance given to each of these needs.

Food. Everybody gets hungry and must eat. But the way in which individuals meet their need for food and satisfy their hunger is influenced by their cultural background, religious beliefs and practices, family superstitions, and where they live. Therefore, how we interpret our need for food—the kind and quantity of food eaten, the time for eating, and the rituals that accompany meals—will be influenced by more than the amount of money we have to spend.

Clothing and shelter. People measure their needs for clothing and shelter differently. There are people for whom clothing means little more than protection and covering; they are content with a meager wardrobe. Other people feel a need for a wide variety of clothing; they dress to fit their moods, or to please other people, or to suit the demands of their jobs or their social lives. In the case of housing, a similar list of influences comes to bear. A family that places a high value on individual privacy will interpret its housing needs quite differently from the family that values "togetherness" and group activity. Some people value space, others value convenience. Some families want to live near relatives, or good friends, or their place of work; others value the distance they can put between their home and neighbors, relatives, or job. Some families consider their housing a status symbol; other families consider housing as simply a shelter. The meanings given to shelter, however, will differ.

People fulfill intangible needs in various ways. Food, shelter, and clothing are *tangible needs*; they are items of consumption and of practical use for day-to-day living. It takes no stretch of the imagination to relate personal and family resources to them. Love, security, and fulfillment, on the other hand, are intangible needs. These are not products that can be manufactured and marketed. Nevertheless, people can use their resources to fulfill these needs, although each person will do so in his own individual way.

An older brother is a girl's best friend, especially when he takes her shopping.

Love.   One person may show his love through service to other family members.   Performing some task—polishing shoes for someone else in the family, or pressing Dad's Sunday trousers, or teaching a little brother how to ride a bike—any of these activities can be expressions of love. Love in another family may be expressed through the "extras" each person brings to family life—surprises, awards for achievement, pride in the accomplishments of others, or assuming responsibilities in order to relieve another person. We express our love through the use of what we have, whether it be possessions—including money—or the abilities, skills, and knowledge that we use in behalf of others. Love for one's family and friends prompts a person to use his resources in a way that brings them pleasure.

The resources we use and the manner in which we show our love to others will depend entirely on what love means to us. Our individual and family values will again be at work shaping our interpretation and influencing the use we make of our available resources. A mother who sacrifices her own clothing needs in order that her children may have better clothes or who prepares dinner with care and patience is expressing her love for her family.

Security.   Love is necessary to another of man's basic needs—security. People find security within their families and are assured of it through the love that is shared in the home. It is love that causes parents to be concerned about the safety and security of their children, as well as of each other.

However, there is more to security than love. There is also a need for each person to feel safe, and each one finds his own way of satisfying this need and of giving it meaning. Security may be checking the tires before driving off in the car; or it may be money in the bank; or it may be a strong lock on the door; or it may be a "thumb and a blanket;" or it may be holding a parent's hand as one crosses the street. An insurance policy represents one kind of security; protection against economic loss. Holding mother's hand represents another kind; emotional security that comes with having confidence in parental protection. Checking the tires may represent still another kind of security: physical security, or protection against danger or mishap.

The need for security is universal, but what we do to create it or in what particular area we feel the greatest need—physical, emotional, or economic—is an individual matter. Again, it is apparent that there is a need which, in order to be met, is interpreted according to personal values.

Self-realization.   Possibly self-realization may be thought of as a value rather than as a need. Nevertheless, we find again that each individual has a personal interpretation of what creates in him a sense of achievement and fulfillment. The hobbies, the professional advancement, the creative activities or work with other people that one person finds significant may be inconsequential to another. Whatever one does with his resources in order to add a dimension of growth and self-enhancement will be determined by his personal value system.

*Investing your time to develop a talent may bring you
satisfaction for the rest of your life.*

FOR DISCUSSION

1. How do values influence the way a family might meet its need
   for food? For shelter?
2. How does the need for self-realization affect the way a person
   might use his money?
3. What are the ways in which people interpret their need for security?

MONEY MANAGEMENT BEGINS WITH UNDERSTANDING ONE'S SELF

All of us measure and interpret our needs differently, according to
our values, our culture, and our attitudes about ourselves, our feelings,
our families, our jobs, and our money. Our effectiveness in meeting

our needs will depend on how well we know and understand ourselves as persons.

Personal attitudes affect the way money is used.   In order to understand how families and individuals live with money, it is important to be aware of the influence of personal *attitudes* on how money is used. An understanding of our own attitudes helps us to manage our money and other resources in a way that will be most satisfactory to us. Consider for a minute your own attitudes: what is your attitude, for instance, about the current hair styles? Or about TV commercials? Or about foreign sports cars? Or about folk music? In each case you reacted either for or against, or you were indifferent, for reasons that are neither right nor wrong but that reflect your own tastes, preferences, and feelings.

Just as you have attitudes about hair-dos, commercials, and sports cars, you have attitudes about money. You have feelings about money that give it a particular meaning for you. And this particular meaning, whatever it is, becomes one more factor influencing how you use the funds at your disposal. Often people whose money income is small and who actually have very little to spend for the basic necessities of living place great importance on money. They are often preoccupied with the struggle to get up enough money for the day's food, let alone anything else. In contrast, people who have considerable money are usually less concerned with it; their attitude about money is matter-of-fact; it is an important resource, but the pressure to acquire more money is not as evident, and their use of it is less compulsive.

The use of money is influenced not only by one's attitude about money, but also by one's attitudes about many other things. Personal attitudes about food, fashion, recreation, transportation, or security enter into the way one uses money to acquire any of these goods or services.

Some spending may seem irrational.   Because money is a limited resource, decisions about spending it usually call for thought, care, and planning. But people being as they are—made up of attitudes and emotions and influenced by culture and values—not all of their decisions appear rational. In other words, people aren't always "sensible" about money. Very possibly you have observed another person spending his money and have thought to yourself how foolish his purchase was. It is possible, too, that you have been observed by someone who thought the same of you.

Spending that appears irrational might make sense if one understood the spender's motives. Often the spender himself realizes that what he is doing makes little sense but may not know why he is doing it. If he could understand his motives, perhaps he would stop his irrational spending or at least accept it without feeling guilty.

People often use their money in such a way as to compensate themselves for personal shortcomings or failures, or for the hurts caused by society. For example, Sarah has more sweaters than any girl in her class. Whenever she has extra money, she buys another sweater. For her, sweaters are more than articles of clothing, they are compensation for being overweight. Sarah's sweaters are to her what the slick luxury automobile is to the family that is denied decent housing in the neighborhood of their choice and makes up for it with a fancy car.

People may use money to satisfy emotional needs, but such attempts are not always the best solutions. Jerry is a person who appears illogical when it comes to spending money. Actually, his spending is a barometer of his moods. When he is feeling "up" and on top of things, he spends his money only as he needs to—for carfare, lunches, and daily expenses. But when he is "down," when things seem to be going against him, Jerry throws his money around. A dollar here and a dollar there, it doesn't matter to Jerry.

Ozzie is another who can't make sense with his dollars. He doesn't have much money to start with, but what he does have he uses to treat any group who will join him after school. You see, Ozzie doesn't have many friends and he uses his money to try to make himself popular. He hasn't yet learned that friendship is not "for sale."

Dolly is well nicknamed. She is a fun-loving doll. In fact, she has so much fun so often that she is usually behind in her school work. When things pile up, Dolly will "buy" her way out. She will pay someone to write her English theme; she will find someone to lend her their book review cards—at a price. Dolly sees nothing wrong in this method of coping with responsibilities. After all, to her it's no different than having a traffic ticket "fixed." For some people, Dolly for instance, money represents power or authority. They use their money to buy their way rather than earn it; which is another way of using money that doesn't seem to make sense.

Whether Dolly, Ozzie, and the others are right or wrong in what they do with money is not the point here; they are typical of people who rely on money to make up for shortcomings in their own personalities. The problems they may have with money can be traced back to problems they may have with themselves.

Occasionally buying a hat on whim won't hurt the budget
and may add just the right touch to a wardrobe.

To be always logical and rational about what we do with money, or time, or any of our resources would be illogical human behavior. Sometimes a person is most human when she buys the new hat, or takes home a surprise to the family, or gives her allowance to a favorite charity, or buys the latest hit record, even when she can't afford it. But, by the same token, to be consistently irrational in using money is also illogical human behavior.

It is important to have a realistic attitude toward money. We should be aware of what we expect of our money. Money, in and of itself, is neither good nor bad. Problems with money arise when our attitudes toward it are not realistic. If we think of money as a source of power, money can be a destructive force in our lives; if we think of it as a ticket to uncontrolled freedom and license, money can be degrading and self-defeating. If we expect money to make up for our own short-comings and personal failures, we are probably going to be disappointed. For the truth of the matter is that money was never intended for these purposes. People have attached these purposes to it and have given it a meaning it neither deserves nor can live up to.

FOR DISCUSSION

1. How would you describe your own attitude about money?
2. Can you think of any situations where you were aware of the attitudes influencing another person's use of his money?
3. What might be some examples of the rational use of money? What would be irrational?
4. Why are money matters said to be personal affairs?

Summary for Chapter 2

Although all people share in certain common basic needs, they measure these needs and interpret them according to their individual values, cultures, attitudes, and emotional responses. These personal factors affect to a large extent the way money is used, and lead to the conclusion that money matters are personal matters. Money management begins with an understanding of ourselves and of the factors that influence our behavior, as well as with a recognition of our needs. Because people are people, not all individuals make the same decisions about what to do with money, nor will the same rules of money management apply to every family.

CAN YOU EXPLAIN?

1. basic needs
2. self
3. emotional and physical security
4. tangible needs
5. intangible needs
6. individual attitudes
7. self-understanding
8. self-actualization

HOW WOULD YOU ANSWER?

1. How do you and your family interpret the basic human needs outlined in this chapter? What factors influence your family to consider some needs more important than others? Which needs appear to be less important?

2. What are some of the ways in which money is used to meet basic needs? What other resources could be used instead of money?

3. Which of the three kinds of security essential to family life seems the most important to you? Why?

4. In what way is self-understanding important in managing money?

OTHER THINGS TO DO

1. Show how basic needs change in the various stages of the family life cycle. Do basic needs become more or less important in the later stages of the life cycle? Are the emotional needs as important as the physical needs?

2. Indicate in what ways you used money this past week or month that might be considered foolish or irrational. Explain why you did it. If you had the chance again, would you make the same purchase? Why or why not?

3. Find articles or magazine advertisements that illustrate types of social pressures that affect the needs of families. Why and how is status sought by individuals?

4. View the filmstrip "Umpteen Ways of Shopping" from the J. C. Penney kit on "Decision Making for Consumers" to learn how external forces contribute to individual and family wants and needs.

5. View the filmstrip "Our Role as Consumers" (Institute of Life Insurance) to gain a better understanding of wants and needs in relation to our role as consumers, and to examine the factors that contribute to needs and wants.

6. On a sheet of paper list in two columns your needs (Must Have) and your wants (Nice to Have). Write down the items that seem important to you in the appropriate column. As a class, prepare a list of needs and wants and let each student separate the items into appropriate columns.

7. Find and bring to class a picture, poem, song, cartoon, or story to show how people are meeting their needs and satisfying their wants. Share with the class.

8. In small discussion groups consider these questions: What is self-actualization? What are some basic principles regarding human behavior? Do the conditions under which a person lives affect his sense of wants and needs? What would be an example of one person's needs that might be another person's wants?

9. Bring to class some of the ads that are popular today. Identify the basic need to which each ad is directed. Are most of the ads appealing to one particular need? If you think this is true, why?

10. When you were very small, what was the finest treat you could have (bearing in mind that "treat" was something nice that happened only on special occasions)? What was the material gift you wanted the most? At what age did you want money as a gift and why? Do you think your values have changed? If so, at what point in time, and why?

3 The Family in the Economy

What this chapter is about

Families live in several worlds. Each family lives in a private world of its own, shared only by those who are invited to share it; each family lives in a social world, that is, the society in which it moves, works, and to which it contributes; and each family lives in an economic world. In this chapter we shall observe that the economic world in which American families live and work is related to the private world of the family: not only does a vital economy contribute to the economic vitality of families, but the economic behavior of families can contribute to the strength and well-being of the nation. Understanding how families function in a money world will further our understanding of the role of money in family life. As you study this section, you will find the following major ideas:

1. Families have an important relationship to the economic world.

2. The economy looks to the family as a market for its goods and services.

3. The economy looks to the family as a source of capital.

4. The economy looks to the family as a source of funds for government programs and services.

5. Our economic system makes possible a high standard of living.

FAMILIES HAVE AN IMPORTANT RELATIONSHIP TO THE ECONOMIC WORLD

In 1964, before the United States became deeply involved in the war in Southeast Asia, the President and Congress reduced income taxes. This move automatically meant more take-home pay for individuals and families. To be sure, the federal government still needed money, but there was a growing indication that the economy of the United States needed bolstering. Customarily when the economy had shown signs of weakness, the prescribed remedy had been to increase government spending. This time, however, a different approach to the problem was recommended: to lower taxes so that American families would have more money to spend and to save. The plan worked. By the end of 1964 the economy had regained its strength; the forecasts for continued growth were reassuring.

The result of the tax cut dramatized the relationship of the American family to the economic functioning of the nation. When families have more money to spend and to save, the whole country benefits. Thus, what families do with their money, how they choose to use it, is a matter of major importance.

Young people too are spenders and savers. Their significance—economically speaking—is now being felt more and more. According to the U.S. Bureau of the Census, youth aged 14 to 24 accounted for 20 percent of the population in 1970. These young people earned $45 billion in 1971, and influenced the spending of an additional $135 billion. By 1986, almost a third of the nation's total spending power will be in the hands of young adults under age 35. With these facts in mind, you can get a better picture of how you and your family relate to the economy of the United States.

What is meant by "the economy"?   As commonly used, the term "the economy" refers to the wealth of the nation. A more complete definition describes the economy as consisting of the total *production, distribution,* and *consumption* of goods and services within the country. For example, an automobile company manufactures (produces) a variety of cars. A local dealer sells (distributes) these new automobiles. A customer buys a new car and becomes a consumer.

The economy includes big business, little business, and people; it includes the shoe repair shop, the bank, the florist, the newsboy; it includes the factory that turns out buttons and the factory that turns out steel. It includes the doctor, the lawyer, the hospital, the school, and the church. The economy is the steady flow of goods and services, generated by the flow of money between all of these individuals and institutions.

Therefore, if people are part of the economy, there must exist some kind of relationship between the family and the economic system. Such a relationship does exist, and it is a relationship that is absolutely essential to the financial health of both family and nation. Thus, it is important to know how it operates because it has a direct bearing on how individuals and families make financial decisions.

The Gross National Product (GNP), calculated annually, measures the health of the economy.   In order to know whether the economy is healthy, some method for measuring it each year is needed. The method worked out by economists many years ago is to put a dollar value on all goods and services produced in the nation and to add up all of these dollars. The sum is called the *Gross National Product.* The Gross National Product, in other words, is the total market value of all the goods and services that have been produced in a given year. Although the GNP is not an exact device for measuring economic health, it is the best so far devised. Our definition here is oversimplified since we have not described how values are derived for each of the goods and services, but for our purpose it is adequate. We are using the GNP simply as a picture of the economy and of our individual place in it.

The following figure shows how the GNP for 1970 might be pictured. Notice how simple the figure is: a circle divided into three unequal parts. As you look at it, remember that it is a picture of the total economy.

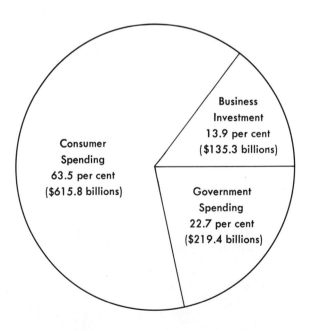

GROSS NATIONAL PRODUCT, 1970

Consumer spending.   The largest portion of the circle, almost two-thirds of it, is labeled "consumer spending." Who are the consumers? You are, and your family, your friends, and your relatives. Consumers are people—families and individuals. Within the economy consumer spending accounted for nearly two-thirds of all the goods and services produced in the United States in 1970.

Business investment.   The money spent by business and industry in order to operate is labeled "business investment." This portion of the Gross National Product represents the money spent for factories, tools, machinery, and equipment. These expenditures are made so that business may expand and grow. One of the functions of the economy is to provide business with the *capital* necessary for such expansion and growth. Here, again, the economy looks to the family for a large portion of the necessary capital. The money that families put into their savings accounts or into savings and loan associations or into the purchase of life insurance forms a great reservoir of dollars that business and industry use to finance the capital investments

*In frontier days family members supplied their own
goods and services.*

needed for continued growth. The family thus represents a source of capital for business and industry, forming another link in the relationship between the economy and the family.

Government spending. Finally, consider the third section of the chart. The money that government spends comes from taxes collected from individuals, families, business enterprises, and from the sale of bonds. The largest source of government money is from taxes, and the largest taxpayer in the United States is the family. Here, then, is the third link in the relationship between the family and the economy.

From this simple explanation of the Gross National Product, the relationship between the family and the economy has been outlined. As consumers, as savers, and as taxpayers, the family has a tremendously large stake in making the economic system operate. This relationship deserves further explanation and analysis.

FOR DISCUSSION

1. What is meant by the GNP? Explain.
2. How does the family contribute to the nation's economy?
3. What is the economy?

THE ECONOMY LOOKS TO THE FAMILY AS A MARKET FOR ITS GOODS AND SERVICES

Families contribute to the economy as producers and as consumers. Early in our national history and until quite recently, the family was described economically as a producing unit. The family was responsible for the production of its own food, clothing, and household furnishings. All family members, including parents and children, grandparents, aunts, and uncles, worked together in the fields and barns, or in the house. Women were expected to do their share of the work, too, for without their help family life would have been imperiled. What was produced by the family was, in large part, consumed by the same family, so the producers and consumers were one and the same group.

Today the family is frequently described as a consuming unit, but this is an incomplete description. To be sure, families go to the *marketplace* for what they need, and thus they are the consumers of goods produced by somebody else. But being a consumer requires money, and in order to have the money to buy goods and services, the family must be productive. In today's highly industrialized world, family members take up their productive roles outside the home in the businesses, industries, and service professions of the country. As producers they earn the money necessary to be consumers. As consumers, the family helps to maintain the high level of productivity necessary to maintain a healthy national economy.

This process may sound complex, but actually it is quite simple. In order to make the wheels of the economy go around—the assembly lines moving, the transportation system in operation, the communications systems open, and the distribution of goods in constant flow—people are employed. In their productive roles people earn salaries and are thereby able to be the consumers of much that is produced; they are contributing to the economy both as producers and as consumers, a dual contribution upon which the economy is dependent. The figure on page 57 illustrates this circular flow of money in the economy. It shows clearly how the expenditures of business and industry become the income of individuals whose expenditures, in turn, flow back into business and industry.

We must not overlook the fact, too, that families are productive, economically speaking, as they perform the numerous tasks necessary to maintain a home. The preparation of a meal is as productive an activity as is the job that earns the wages for buying groceries. Whatever an individual or family does in the way of conserving goods, or extending financial resources through savings, or maintaining property by careful upkeep is a productive activity. Such activity benefits the family and also promotes the economic well-being of the whole society.

Being a consumer means making decisions. As consumers, the family faces a host of daily decisions. Suppose you receive $10. You now have the capacity to be a consumer; you can buy $10 worth of goods or services. You can buy two record albums, or you can buy a blouse, or a pair of jeans, or a dozen paperback books, or groceries for the family dinner. You can decide not to spend your $10, or you can allocate part for spending, part for saving, and part for giving. The choices are endless.

In making consumer decisions more is involved than simply selecting the brand or the store. You have that $10. In deciding what to do with it, you must consider what will give you the greatest satisfaction; will your purchase be something that you can use right away

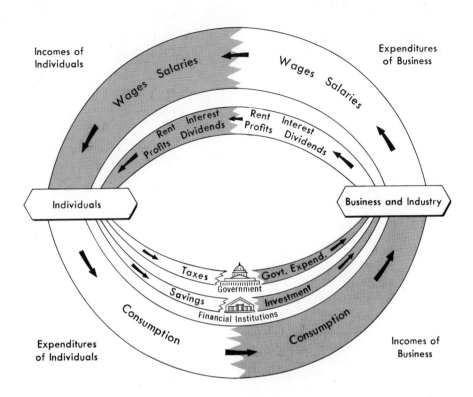

Incomes of
Individuals

Expenditures
of Business

Wages Salaries

Wages Salaries

Rent Interest
Profits Dividends

Rent Interest
Profits Dividends

Individuals

Business and Industry

Taxes

Govt. Expend.

Government

Savings

Investment

Financial Institutions

Consumption

Consumption

Expenditures
of Individuals

Incomes of
Business

CIRCULAR FLOW OF MONEY IN THE ECONOMY

and enjoy, or will it be something that you will use over an extended
period of time, such as shoes, in which case the wearability and dura-
bility of the product must be considered? You wonder if your $10
should be spent on something that will give you *immediate satisfaction,* but only temporarily, or should go for something that will
give you *continuing satisfaction* over a period of time. If you decide
not to spend your $10, but to add it to your savings account, you have
deferred satisfaction from your money until a future time. These
choices are typical of the consumer decisions families have to make
with every paycheck. And with each decision to spend or not to spend,
the economy is affected.

As was pointed out in the previous chapter, families and individuals
have their own values, interests, needs, obligations, tastes, and other
differences that influence their decisions as consumers. The economy
is geared to produce a staggering variety of goods and services in order
to meet the various demands of the consuming public. With such a vast

assortment of products from which to choose, life as a consumer in our economy becomes one long series of decisions, some more difficult than others. But the chances for satisfaction—whether immediate, continuing, or deferred—are very good.

Our decisions as consumers affect the economy. Looking back into the past it is evident that the frontier family was very independent. Each family was self-sufficient and relied on the economy for very few of the goods that it needed. The family maintained itself through the efforts of its own family members.

Today we are far more dependent on the economy than was the frontier family. During periods of recession or depression, people have less money to spend and as a result productivity and consumption drop and unemployment rises. With a high level of productivity and a high rate of employment, families as a whole are well off and can maintain a high rate of consumption. As much as we pride ourselves on

This deserted station is the forlorn survivor of a once great railroad that came upon hard times, causing inconvenience for some and unemployment for many.

The economy is geared to produce a staggering array of goods and services in order to meet the countless demands of consumers.

our independence, we have come to recognize that we cannot directly control our economic lives in quite the same way as did the family on the frontier. We are dependent on each other, on government, and on institutions and organizations quite removed from us.

But Americans still retain their independent character, although it has a different shape than it had for the frontier family. Our influence and control is exerted now by our vote, by our behavior as citizens, and by our behavior as consumers. Today's consumers can spend their money in the stores they prefer; they can, by their choices, decide what products will continue to be marketed and those items that will fail. This controlling influence is a result of the increased buying power of the individual family.

Family donations help the economy.   Although it is not clearly outlined in the picture of the Gross National Product, the money that families donate to charities and to private institutions is of great importance in the economy. Family money is the main support of churches and synagogues throughout the nation. Families contribute to hospitals, to important medical research, and to charitable institutions and organizations that care for the less fortunate or those hit by such disasters as tornadoes, hurricanes, or floods. Their money helps many programs and institutions not supported by public funds, but that provide for the welfare of people and help make better communities.

When all of these funds that are contributed principally by individuals and families are totaled, the amount reaches many millions of dollars annually. By the late 1960's our religious and charitable contributions came to more than seven billion dollars. Seldom do we think of our contributions in economic terms, but rather as an expression of our religious faith or of our concern for others. Nevertheless, family dollars given away become part of the total economy, and are essential to the institutions performing these many services.

FOR DISCUSSION

1. Explain how it is that the family is both a producing and a consuming unit.
2. In what ways do you contribute productively to your family?
3. In what ways do consumers have considerable power in the economy?
4. Is it possible for an individual family to have complete control of its economic life? Give reasons for your answer.

THE ECONOMY LOOKS TO THE FAMILY AS A SOURCE OF CAPITAL

When families decide to defer satisfaction from the use of their money or a portion of it, they usually select some method for saving it. They may open a savings account in a bank, or in a savings and loan association, or in a credit union; they may choose to buy government savings bonds, or stocks and bonds, or life insurance. As a matter of fact, families may use several of these methods over the years. Later in this book attention will be given to the methods of saving available to families; our concern here is with the role of family savings, by whatever method, in the national economy.

The children in this family learn at an early age that money put in a savings account earns more money.

American families and individuals have established a good record as savers. In 1970 total personal and family savings amounted to $54.1 billion for the year. As was pointed out in the discussion of the Gross National Product, money is a source of capital for business expansion and national growth. Let us see how this process works.

The $10 you decide to add to your savings account doesn't lie dormant after it has been deposited in the bank. It becomes part of the bank's resources from which loans and investments are made. Possibly your $10 was part of the loan to your neighbor for his new car; or to the family down the street for their house; or to the cheese factory for the purchase of new trucks. Maybe the bank purchased municipal or state bonds in order that a new school could be built or a new highway constructed. At any rate, your $10 was put to work somehow, and for the use of your money the bank pays you *interest*. Interest is the money that money earns. This interest is added to your savings account at regular intervals during the year. By the time you are ready to use your money on deposit, it will have amounted to more than you put into the bank.

So by saving, you helped yourself and your money helped the economy. You have the funds for your particular savings goal; your money grew in amount through the interest it earned; and the economy was enabled to expand.

FOR DISCUSSION

1. What does the word "capital" mean?
2. How does it happen that money deposited in a savings account can benefit national growth?
3. What is interest? What is the rate of interest paid by the savings institutions in your community?

THE ECONOMY LOOKS TO THE FAMILY AS A SOURCE OF FUNDS FOR GOVERNMENT PROGRAMS AND SERVICES

As taxpayers, families are a source of revenue for the government. Recall again the Gross National Product and the portion labeled "government spending." In 1970 the dollars spent by all levels of government totaled over $219 billion. Where did these government dollars come from? A very large portion came from taxes paid by American families.

When taxes are mentioned, people usually think first of the Federal Income Tax, which for most employed people is withheld from their paychecks. The Federal Income Tax represents the major source of funds for the United States government. Families in some states pay a state income tax also. It too may be withheld from the paycheck. Although taxes on income are the largest portion of the total tax expenditure for most people, there are other taxes that a family usually pays. The government also collects sales taxes, property taxes, and taxes on special goods and services such as gasoline, cigarettes, liquor, and plane tickets, to mention a few.

Taxes provide families with many services. Not many people like to pay taxes. But what we sometimes forget is that we are the consumers of practically all of the services performed by the government and paid for with tax funds. If we are to enjoy these services, we must share in paying for them. As a matter of fact, it is the family for whom the services were intended in the first place.

On the local level, taxes provide police and fire protection, schools, community colleges, streets, sidewalks, libraries, sewer systems, parks, and swimming pools. On the state level, tax money provides a highway system, recreation areas, schools, colleges and universities, hospitals for the mentally ill, special schools for the handicapped, and public assistance and welfare service. On the federal level, taxes pay for highways, national parks, numerous educational services, public health and welfare services, agricultural and medical research, and of course, the national defense program. Through taxes to the federal government we are participating in aid to underdeveloped countries and sharing in the exploration of outer space.

Our tax money, therefore, is buying countless services that would be quite impossible to obtain in any other way. For example, suppose that all the roads and highways in the state had to be built and maintained by those families who lived along the roadway. In such a case, if a farmer wanted a road to town, he would have to pay for it. What kind of highways do you suppose we would have? If families in a city

The taxes we pay make possible national and state parks,
vacation meccas for thousands of families each year.

block or on one street had to hire their own policeman and their own fireman, how effective would such a plan be? If there were no city parks or playgrounds, where would children play and where could families picnic?

All of these services contribute to family life. They are among the resources available to individuals and families that either directly or indirectly help meet needs and goals. The money paid in taxes by families, therefore, returns to the family in the form of services. However, the greater the number of services we demand from government, the greater will be our individual and family tax bill. It is well to keep in mind that as families we are the chief consumers of government services, but it is our dollars that pay for everything we receive.

FOR DISCUSSION

1. In what three ways is the family an important part of the economy?
2. Does your state levy a sales tax? If so, how does it operate?
3. What other kinds of taxes are levied in your community? What are these tax funds used for?

OUR ECONOMIC SYSTEM MAKES POSSIBLE A HIGH STANDARD OF LIVING

American families, taken all together, live very well. They own automobiles, houses, television and radio sets, and a variety of other electrical appliances and equipment. For recreation they attend movies, ball games, or participate in any number of sports: golf, bowling, boating, tennis. They eat steaks, ice cream, peanut butter, fresh oranges, bananas, and apple pie; they drink milk, colas, tea, and coffee. They have telephones and bathrooms. All of these goods are indicative of the *standard of living* in the United States.

Standard of living is the term used to indicate the level at which families aspire to live, as represented by the quality and kinds of consumer goods they seek to enjoy. *Level of living* indicates the level at which families actually do live, based on the amount of money they have to spend. The standard of living is, for most families, somewhat above or ahead of the level of living; in other words, as a family achieves a standard of living, the standard moves upward. It is rising

This kitchen, with its wide variety of electrical appliances, is an indication of the American standard of living.

constantly; each generation has a standard of living higher than the previous generation.

The high standard of living in the United States is made possible because so many families are earning substantial amounts of money, as a result of the high level of productivity maintained by the economy. The quantity and variety of consumer goods that Americans take for granted are considered luxuries in many parts of the world: television, cars, bathrooms, telephones, and washing machines, for example. Yet for most American families, these items are considered indispensable for everyday living.

FOR DISCUSSION

1. What factors affect your standard of living? How is the standard of living different from your level of living?
2. What accounts for the high standard of living in the United States?

Summary for Chapter 3

In considering the relationship between the family and the economy, we have found that the family is essential to the functioning of the economy. Binding the two together are three links:

1. Individual and family spending for consumer goods represents the largest portion of the national wealth.

2. Individual and family savings represent a major source of investment capital necessary to business and industrial expansion.

3. Individual and family tax dollars furnish all levels of government with funds needed to provide essential services, many of which directly benefit the family.

Finally, the dollars that families give to the support of religious and charitable institutions form another stream of income adding to the operation of the economic system.

Much that happens to us as individuals is the result of our economic system at work. The strong stable economy that we enjoy permits our high standard of living; families and individuals are secure in planning their future; they are free to make long-range commitments. Our economic system is not something outside our personal and family lives, remote from our day-to-day activities; rather it is the system that makes possible much that we do, achieve, and possess. As participants in this system, we are responsible to it.

CAN YOU EXPLAIN?

1. Gross National Product
2. production and consumption
3. the marketplace
4. deferred satisfaction
5. economy
6. capital
7. interest
8. standard of living
9. level of living
10. consumer

HOW WOULD YOU ANSWER?

1. In what ways is family money important to the economic life of the nation?
2. People sometimes believe that the money donated to religious and charitable institutions is of little importance. What do you think?
3. When people demand more services from government, how are their demands reflected in the taxes each family or individual must pay?
4. How will the level of living change at different stages of the family life cycle?

OTHER THINGS TO DO

1. Find in magazines or newspapers articles that discuss the standard of living. Talk with your parents and grandparents about the changes that have occurred in the standard of living since the days of their youth. In what respects do you think our standard of living is more desirable than that of twenty or fifty years ago? What causes the standard of living to change? Write a paper describing the changes that have occurred.

2. Review the discussion of teenage spending in the opening section of this book. In what ways do you think young people contribute to the national economy?

3. Suppose there were rapid scientific advancements that would enable most labor and work now being performed by people to be performed by machines. Great numbers of people might thus become unemployed. What might this do to the economy? What might the consequences be if there were no opportunities for the family to function productively in the economy.

4. List some services in your community that are supported by taxes or voluntary contributions. How do these services aid or enrich your community and family life?

5. View the filmstrip "The Exploited Generation" (Guidance Associates) to see the importance of teen-agers in the marketplace. What are some of the characteristics of the Youth Market? Do you agree that youth are exploited in the marketplace? What can young people do to respond to the pressures of exploitation?

6. From newspapers and periodicals, identify the current consumer issues and areas of concern.

7. View the filmstrip "The Consumer in the Marketplace" (Institute of Life Insurance) to see what influences an individual has upon the production of goods and services.

8. Discuss what factors influence our standard of living. What is the difference between level of living and standard of living? How do certain standards originate? What standards are typical in your community? What is meant by living on one level but dreaming on another? What is one's mental standard of living? How can flexibility in standards result in greater happiness and satisfaction for the individual?

9. Read CHILD OF THE DARK by Carolina de Jesus (Dutton) and identify the relationship between the values, goals, and standards of the main characters.

10. Read THE SILENT LANGUAGE by Edward Hall (Fawcett) to see how standards differ from culture to culture and also what is being communicated to other people by actions or behavior.

2

Management in Family Living

4 The Ways Families Live with Money

What this chapter is about

The ways families live with money vary, just as families themselves do. This chapter will examine some of those ways. Our exploration will introduce some of the puzzling problems families face, and we will observe how the solutions to these problems often dictate the way in which money is used. Finally, we will look for an approach to family problems that might prove applicable to a variety of situations. This chapter focuses on three major ideas:

1. There are many ways of living with money, some more effective than others.

2. Families are effective in using money when they achieve their goals.

3. Effective economic management uses resources to solve problems and to achieve goals.

THERE ARE MANY WAYS OF LIVING WITH MONEY, SOME MORE EFFECTIVE THAN OTHERS

In the preceding chapter we saw that individuals and families have an important relationship to the larger economy and, in turn, that the economic functioning of society has a significant effect on how families function economically.

We must keep in mind that the nation's economy operates so as to permit society to achieve national goals. In achieving them, the economy uses whatever resources are available and allocates these resources on the basis of decisions made to provide the greatest good for the greatest number. The stuff of economics therefore can be said to be resources, and the process of economics is decision-making.

It would be accurate to say that a family is a miniature economic unit. In the family, too, the stuff of its economy is its resources, and the process of its economy is deciding how to use these resources for the achievement of its particular goals. Just as no two nations have adopted exactly the same economic system, no two families have either. Goals are not necessarily the same for nations, nor are they for families. Resources are not duplicated in amount, and methods for using what is available will differ. Therefore, we find that families and individuals have different ways of managing and using their resources, including their money. These differences arise not only because of differences in financial resources, but even more because of differences in the extent to which goals and purposes serve as points of direction in making financial decisions.

Phyllis will never forget the day she received her first paycheck. Never before had she had so much money all at once. During her lunch hour she cashed the check so that she could go directly to the shopping center after work. There, in less than an hour, Phyl bought a new coat, new shoes, a gift for her mother, a lipstick, and a model plane kit for her brother. Suddenly she realized there is a limit to what one paycheck will buy. Phyl was broke. Fortunately for Phyl, her lack of foresight as far as her money was concerned wasn't too serious. After all, she still had a place to eat and sleep, and no one was depending on her for support. She could borrow lunch money and carfare from her mother and get along for another two weeks.

Phyl is not unique. There are many young people whose thrill with their first paycheck causes them to go overboard in the shopping center. But when this kind of frenzied spending happens in families, the results can be disastrous. Sooner or later, another method of living with money will have to be found.

Families and individuals have different ways of living with money. Although no one way is right for all persons or families, some ways are more effective than others. The most effective way will be the one that takes into account those qualities that are unique to a particular family, those characteristics that make each family different.

Living from day to day is one way of living with money. In her diary, *Child of the Dark*, Carolina de Jesus vividly describes the day-to-day existence of families living in utmost poverty. She tells of her life in the slums of a Brazilian city, where she eked out a bare living for herself and her three children by gathering up scrap paper from the streets and selling it. The few cents she earned had to go for food. Financial resources were acutely limited and so were all other resources. The unstable economy of her government held little promise for better days to come; only Carolina's pride and determination to "get out" kept her from complete despair and helped her to maintain a dimly flickering hope that days might eventually be better. But for the present, she saw no other way to manage except from day to day, and from meal to meal.

Even among families where poverty is less acute than in a South American city slum, there are those who are forced by circumstances outside the family to live on a day-to-day basis. Limited in resources, these families have had to accept a day-to-day existence and may have come to believe that there is no other way to live. For such families, life is a matter of "feast or famine," of continuous demands to be met out of a fluctuating income. When money is on hand they spend it freely; when money is scarce they make do the best way they can.

Living from paycheck to paycheck is another way of living with money. Very simply, paycheck-to-paycheck living is using up all of the money as it comes in so that by the time payday comes again, there is nothing left, nothing to show for the money, and nothing that brings one closer to a goal. Although statistics are not available to prove it, the number of paycheck-to-paycheck households may be surprisingly large, especially among young families and young single adults. This observation has been made by financial advisers in banks and other agencies where people seek financial counseling.

A family may not meet any problems in living from payday to payday —if there are no emergencies, or if there is a comfortable financial reserve available, or if the individual or family has no specific goals. However, the reports of those who have experienced this kind of living for a time indicate that such a pattern eventually leads to dissatisfaction among family members. They say, "We aren't getting any place" or "We just use our money as it comes along and have nothing to show for it" or "Our income is okay, but we never can afford to do the things other families do."

A family may seem to live from paycheck to paycheck if by the end of the pay period their cash on hand is gone, but they may have allocated their income for vacation funds, or for a new car, or for insurance, or for other special purposes and needs. These families are not paycheck-to-paycheck managers.

Living "in the red" is a third way of living with money. When expenditures consistently exceed income, a family is living "in the red." If now and then a family spends more money during the month than it earns, the consequences may not necessarily be serious. It becomes a matter of real concern, however, when this over-spending is consistent and occurs month after month. What usually happens is that the family incurs debts that become unmanageable.

It is very easy in our kind of economy where consumer credit is readily available to fall into this particular pattern of living. It happened to the Greggs. Ray Gregg went to work for a utilities company following his military service. He had a good job and was earning about $9,000 a year. The family bought a new house and also a car, both of which involved monthly payments. They needed a new washing machine when Randy was born, which meant another monthly payment. Shortly after buying the washing machine they had a chance to buy a food freezer, which added a fourth monthly payment; then the wall-to-wall carpeting, a fifth monthly payment. Before they knew it, they were in trouble. In less than one year their monthly payments consumed over half their monthly income. What remained was not enough to pay for their food bills, gas and oil for the car, utilities, and for the other necessary living expenses. The Greggs were "in the red."

Living creatively with money is a more effective approach. The ways of living with money mentioned so far do not appear to be particularly satisfying. There is another approach that families find more rewarding. It may appear in a variety of patterns because no two families do things exactly alike, but it has certain characteristics that are always present. Families and individuals who use money creatively are free of money worries; they are comfortable about how they use their money; and they see themselves moving ahead toward their goals. These are people who have come to understand themselves as people, who understand what it is they are working toward. They understand the limits of their financial resources, and at the same time they recognize that they have many other resources that can be used to advantage; they realize that their income consists not only of the money they receive on payday, but also of the income value to be derived from the use of their other resources. For example, the girl who uses her skill and her hairdrier to set her own hair every week rather than go to a hairdresser is adding to her income. Such people are living creatively with their money. We say "creatively" because this way of living with money calls for some ingenuity and imagination, as well as common sense.

This girl is adding to her real income by using her resources creatively to meet her clothing needs.

Economists have another way of measuring how effective one is in using money. Their measure, which they call *real income*, is the total amount of goods and services enjoyed by the individual or family. It is everything that the paycheck will buy. Economists explain that in . order to know how effective a person is in using his money, we have to look at all the goods and services he is securing with it.

FOR DISCUSSION

1. What is the justification for some families to use their money on a day-to-day basis?
2. If a family uses up its available money by the end of a pay period, is it necessarily true that they have nothing to show for it? Explain your answer.
3. "In the red" is a term often used in conversation or in newspaper stories. What does it mean?

FAMILIES ARE EFFECTIVE IN USING MONEY
WHEN THEY ACHIEVE THEIR GOALS

Perhaps this concept of creatively living with money can best be clarified by knowing a family who has such a record. The Jeffersons live in a modest walk-up apartment in what was once a rather stylish section of Chicago but is now showing signs of age and deterioration. Mr. Jefferson, a hearty man who loves laughter and good fun, is a truck driver for a store delivery service. Mrs. Jefferson, a quiet motherly woman, is employed in a dry-cleaning establishment. Their three children, Joe, Jack, and Judy Ann, are all in high school. The Jeffersons have never had much money. Even now, with both parents employed, their income is well below the national average. However, their achievements have been remarkable.

Money is being used to meet needs and to achieve goals. The Jeffersons have always had enough money to meet their family needs. Food, shelter, clothing, medical and dental care, transportation, education, church—these have always been paid for out of the weekly wages. But in order to do it, the Jeffersons had to know what they wanted—what their goals were, and what they had to work with—their resources. Then they had to think and plan in advance.

The Jeffersons have found ways to achieve some of their goals. The most remarkable, perhaps, was Mr. Jefferson's determination to finish high school in order to get a better job. He gave up his full-time job, returned to school, worked part-time in a filling station, and graduated from high school the same day Jack was born. This experience taught the Jeffersons that goals can be realized if, first, they are firmly set, and second, if all "pitch in and set to," as Mr. Jefferson says. Since then, they have never hesitated to set their goals high. As a result, their three children will attend college. Jack has had music lessons for six years. Judy Ann has gone to day camp the past four summers. "We learned way back that for us it's better to invest in us than in things," Mrs. Jefferson explains.

The family is free from concern about money. The Jeffersons use money to free themselves of money worries. They make a point of putting some money into their savings account every month, and thus their money earns money. Then too, they have tried, to the best of their ability, to protect their income against economic loss by the use of insurance. They have never once failed to set some money aside each year. This "set-aside" money is their risk capital, in a way. Some of it is used to pay for their insurance premiums and the rest goes into the college fund. On occasion they have borrowed from this account, but they conscientiously pay it back as soon as possible. To be sure, there isn't enough in the account to fully finance three college educations, but with what the children earn in the summers, and on part-time jobs during the school year, and possibly from scholarships, there is little doubt that college will be paid for.

The family uses all of their available resources. The Jeffersons have used their money in combination with other resources. Mr. Jefferson says it this way: "We've had a lot of things going for us," and he lists his "strong back," his wife's skill in the kitchen and at the market, the good health each of the family members enjoys, and the willingness on the part of the children to work and to help at home.

The family recognizes that their economic status can improve. The Jeffersons have recognized that money can be used to move the family ahead. "Some folks can't see it this way," says Mr. Jefferson. "They figure that if you're poor folks, you'll always be poor folks. But I say folks don't have to stay poor if they'll just make some effort and whatever else it takes to improve themselves." Mr. Jefferson has recognized that there can be mobility in economic status; the way people choose to live with money can move them up economically or it can move them down. "Making life better for ourselves is what we've tried hardest for," he says.

The Jeffersons are a good illustration of how families can live creatively. with money. They have met their needs and achieved major goals; they have avoided financial worries by letting some of their money work for them; they have put other resources to work along with their money; and they have remained masters of their money matters.

FOR DISCUSSION

1. The Jefferson family lives creatively with money. Why is this so? What did they do that could be called "creative"?
2. Explain the idea that money can be used in combination with other resources. Give an example.
3. What did Mrs. Jefferson mean when she said it is "better to invest in us than in things"?
4. How is it possible to use money to free oneself from money worries?

A boy's dream came true because his parents included summer camp in their financial plans.

EFFECTIVE ECONOMIC MANAGEMENT USES RESOURCES TO SOLVE PROBLEMS AND TO ACHIEVE GOALS

The sketch of the Jeffersons suggests some of the principles that guide families in achieving goals. In the process of making a good life for themselves, the Jeffersons undoubtedly were confronted with some complicated life problems. In solving these problems, they had to make decisions about how to use their money. Their economic decisions were directed toward the solution of their problems as well as toward the achievement of their goals.

Families are faced with many problems. It is reasonable to expect that the Jeffersons, like other families, had to find satisfactory solutions to puzzling questions like these:
- What should we do about housing? Shall we rent or buy?
- How can we make our food and clothing dollars go farther?
- How can we get out of debt? How can we stay out? Is being in debt a bad thing?

- How can we keep ahead of the bills when the family is growing and needing so many things?
- What will we do if one of the family members becomes seriously ill?
- How can we finance a car?
- What will we do if our income stops?
- How can we send our children to college or to a vocational school?
- How do we know if we are saving enough money? How can we save on our small income?

These are important questions. The answers to any one of them will differ from family to family. To questions suggested here there is no one answer that will suit every family or individual. If such were the case, people could learn a set of rules, just as they learn the rules of grammar or formulas in chemistry, and thus be prepared to meet life head on, assured that they had the answers. The excitement in living, however, comes with solving problems one by one, thus creating a life for ourselves and our families that is productive and satisfying.

Although the answers to the questions that families face will differ, the method of arriving at the answers can be described and can be relied on to serve in countless situations. Each problem solved should move a family a step or more nearer its goal or goals. If goals are not reached, then possibly not all of the problems have been completely solved. The success of the total process of *problem-solving* hinges on how it helps move the family toward a goal or network of goals. Let us see what the steps in this process are.

Problem-solving begins with knowing that a situation can be better. The process of problem-solving starts with realizing the difference between what is and what ought to be, and wanting to do something about it. Like the fellow who recognized that something was out of order because he never had cash for the things he really wanted; or the girl who knew that something was wrong when her baby-sitting earnings of $12 a week never reached from payday to payday. If a person doesn't know that a situation can be better, he will hardly be ready to solve his problems, for he is not even aware that he has any that need solving. Once he knows a problem exists he is ready to find the answer.

It is necessary to have a clear definition and understanding of individual and family goals. Recall the Jeffersons. ''Making life better for ourselves is what we've tried hardest for,'' is how the Jeffersons

Problem: How can we improve the appearance of our
street? Solution: Organize a group to clean up the litter.

stated the major (often called "ultimate") goal for their family. In accomplishing that objective, recall the other goals they set for themselves along the way: music lessons, day camp, college. There are undoubtedly many other goals not stated in the account. The Jeffersons could measure their success in terms of goals achieved, which is the very reason a careful definition of goals is necessary to start with.

Once the goals are known, the problem needs to be defined.　After a person knows beyond a doubt what he is aiming for, he is ready to state the problem that stands in his way. Maybe more than one problem becomes apparent. Possibly several solutions will have to be found. Problems need to be defined carefully. If they are formulated only in vague and general terms, the solutions are apt to be vague and general, too. Also, problems can be studied more easily if they are stated in relation to goals. For example, assume the Jeffersons were considering the problem of housing. They may have stated the problem, as they saw it, as follows:

If we're going to send the children to college, can we afford to buy a house, or will we be better off renting an apartment?

A do-it-yourself decorator uses his energy, skill, and know-how to save money for other things.

The problem of housing was related to the family goal of sending the children to college. Stating the problem in this way helps keep the goal in focus and the problem in perspective.

As families deal with one problem, they soon find themselves having to deal with many others. For instance, in working out a solution to the question of housing, it is quite likely that the Jeffersons also found themselves trying to find solutions to the problem of savings, the problem of college education, and problems concerned with the risk of illness or of loss of income. Seldom can a problem be dealt with in isolation; the solution to one puzzle may alter other solutions or it may introduce new problems. The matter of problem-solving goes on and on.

After the problem is stated, the available resources need to be determined. What resources are available or can be made available that might contribute to the solution of the problem? Recall the discussion earlier in the Prologue about resources. How were resources defined? What are the resources that a person has available? It was suggested that resources may be classified into two categories: *human* and *material*. Human resources are intangible and are to be found within or among family members: skills, talent, knowledge, health, and energy. For our discussion, we will also include time among the human resources. Material resources are tangible and consist of money, house and other property, household equipment (washer, sewing machine, freezer, vacuum cleaner, lawn mower), other possessions (camera, car, trailer, typewriter), and community facilities and services (school, library, park, playground, social services).

It is important for families and individuals to be aware of all of their resources. Resources are the tools that will help them reach their goals. Too often, however, there is the tendency to assume that a goal is achieved only by the use of money. But frequently a goal can be reached more effectively if other resources are used as well.

To use human and material resources most effectively, it is necessary to understand two characteristics about them:

1. All resources are limited. Each family has only a limited amount of time, of money, of equipment, of energy, of skill, and so on. It would be a dream world indeed if unlimited supplies of any of these resources existed. If, for example, a member of the family had an unlimited store of skill and know-how, plus energy and time, backed up by a huge bank account, this family would undoubtedly have no trouble in achieving goals. The truth of the matter is that no such family exists.

Furthermore, the quantity of any one resource that a person has will vary with time. That is, a resource may be scarce at one stage in family life, but at another time it may exist in greater quantity. For example, money may be in short supply during the early years of marriage when the household is getting established and the family is growing, but in the middle years, when earnings reach their peak, money may be more abundant. Therefore, because of the limited resource supply, it is necessary to assess all available resources and to decide how they may best be used at a given time in order to achieve family goals.

2. Resources are interrelated. A resource is used according to the availability of other resources. When one resource is in short supply, another can be used in its place. That is, resources may be used interchangeably. For example, Ann Iverson's mother who is a nurse at the local hospital comes home from work with her energy depleted and with little time left for housework. Therefore, Mrs. Iverson employs a woman one day a week to help with the cleaning and the laundry. She is converting one resource, money, into the skills necessary to make up for her own limited time and energy.

The Merrills puzzled over the problem of redecorating the living room. They had the choice of buying a new sofa and having the walls painted or of doing their own painting and making a slipcover for the sofa. With the money saved in that way, they could buy a new rug. They chose the do-it-yourself method, utilizing their own skills and know-how to redecorate the living room. They realized that in making this decision they would be giving up their bowling time, television time, and "spare" time for several weeks. It is this kind of resource study and allocation that is necessary to effectively achieve family goals and solve many family problems.

The alternative solutions to the problem need to be outlined. Consider the Merrills again. Their problem was how to redecorate their living room. They found two possible solutions to choose from, either of which would have provided the "new look" they wanted. These two solutions were the *alternatives* the Merrills identified as the possible ways to solve their problem. Once the problem has been identified, the goals defined, and the resources evaluated, all of the alternatives need to be outlined, thus providing an opportunity to select the most satisfying solution.

This process may require additional information. Possibly Mrs. Merrill had to locate instructions for making slipcovers; she had to find out how much paint and fabric would be needed and what they would cost. These answers were necessary before the Merrills could know how much money would be saved if they did the work themselves. Then they were ready to look at rugs to see what quality they could afford with the money they were saving. There was need for a good bit of information before a choice could be made that would prove satisfying to them.

After the alternative solutions to a problem have been outlined, each alternative must be evaluated in terms of its outcome. When the Merrills gathered information about the cost of the materials and calculated the amount of money they might save, they were studying the outcomes of the possible solutions to the problem of redecorating the living room.

The Merrills' problem was considerably less complex than the problem of what to do about housing, or about economic security, or about some of the other important issues in family life. The need for factual and instructive information becomes even greater when dealing with these problems, and in many cases there is need for special help and assistance from experts. Until such information is obtained, the family is not in a position to define the choices and to make decisions in which they can have confidence or which they will "make stick."

Shall she buy a dress or make it herself? Prices on the fabrics available will help her make this decision.

After the alternatives have been analyzed, it is time to make a decision.   The moment has come to decide on adopting one of the possible solutions. Because decision-making is so important in the problem-solving process, it will be discussed in greater detail in the next chapter. Here we mention only that it is part of the method we have been examining; it is of central importance to the process because until a decision is made and carried out, no problem will be solved. Nor can the final solution of the problem be "proved" right or wrong until the decision has been made, acted upon, and the results evaluated.

Let's review the method for problem-solving.   It may be helpful to summarize this method for problem-solving and see again just what goes into finding solutions to the problems of personal and family living.

To start with, we must (1) realize that a problem exists, that something about our present practice or procedures isn't satisfactory. We know it isn't satisfactory because we aren't accomplishing anything, or so it seems. So in order to know what we want to accomplish, we must (2) define our goals. The real purpose for solving the problems confronting us is to achieve particular goals.

In light of our goals, we can now (3) state the problem. Then, after seeing more precisely what our problem is, we must (4) determine what we have to work with by taking an inventory of our resources. With our resources in mind, we are now ready to (5) outline the possible solutions to the problem (identify the alternatives) and how each solution is likely to work out. On the basis of our analysis of the possible outcomes, (6) we make a decision as to what solution we will adopt.

Before the problem is solved, however, (7) the decision must be acted upon, that is, it must be carried out. When it has been allowed to operate (8) we can evaluate the results and decide if the solution is satisfactory. It will be satisfactory if it helps achieve a desired objective or goal with a minimum of cost in resources.

Effective home management uses the problem-solving process.   We have analyzed the flow of mental and physical activities that have as their major function the achievement of goals. The name for this flow of activities is *management*. It is a flow that requires thoughtful and informed *planning*, careful *control* of the resources and activities necessary to carry out a decision, and it calls for continued *evaluation* along the way in order to judge outcomes and to know if the events taking place are accomplishing what was intended.

The term "management" implies two understandings: (1) something is being managed (resources); and (2) someone is doing the managing. A further assumption is made: management takes place in order to accomplish something (a goal). Thus, in speaking of money management, it is understood that money is being managed by someone in order to achieve a particular goal. The aim of management within the home is to achieve a satisfying life for family members, a life in which each person will be helped to realize his potential as a person. Family money management is but one part of this total process, but it is an important part. It operates toward the achievement of specific goals or toward the solution of specific problems, each of which contributes to the ultimate goal of the family.

Contrary to what many people believe, money management is not simply planning expenditures, nor is it the same thing as budgeting. As soon as we use the word management, we suggest a way of doing things that grows out of decisions directed toward achieving a goal. Money management involves an endless series of decisions, many of which affect the family and its use of resources over a period of many years. Young wage earners like Phyl, whom we introduced in the beginning of this chapter, have had to learn this lesson. Although Phyl made several decisions about what to buy with her first paycheck, she failed to consider the consequences of her decisons until it was too late. Living with money requires something more than the immediate gratification of wants and needs.

FOR DISCUSSION

1. What are some of the problems with which families must deal?
2. Is there a process that can operate to help families solve these problems? If so, what is that process? What are the steps included in it? These steps are said to constitute a flow of activities. What is this flow called?
3. What are two characteristics of resources? Explain, by example, what these characteristics mean.

Summary for Chapter 4

We began the chapter by looking at the ways families and individuals live with money. We ended with an explanation of management. In arriving at the explanation, it was necessary to examine how goals are achieved in family living. Goal achievement, it was learned, is the purpose of management.

Understanding how goals are achieved means understanding the flow of activities that revolve around how resources are used. These activities start with a recognition that things can be better. More effective use of resources, including money, can be achieved by keeping goals in focus and by making decisions that point the way toward achieving goals.

Management is a way of doing and thinking that involves planning the use of resources and how they are to be allocated, and planning a course of action that will lead to one's objectives; it involves controlling the use of resources and also the activities necessary to carry through the plan; and it requires a constant evaluation of how things are proceeding as well as an evaluation of the final outcome.

Money management is only one part of management. Because resources are limited, and because they may be used interchangeably, money is managed together with all other resources.

CAN YOU EXPLAIN?

1. real income
2. human resources
3. material resources

4. problem-solving
5. alternative solutions
6. management

HOW WOULD YOU ANSWER

1. Several ways of living with money have been described in this chapter. Which way is the one you would prefer for yourself? Why?
2. Why is it necessary to know precisely what one's goals are? How can knowing goals increase one's effectiveness as a manager?
3. In attempting to find a solution to a problem, it is advisable to identify as many solutions as possible so as to enlarge the field of choice. How does one go about making a selection?
4. Explain why the supply of resources may vary over the family's life cycle. What resources are apt to increase in supply over time? What resources are likely to decrease in supply as the family ages?

OTHER THINGS TO DO

1. Describe a situation in which you have participated where management of resources appeared particularly effective. Why was it effective?

2. Select a family, either your own or one you know well. Are you aware of its goals? If so, list its goals and how it is working toward achieving them. Make a list of resources that the family would be able to use in reaching its goals. List what goals you want for the family. Which are the short- and long-term goals?
3. Write a short character sketch of a good manager. What makes him a good manager? What is his relationship to others? How would you describe yourself as a manager? What effect do you have upon others?
4. Make a list of all the resources you have available. How can you extend your financial resources by using other resources in place of money to accomplish some of your goals?
5. Make a list of goals you have set for yourself or would like to set. Select one of the goals, and using the management process, illustrate the steps that might be taken to achieve the goal.
6. To help you see that resources are all around you, list those in your Homemaking room that save time; save energy; are free; decrease when used; increase with use; are strictly material; can't be saved; are resources only when available at the right time; are resources you can't give away. Discuss, as a group, your lists.
7. Review the filmstrips "Our Role as Consumers" and "Consumers in the Marketplace" (Institute of Life Insurance) to see the role of a consumer in relationship to his needs, wants, and resources. Discuss such questions as: What roles do we perform? What are some types and examples of community resources? How can a person use skill in the marketplace?
8. Find a cartoon, short story, poem, or song to show how a particular individual (family) used resources. Discuss whether you feel that that individual (or family) made "wise" use of resources.
9. Select a case study from CONSUMER AND HOMEMAKING EDUCATION (A CASE STUDY APPROACH), by Bell and Fallow, or THE SPENDER SYNDROME (University of Wisconsin) to see what resources are available to that particular individual or family. Identify the resources that might be available five years from now if they would continue their education. Would their resources be different if they restricted their education to what they now have?
10. What resources might be available to different ethnic or cultural backgrounds? Different stages in the family life cycle? Different jobs? Different sections or parts of the country? To a retired couple?
11. See the film "Of Time, Work, and Leisure" (NET), based upon the book by Sebastian de Grazia, who claims that man is best measured by his capacity for life when he is not working. What is free time? What is leisure time? What is the good life?
12. Discuss the reasons why the number of housework hours have decreased sharply since the early 1920's. What resources do homemakers have now that they didn't have then? Have we really saved time?

13. Is your use of time based on your own free choice, governed by advice from an older person, or dictated specifically by a higher authority, such as your mother?

14. Interview an elderly woman in your community—one who is considerably older than your own parents. Find out the resources she had available in her youth that took the place of these commonly accepted modern-day "necessities:" facial tissues; bathroom tissue; paper towels; scotch tape, foil wrap; deodorants; "whiter-than-white" laundry detergents; frozen foods; radio and TV home entertainment.

5 Decisions, Money, and Family Goals

What this chapter is about

Decision-making is a mental activity that cannot be avoided. It is a process we must engage in every day in order to function effectively as a family or as an individual. Making decisions about financial affairs demands conscious attention to one's goals as well as to one's money.

This chapter will examine some characteristics of decisions in order to observe what a decision consists of and how it affects what we do with our resources. We will look at the steps involved in making decisions, and outline the sources of help available to people in making financial decisions. Here are the major ideas to be discussed:

1. There are five characteristics of decisions that help us understand what decisions are and how they operate.

2. Family financial decisions are satellite decisions that implement central decisions.

3. The decision-making process consists of three steps.

4. Financial decisions often require specific knowledge and information.

5. Decisions, once made, need to be reviewed.

FIVE CHARACTERISTICS OF DECISIONS TELL WHAT DECISIONS ARE AND HOW THEY OPERATE

You will recall reading in the previous chapter that management cannot take place without decision-making. Decisions form the hub around which all of management takes place. Here we will examine in greater detail what is known about decision-making in general and financial decisions in particular.

When is a decision not a decision?   Although decisions call for some kind of action in order to be completed, not all actions are the result of decisions. When you get up in the morning, you go through a series of activities: you wash your face, brush your teeth, dress, comb your hair, and eat your breakfast. These actions you perform out of habit. Habitual behavior is not the result of decisions, at least not of decisions that are made each time the act is performed.

The same can be said about many expenditures of money. Often we spend money not as a result of a decision just made, but as a kind of habit necessary to our daily living, or as a result of a decision made by an authority. In order to get to school in the morning, it is necessary to pay 15¢ to ride the bus. That 15¢ expenditure does not call for a decision each time one boards the bus.

A decision is a decision when it is a judgment made consciously after weighing the facts and examining the alternatives and their outcomes. Recall from the previous chapter the discussion about identifying the various solutions to a problem. These possible solutions are the alternatives. The decision is the choice one makes from a field of alternatives. The decision is complete when it is acted upon—that is, when we do what we have decided to do (or be, or obtain, or change, or begin). Until some action is taken, the decision is not a decision; instead, it is still an idea or notion or unsettled problem in one's mind.

Decisions often must be lived with for some time; many times they have a way of altering lives, even when they are least expected to. Therefore, in order to see how decisions operate, it may be helpful to identify some of their characteristics.

1. Decisions are interrelated.   A decision has a history; that is, it is related to a past and to a future. Something has occurred prior to the decision that related to it, and events will occur in the future as a result. Think of a row of dominoes standing on end. When the first domino is knocked over, the entire row falls in orderly succession. Decisions work in a similar way—once a decision is made, it sets in motion a chain reaction of further decisions.

Here is another way of looking at the relationship of decisions. Take, for example, a class decision to have a picnic. This decision came about because the class wished to celebrate winning the school award for scholarship, a goal set at the beginning of the school year. Once the picnic was decided on, the class had to plan where to hold it, how to pay for it, what transportation to obtain, what entertainment to plan, what food to serve and who would be responsible for it, and when to schedule the picnic. The decision to have the picnic may be called the *central decision*; the decisions that relate to it may descriptively be called the *satellite decisions*—they are those decisions necessary to carry out the central decision.

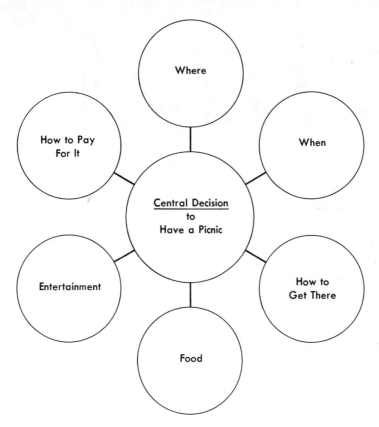

The relationship of the central decision to the satellite decisions needed to carry out the major decision.

This interrelationship of decisions may be viewed in another way. For example, the Coopers decided to build a house that came as near to being their dream house as they could find. It also cost more than they had planned. With that decision, therefore, it was necessary to make a

Let's have a picnic! Once this central decision was made, many satellite decisions had to be made in order for the picnic to become a reality.

series of new decisions as to how other costs of living could be reduced: how to cut down on food costs, on clothing costs, on transportation. Should Mrs. Cooper find a job? Should they rent out space in the garage? The decision to buy the house, therefore, called for many additional adjustments in living, each one requiring new decisions. Here the central decision is to buy the house. Surrounding this decision, and necessary to carry out the purchase, are a series of other decisions that will make possible the monthly payments.

2. Making a choice involves risk.   There is no way of knowing for sure how a decision will turn out. Although we may base the decision on all the facts available and obtain the most expert advice, there is still the possibility that the results of the decision will not be what we anticipated.

Cora and Dick did not anticipate the outcome of their decision. After they were married a short while, Dick was offered a position in Denver with a new engineering firm. To accept the offer would mean leaving New Jersey, moving to a strange community far from relatives and friends, and giving up Dick's present job with an old well-established company. After much thought, consultation, interviewing, and study, Dick and Cora took the Denver offer. After living in Colorado for only a few months, Cora was told by her doctor that because of the high altitude it would be advisable to leave. The decision to move to Denver, therefore, did not turn out as they had expected.

The decision to buy the off-white silk raincoat didn't turn out as Joyce had planned either. She knew that she was taking a big risk in spending $55 for the coat in the first place. She realized that it would be difficult to keep it clean and the salesman had pointed out to her that the label warned against dry-cleaning too often. But Joyce bought the coat. The first time she wore it, a bus splattered greasy muddy water on her as it drove past while she was standing on the curb. The front of the coat was permanently stained. Only a dye job could repair the damage, and this would cost Joyce $18. Her new coat now cost her $73 and was no longer the coat she had decided she wanted.

The night before the social studies exam Jack decided to go to the movies. He was fairly sure he would do "all right," even if he didn't review. But he failed the exam; his decision didn't turn out as he had planned. That's how decisions are—the outcome cannot always be predicted. The risks involved are often the reasons people find it very difficult to make decisions, particularly big ones.

3. Decisions cause change. It is true that some decisions may not involve change. Possibly the class picnic decision caused no change, although there is every chance that some changes were necessary: changes in schedule, for instance, or changes in the use of time by those class members responsible for the food or entertainment.

Decisions that require the use of resources in order to be carried out, as most decisions do, call for change. Burt, a senior at Jackson High, decided that he would buy a used car as soon as he had saved enough money for the down payment. If the car was to become a reality for Burt, he would have to start saving in a regular and systematic manner. Furthermore, he would get a part-time job. To carry out his decision to buy a car, Burt had to change his way of using money and time.

Decisions often require one to "do things differently." Don decided to lose weight, which meant a change in his eating habits and also required him to get more exercise. Kris decided to enter the competition for a music scholarship. From that moment on, her spare time was devoted to practicing, which meant that she could not join the gang for cokes after school and would not have time to baby-sit.

A change in attitude usually precedes the actual decision. Often the decision cannot be made until a change in attitude occurs that will permit one to accept the results of the decision. Many people who have stopped smoking will testify to this. The decision to stop had to be preceded by a change in attitude regarding the habit, a change that finally permitted the smoker to say, "Yes, I want to stop."

4. Decisions require commitment.   When we speak of commitment, we are talking about a pledge we make to another person or to ourselves; this means that we make an agreement to do something, to take some course of action. It further implies that we will accept the results of what we do as well as the conditions under which we must act. Commitment, therefore, is a rather imposing idea.

When the whole notion of commitment is related to decision-making, we find that two commitments are involved: (1) the primary commitment to a goal; and (2) the commitment to carry out the decision and accept the results. Consider first the matter of goals. Without a serious and determined commitment to a goal, one often lacks the incentive and courage to make major decisions related to the goal and to follow through on them. Recall the man who wanted to lose weight. He was tired of his nickname, Tubby, and he was embarassed each time he had to shop for clothes in the "Fat Men's Store." To accomplish his goal, he knew that he would have to change his eating habits. It would mean giving up sweet rolls with his mid-morning coffee and pie à la mode for dessert every noon. He would have to be more moderate in his favorite pastime, eating. Without a serious commitment to his goal, do you think he could make the decision that called for such a drastic change in his way of living and stick with it?

A secretary in one of the offices at the courthouse made up her mind to go to Sweden, the country from which her grandparents had come. To visit their homeland had long been one of her dreams. Finally, she decided to make it come true the following summer. To do it she would have to save several hundred dollars. From the moment of her decision to go to Sweden, she had to make a series of decisions about money in order to be able to deposit at least $50 in her savings account every month. Her commitment to the goal, however, made it easy to accept the austerity program with which she would have to live.

Consider the commitment involved in carrying out a decision and accepting the results. More often than not a decision, in order to be acted upon, calls for a course of action that means work of some kind, or that alters habits, or that limits the use of certain resources. In other

*To make the best use of her travel time, a vacationer
studies alternative routes and tours.*

words, a decision makes demands that require self-discipline. Unless
there is a firm commitment to the decision, we will be tempted to
"throw in the sponge," to give up rather than to follow through. If
the secretary doesn't persist in the saving program to which she is committed, if she can't accept the austere pattern of living necessary to
build a travel fund, she will not achieve her goal. She is committed to
the trip and in order to achieve it, she must be committed to her course
of action.

5. Decisions involve cost. The cost of a decision may be measured in
terms of money, but not necessarily. The cost may also be measured
by what has to be given up as a result of making the decision. For Don,
the cost of his decision to lose weight was measured in terms of what

he could no longer eat; Kris paid in terms of the spare time with her friends that she gave up in order to practice for the music competition; for the secretary the cost meant bringing her lunch to work instead of eating out, fewer movies, fewer new clothes, and no treats. In each case, the cost of the decision can be identified by what each person had to give up.

With financial decisions the cost in dollars and cents can be easily recognized. When it became necessary for Jimmy to have his teeth straightened, the family was faced wih the prospect of a dental bill that would total well over $1,000 during the next two years. The family would have to get along on $1,000 less than they normally would.

Once he commits himself to his sport, the athlete must be prepared for the cost —long hours of training.

Orthodontia for Jimmy was worth the cost, however, and the decision was not so difficult to live with. For the family who bought the dream house, the decision was more complex and the cost far greater, because it would make itself felt for many years to come. After all, there is just so much money, and when some of it is used for one thing, there will be less to use for other things. This cost of a financial decision is often overlooked, and yet it is what can make the decision a difficult one to accept and to live with.

FOR DISCUSSION

1. What do we mean when we say that a decision is a judgment made consciously after weighing the facts and examining alternatives and their outcomes?
2. Explain the relationship between *central* and *satellite* decisions. Give some examples.
3. In what way is risk involved in decision-making?
4. How do decisions cause change? Give some examples from your own experience.
5. What two commitments are demanded in making a decision?
6. How is the cost of a decision measured?

FINANCIAL DECISIONS ARE SATELLITE DECISIONS THAT IMPLEMENT CENTRAL DECISIONS

The five characteristics of decisions just discussed are true of all kinds of decisions, including those we call financial. Financial decisions are those that involve the use of financial resources—money. Whether to buy a 50¢ lipstick or one costing 59¢ would hardly qualify as a financial decision, but determining the amount of money to allocate for cosmetics and for grooming aids over a period of time might logically be classified as financial.

There is another way of looking at financial decisions that helps keep money in its proper perspective. Recall the comments describing the interrelatedness of decisions and how the central decision is surrounded by satellite decisions, those decisions necessary to carry out the central decision. Remember that the central decision is directly related to one's goals or to the solution of a particular problem. Examples of some typical central decisions would be the decision to go to a technical institute to learn electronic data processing; or to accept a job in a distant community; or to go into business for one's self; or to marry the boy next door; or to move to the suburbs. None of these decisions are financial. However, in order to carry each of them out, a series of financial decisions must be made. The big life-shaping decisions people must make involve money, but only as a tool in carrying through the central decisions. So when families or individuals are pondering how best to finance a home, they are actually trying to decide how to carry out a decision related to their personal and family goals, which are non-financial.

The fact that financial decisions are satellite decisions does not mean that they are any easier to make than central decisions. After all, financial resources are limited for every family, even those we think of as being wealthy, and the ways of solving financial problems are varied. Therefore, to decide how best to use family money to achieve family goals can be difficult and often confusing, unless one is armed with reliable information and supported by reliable advice.

FOR DISCUSSION

1. Explain the statement that financial decisions "implement" central decisions.
2. How are financial decisions related to one's central decisions?

THE DECISION-MAKING PROCESS CONSISTS OF THREE STEPS

The decision-making process pertains only to rational decisions. Before discussing the steps involved in decision-making, a distinction must be made between *spur-of-the-moment* decisions and *rational* decisions. As people, we don't always behave in a logical and rational manner, nor do we make all decisions in that way either. There is much to be said in favor of occasionally acting on the "spur of the moment." This kind of human behavior is what lends excitement to what we do and gives warmth to our responses.

Sylvia, for example, is a spontaneous, spur-of-the-moment hostess. She loves parties, loves giving them, and finds an excuse at the drop of a hat. She doesn't spend time deciding "should she or shouldn't she" or "is the time right?" or "does the occasion warrant celebrating?" She just gathers people together and they have a party. If you were to ask Sylvia to outline the steps in her decision to have a party, she wouldn't know what you were talking about. Not everyone is like Sylvia. But we all make some spontaneous decisions, and often these turn into delightful experiences. There are times when the best thing to do is to buy the red dress, or the "silly" shoes, or paint the bedroom. Such spur-of-the-moment decisions give one a lift and brighten one's mental attitude.

The concern in this discussion, however, is with rational decision-making. Many concerns in family and personal living will not yield to spur-of-the-moment thinking and top-of-the-head decisions. Rational decisions are related to one's goals; they are necessary in order to find the solutions to perplexing problems concerning the major issues in the life of each family and individual. What is involved in making rational decisions?

An after-school job means less time for other activities,
but young people are often willing to make this sacrifice
in order to meet their goals.

1. Seek alternative solutions.   In the previous chapter it was pointed out that decision-making is at the very center of management. You will recall the Merrills, who had the problem of redecorating their living room. What did they do in arriving at their decision? After studying their available resources, they set about identifying all the possible solutions to the living room problem. At this point they began to make a decision.

"There's more than one way to skin a cat" is an old saying that means there's more than one way of doing things. To make a decision with some confidence, it is helpful to look at all the possible ways of solving the problem. Thus one can better measure his resources against the alternatives and examine more clearly the possible solutions in terms of his particular circumstances.

2. Weigh the alternatives.   The Merrills saw two alternatives: they could hire decorators to do the work, or they could do it themselves and use the money they saved to buy a rug. But before they could make a choice, they had to gather information about costs and materials in order to know if they would save enough for the rug. They had to consider also the value of their time and how much they had available. The facts and information they gathered were necessary so that they could weigh the alternatives; they would compare the possible solutions, know what resources would be used in each case, and have an understanding of the outcomes of each solution.

Very often the alternatives cannot be judged very accurately unless more is known about them. It is impossible to decide from among several methods if one does not know what each method involves. Take the matter of financing the purchase of a new car. The alternatives may include: financing through the dealer; borrowing from the bank; or using savings to pay cash for the car. For example, what will it cost to finance the car through the dealer? What will it cost to borrow from the bank? What will be lost in interest earnings if one uses his savings? How does the interest lost compare to the charges required to pay for a loan? Unless the car buyer knows what is involved in each method, he will find it difficult to weigh his choices and come to a decision that will best suit his financial circumstances and at the same time meet his needs.

3. Make a choice.   After studying the alternatives, one is ready to make a choice. The choice is the decision one makes after carefully examining the several possible courses of action. What one chooses will be based on his own goals and the availability of resources. The

Merrills decided on the do-it-yourself method of redecorating. After investigating the costs and assessing their own time and skills, they decided that this method would serve them best and provide the most satisfying results (they could buy the rug, too). On the other hand, if they had been limited in time, or if they had felt their skills would produce only an amateurish job (after all, slip covers need to be accurately fitted and tailored), they might have chosen to do without the rug and have the work done.

The decision is carried out and the results are analyzed. Three elements go into the making of rational decisions: seeking the alternatives; weighing the alternatives; and making a choice. But until the decision is carried out, it doesn't really help solve anything. Now it becomes a matter of management—managing the resources and activities necessary to put the decision into action.

Having made a decision, one must assume responsibility for it and follow through with it. Even though there may be some risk in whatever is chosen, a person must be ready to accept and live with the consequences of a decision. People often spend time worrying about their choice and wonder if another decision would have been better or more to their liking. This kind of concern, however, only hinders one's effectiveness in living with a decision. The mature manager can make decisions and put them into effect without worrying about "what might have been."

The effectiveness of a decision is measured by whether or not it helps accomplish whatever one sets out to do. If the course chosen turns out to impede progress toward a goal, probably that choice will not be made again. Instead, it may be necessary to stop and find out what is hindering the desired outcome. When the course of action takes more money than anticipated, another way may have to be found. Otherwise the drain on income may do harm in other areas of day-to-day living. Evaluating the results of a decision is important, too, in preparing one for future decisions. We can learn from our own experience if we stop to examine what our experience is teaching us.

FOR DISCUSSION

1. Why is it necessary when making a decision to outline alternatives?
2. In "weighing alternatives" what is one actually considering?

3. On what basis does a person finally make a choice? From what does he choose?
4. After a choice has been made, is the decision finished? What takes place now?
5. How does a person know if his decision is a good one?

FINANCIAL DECISIONS OFTEN REQUIRE SPECIFIC KNOWLEDGE AND INFORMATION

Any decision that involves the use of financial resources requires careful thought, particularly a decision that may affect one's life for a long period of time. To buy Brand A or Brand X detergent is not a very serious problem, perhaps, for the expenditure involves only a few cents. If the decision is a poor one, the loss will not seriously affect family relationships nor delay the achievement of a particular goal. But a decision to finance a college education, or to move to another community, or to purchase a home, or finance a car, or plan an investment program or a life insurance program—any of these decisions will have consequences that extend far into the future. Such decisions call for more than spur-of-the-moment conclusions based on emotional impulses.

Because of the long-range effects of so many of the decisions that families and individuals must make, most people are anxious for help in the form of advice or information. Anything that can help them make a rational decision, a decision that can be lived with comfortably, is usually welcomed. Unfortunately many people do not know where to go for help or what help they need. Here, then, are some sources that may be useful to persons making financial decisions.

Recall past experience.   One's own experience is not foolproof, but if it is true that "experience is the best teacher," then at least we can use what we have learned to avoid making the same mistakes. The Randalls relied on their past experience in buying a house and were pleased that they had something to guide them. Their first house was handsome, outside. It made a beautiful picture. But once the five of them had moved in and were settled, it became apparent that the house in the picture was not exactly a house for living. The closets were too small, the main traffic area led past the bedrooms, the living room was too dark, and the family room too small. So when Bob Randall was transferred to another city, they had a far better idea of what to look for in housing.

Keep financial records. Financial records may not provide answers to new problems, but they can give a clue to how much money is available to work with. Even the most elementary records can reveal a great deal about one's financial situation. In considering a venture that requires a financial commitment of some kind, it is necessary to know how it may affect commitments that have already been made. From one's records it is possible to determine how much income has already been committed, how much is required for daily living expenses, and how much will be available for new expenses. And perhaps most important of all, financial records provide a picture of a life style that may be essential for the family to maintain.

Borrow experience from people you know. Often our own experience and our own records do not relate to the problem we have to solve. Jane discovered this fact when she decided to set up a savings program for her retirement. Nothing from her past experience seemed to help her. She asked some of her friends what they had done and learned that Ruth had invested in mutual funds, Charlotte had purchased retirement annuities, and Donna had invested in real estate and common stocks. Although Jane still didn't know what she should do, she did learn from her friends that there are several ways of building a retirement fund and that each method seems to work. Other people's experience may not always suit one's needs or situation, but it does suggest some possibilities and can serve as a starting point.

Look up specific information. Jane went to the library to look up material that would explain to her retirement annuities, mutual funds, and common stocks. She found several books written for laymen explaining how people provide for their retirement. The librarian also called Jane's attention to pertinent articles in several current magazines. Evidently financial questions were on many people's minds. Although Jane was still uncertain about how the various investments might relate to her, she at least understood how these forms of investment work and felt knowledgeable enough to ask further questions. It is this kind of background information and understanding that is essential in choosing a course of action.

Consult experts. There finally comes a time when one must consult an expert on financial matters. Jane chose to talk with the manager of the bank where she had a savings account. After all, he was skilled and experienced in matters relating to money, and furthermore, he was impartial. He was able to help Jane assess her retirement needs and to

*Before making a major financial decision, advice may be
needed from a financial expert.*

suggest the best way to meet them. Jane might have obtained similar advice from an attorney, as many people do. Other specialists such as life insurance agents or stock brokers can give sound advice; their business consists of helping people solve critical and perplexing financial problems. Usually they are the people who must help one make the final move—to act on one's decision.

FOR DISCUSSION

1. Why is it sometimes necessary to have special advice or information prior to making a decision?
2. How does past experience help in making a decision? Why are financial records an account of one's past experience?
3. Is it safe to rely on other people's experience? Why?

4. How can the library provide help in decision-making?
5. What experts would you call on for help in making a financial decision?

DECISIONS NEED TO BE REVIEWED

Decisions seldom remain fixed for all time. Because a problem has once been solved and the solution seems to be functioning as planned does not mean that the problem will never have to be solved again later on. Families sometimes forget this point, and the result is a new set of anxieties and perplexities, simply because the old solution doesn't fit the present situation. Decisions need regular tending and even transplanting from time to time. This decision review is identified as *evaluation* by managers.

Nothing about family living remains static; the family is changing constantly, and as the family changes, so do its problems. It is impossible to predict accurately what we will face next week or next year, and to forecast what problems will confront us ten years from now is out of the question. The best guide devised so far for estimating future needs is the family life cycle. This guide can be used to forecast, in general, what the family needs are likely to be and what problems may demand attention. It helps families decide on solutions not only to today's problems but also to those problems that are likely to occur in the future.

It is easy to see that the central decisions made in the first year of marriage may not be suitable by the time the family includes adolescent children. A solution to the problem of housing, for example, may need to be altered more than once. Decisions concerning the problem of economic security made during the first year of marriage will surely have been outgrown by the time there are children in the home. Possibly the family is maintaining an investment program of some kind, or a life insurance program, or a savings plan that no longer serves the family's needs. Because life's problems change, as do family situations, decisions relating to them must be kept current. Financial decisions must be reviewed regularly.

FOR DISCUSSION

1. Why do decisions need to be reviewed?
2. How does the family life cycle serve as a guide in estimating future needs?

Summary for Chapter 5

Far-reaching effects in personal and family living result from decisions—those conscious choices that bring about a course of action directed toward goal achievement. The success of a decision can be measured only in terms of one's goals, and not necessarily in immediate satisfaction or pleasure.

Five characteristics of decisions help us to understand what decisions are and how they affect us: (1) decisions are interrelated; (2) decision-making involves risk; (3) decisions result in change; (4) decisions require commitment; and (5) decisions have a cost. Financial decisions have one further characteristic: they are the decisions that implement central decisions.

The decision-making process is an integral part of management. It consists of three procedures: (1) seeking alternatives; (2) weighing alternatives; and (3) making a choice.

Because solutions to many problems are complex, people often need help in making suitable decisions, particularly decisions relating to the use of money. Aids to decision-making include one's own past experience and financial records; the experience of others; specific facts and information; and advice from experts.

Decisions do not remain permanently settled. They need reviewing from time to time to be certain that current practices are in line with one's goals and circumstances.

CAN YOU EXPLAIN?

1. judgment
2. alternative
3. central decision
4. satellite decision
5. commitment
6. rational decisions

HOW WOULD YOU ANSWER?

1. Explain the relationship of decisions to management.
2. When is a decision not a decision?
3. It has been pointed out that many of the decisions that families or individuals make have far-reaching results. Can you explain this idea?
4. In what ways are decisions related to goals?

OTHER THINGS TO DO

1. Identify three central decisions you know your own family has made. What satellite decisions surround each of them? What is the relationship between central and satellite decisions?

2. Make a list of all the sources in your community where people can obtain specific information to help them make financial decisions. List the experts that families can conveniently and safely consult.

3. List the decisions you have to make about what you will do after graduation from high school. How do you expect to make these decisions? What are the circumstances you will have to consider? It is possible that you have already made a decision concerning your next step after finishing high school. What steps led you to decide as you did? What further decisions must be made now in order to carry out your major decisions?

4. View the filmstrip "Marriage and Money" (Institute of Life Insturance) and make a decision for the young couple based upon what you believe is their value system. Be sure to consider all the possible alternatives before making your choice.

5. Read DID I EVER TELL YOU? by Dr. Seuss. Here is an illustration of a decision. Is it on the conscious or unconscious level? Justify your answer.

6. Here are some questions for discussion: How does a person's environment or his personality affect his decisions? On what factors do people base their choices? How is management like a mobile? How is decision-making the key to the good life? When and why are individuals motivated to make deliberate decisions?

7. Discuss the statement, ". . . a person probably makes around 10–15 central decisions in his lifetime." Identify some of the central decisions you believe a person makes.

8. See the film "Phoebe" (McGraw-Hill). Identify the central decision and the satellite decisions. How would *you* advise Phoebe in making her choices?

9. Watch a current television program that deals with family situations to see how that particular family made a decision. What factors were considered in planning? Who initiated the plan? How many alternatives were actually considered? What appraisal of resources took place? Was the decision satisfactory?

10. Read the book THE STORY OF THE TRAPP FAMILY SINGERS, by Maria Augusta Trapp (Lippincott), to see how the interrelatedness of values, goals, and standards is demonstrated in the decisions that were made.

11. Prepare a bulletin board, or use the bulletin board puzzle from the J. C. Penney kit on "Decision Making for Consumers" to see the different steps in making a decision.

12. Identify the central and some of the satellite decisions made by MR. AND MRS. BO JO JONES, by Ann Head (New American Library). Discuss the alternatives you think they took into account when making the central decision of getting married. Why do you think they chose the alternative that they did? How was this decision affected by environment and family? What were the negative and positive outcomes of this central decision?

6 Design for Family Spending

What this chapter is about

In the previous chapters you learned something about decision-making and how it relates to and is an essential part of management. Here we will examine an aid to financial decision-making: the financial plan or design. In order to make realistic decisions about family financial resources, the family manager must operate within some kind of a framework. This chapter will discuss the purposes of a financial plan, the elements that go into it, and how it operates. There are five major ideas discussed here:

1. A financial plan is a necessary tool in managing money.

2. The four parts of a financial plan are related.

3. A successful financial plan fits the specific needs of the family.

4. A successful plan is based on realistic facts and figures.

5. Good consumer habits help make a budget work.

A FINANCIAL PLAN IS A NECESSARY TOOL IN MANAGING MONEY

A financial plan helps in making realistic decisions. Workable decisions, whether financial or any other kind, are made within some kind of framework or design. Such a design provides guide posts that mark the limitations or boundaries within which the decision-maker must operate; the design helps him make decisions that really work.

In making a career choice, for example, one must observe the stated requirements for entry into a profession or the job qualifications outlined by a trade union or by an employer. To decide, therefore, that you are going to be an x-ray technician without considering any of the requirements and then to discover that you can't meet those require-ments would make a failure of your career choice. *Successful decisions must be made within a framework that outlines what is possible.*

Financial decisions, too, must be made within a framework that out-lines the possible. Without such a design, decisions regarding money and how to use it could lead to despair. In fact, they very often do.

Perhaps among your acquaintances you've known someone like Harriet. She couldn't resist a bargain. When the Bon Marché adver-tised a "spectacular fur event," Harriet was among the first in line when the store opened. In no time at all she had selected a stunning fur jacket and jubilantly made a deposit on it, agreeing to pay the balance over the next six months. It was such an easy decision, but she later remembered that she was still making payments on a TV set, that her apartment rent would go up next month, and that she had already signed up for a vacation trip with two other girls from her office. The money for the jacket wasn't there and it wouldn't be available in the foreseeable future. Her decision was impractical and impossible to carry out. She had failed to consider the total design within which she could make financial decisions. Some kind of a pat-tern or framework must exist for individuals or families, otherwise financial troubles may overtake them.

A design for family spending gives order to family money. Webster's dictionary defines "order" as meaning a regular arrangement, a method or system. The definition suggests further that order means "harmonious relationships between parts or members," in other words, balance. So when we talk about order in the use of money, each of these ideas is implied: a regular arrangement, a method or system, and balance.

Living effectively with money—that is, getting satisfaction from the use of one's money—calls for some regular arrangement for managing it. Regularity should exist in whatever method or system we adopt for paying bills, saving, providing for daily living needs, and accomplish-ing goals. This regular and systematic arrangement will save time and will tell us what financial resources we have available.

Order also suggests balance. No one area of our financial lives should outweigh other areas to the point of weakening them or putting them out of focus. Order, meaning balance, helps keep expenses on a car, for example, in line with the total budget, so that essentials like food and clothing are still adequately provided. Regular arrangements and balance, as they relate to the use of money, help us attend to first

*A couple studies the blueprints for their "dream" house,
a goal that will be realized because they have another
blueprint—their financial plan.*

things first, thus making sure that family needs are met and goals realized.

A design for family spending provides a blueprint for building bridges to family goals. A financial design might be compared to a blueprint or to a road map. But whatever picture we call to mind—blueprint or map—it suggests a plan or a route for getting from where we are to some other place. A financial design shows us exactly this: where we are now and how we might gain what we want to accomplish.

If you set out to make a new dress, you start with a pattern or design. You use your material according to pattern instructions. You proceed from pattern and yard goods to completed garment in a logical order. Your objective, a new dress, is soon realized.

A financial design works like a dress pattern. It, too, leads to objectives or goals. It certainly did for Tom and Lila. One of their goals at the time of their marriage was to own a stereo system. The kind of equipment they wanted would cost several hundred dollars, and even with their combined earnings it was a great deal more money than they had. Furthermore, there were many other things to acquire that first year, things that were essential to housekeeping and daily living, such as a bed and table and chairs. When Lila figured out what she needed in the kitchen, just "little things," her list was impressive: ironing board, dish drainer, pots and pans, heavy skillet, kitchen knives, a butter dish, measuring cup—her list went on and on. The total cost made her blink and Tom gulp. The stereo system looked hopelessly remote.

Then and there they decided that if ever the stereo was to be theirs, they would have to plan for it. It would have to become part of their financial design. A study of their financial situation at the time showed them how they were using their income. They could see how much money was committed every month for rent, insurance, car payments, and other payments in fixed amounts. They could estimate the amount of money they needed for food, clothing, and running expenses, and they could see that in a very small way they could begin to build a stereo fund. It was a small beginning, but it was firmly built into their financial design; they knew that eventually they would have the stereo. And they did—several years later.

FOR DISCUSSION

1. What do we mean when we speak of "workable decisions"? Have you ever made a decision that wasn't workable?
2. Why is it helpful to maintain some system in managing financial affairs?
3. What might happen if one's financial plan were out of balance?
4. From the story of Tom and Lila can you suggest how they built the stereo system into their plan?
5. In your own words, how would you define "financial design"?

THE FOUR PARTS OF A FINANCIAL PLAN ARE RELATED

If you have been reading this chapter thoughtfully, you probably have been asking yourself if a financial design is the same thing as a *budget*.

Of course it is! A budget is a financial plan that systematizes one's money affairs and aids one in accomplishing goals. A budget, or plan, is a tool that one uses in managing money, but it does not do the managing.

Budgets for some families and individuals are intricate designs composed of countless details. For others, a budget is very simple and uncomplicated—perhaps a brief outline of income and how it is to be allocated. There are even some people who rely on a mental budget and never commit their plan to paper. Still other families choose a middle way, a plan in outline but with some detail added where it helps clarify or keep straight certain financial obligations. Financial plans can differ substantially; it depends on what will serve the family best.

To understand how a design for family money can serve the purposes it does, it will be helpful to examine what such a design consists of. You will observe that there are four basic parts in the design and that the parts are related.

1. A budget begins with a statement of family income.   A statement of your *income* tells you exactly what financial resources you have to work with. It tells you what money you will receive weekly, or monthly, or annually. It should indicate any funds you receive in addition to your earnings, such as interest on savings, or rent due, or the benefit payments a family member may receive. Once you know your total income, you know one of the limits within which to do your financial planning.

2. A budget informs you of the fixed expenses to which the family is committed.   Rent or mortgage payments, insurance premiums, contributions to your church or synagogue, installment payments on any debt the family owes, taxes, and all other payments made on a regular basis and in fixed amount should be indicated in the budget. A listing of these *fixed expenses* shows what you already have promised to pay and provides another set of limits within which to do further planning. Now you are in a position to plan more realistically and to use your resources to greater advantage.

3. A budget provides for the necessary flexible expenses.   Expenditures for food, clothing, personal allowances, household operations, automobile operation, dry-cleaning, laundry, recreation, and other needs are called *flexible expenses*, because they can be controlled to a certain extent. The food budget can be minimized by buying fresh fruit and vegetables in season, day-old bread and other baked goods, less expensive meats, fewer convenience foods, and by shopping for the "best buys" each week—all without endangering the health of the family. The clothing budget can be controlled also by shopping carefully, by doing without extra garments, and by carefully altering last year's skirt or jacket.

4. A budget provides for emergencies and special goals.   Sometimes people become discouraged with budgeting because an emergency arises and there is no money. The roof leaks, the front tire blows out, mother's glasses break, or some other minor disaster occurs that wrecks the budget. These emergencies cannot be determined in advance, but provision can be made for them in the budget. No one can say for sure just how much money should be kept in this *emergency fund*, but financial experts suggest that it should probably amount to two or three months' income.

Special goals—next year's vacation, painting the kitchen, a bar mitzvah or confirmation, a wedding in the family, or drapes for the living room—must be provided for systematically. If the amount of money needed for a special goal or coming event can be determined in advance, it may be practical to include a regular payment for this event in "fixed expenses." Then the money will be on hand when it is needed.

On pages 116 and 117 is reproduced an outline for financial planning called the *Family Money Manager*. It incorporates the four elements suggested here and includes working instructions. This particular arrangement is a simple one, yet it provides the guide lines that families often need to help them make decisions resulting in financial commitments.

The parts of a budget are related.   The elements in a financial plan are related to each other. A change in one part of the budget—in family income, for example—will quickly be reflected throughout the other parts of the plan. More money will be available in the budget if income goes up, and cuts will be necessary somewhere in the plan if income goes down. Whatever happens to the family financially, whether from a source outside of the family or as a result of a decision made within the family, it will be felt throughout the budget.

If, for example, a family decides to move out of an apartment and into a house of its own, the decision will be reflected in how the family plans expenditures for food, clothing, recreation, transportation, savings, and probably many other items. The house payments may be no more than the amount they were paying for rent, but it costs money to move; possibly the family will need some additional furniture; operating and maintenance costs will be higher; and insurance protection will be needed on their property. In order to meet these expenses they will have to spend less on several other items. In the budget, provision will have to be made for increasing expenditures in certain areas and decreasing expenditures in other areas. The solution to their housing problem, therefore, is reflected throughout the budget. Financial resources are limited; people have only so much money with which to work. Therefore, if they choose to spend more for housing, alterations will be necessary in their financial plan.

How one chooses to make these necessary changes will depend on the family. Some people may temporarily forego making any provision for savings; others may choose to reduce the cost of food for a period of time, or to use the car less; one family may decide that an additional income in the family would help, so the mother takes a job; another family may decide to give up allowances for the teenage children. Whatever a family decides to do in order to accommodate an added cost—of housing, for example—will be compensated for by their satisfaction in the new house and by their conviction that this is what they want. "Pinching" or going without is not so difficult when we know it permits us to have something we really want.

FOR DISCUSSION

1. How would you explain what a budget is?
2. List the four parts of a budget. Why is each part necessary? What items belong in each part?
3. In what ways are the parts of a budget related?

A SUCCESSFUL FINANCIAL PLAN FITS
THE SPECIFIC NEEDS OF THE FAMILY

Studying ready-made budgets may be helpful.   Developing a family or personal budget takes time and thought. Families and individuals sometimes seek additional help as they attempt to work out their own financial plans or budgets. They may find it useful to study standard budgets to see how their expenses compare with those of

FAMILY MONEY MANAGER

Step 1: INCOME

Write down in this chart all the money you expect to receive in the next 12 months. If your income is from wages or salary, include only your "take-home" pay. If it is from a business, farm, or trade, make the best estimate you can. Remember to include any extra income you may receive — interest, dividends, money which the children may contribute, rent from property you own. Add up your figures and divide by 52 to determine your average weekly income for the year. (For a monthly budget, divide by 12.)

ESTIMATE OF OUR TOTAL CASH INCOME

Annual Wages or Income from Farm or Business   _____
Interest or Dividends from Bonds and Investments   _____
Income from Other Members of Family   _____
Other Income   _____
_____   _____

Total ANNUAL Income $_____a year
Total WEEKLY Income (Divide Annual Income by 52) $_____a week

This is the money which we have to spend and save during the next 52 weeks. Enter the amount in the "Family Balance Sheet" at the bottom of the page.

Step 2: FIXED EXPENSES AND OBLIGATIONS

Write down what your fixed expenses and obligations are — housing payments, insurance premiums, taxes, contributions, installments, and so on. Indicate when these are due. Add all your items and divide by 52 to determine your weekly set-aside. This money goes into a special fund every pay-day. When your fixed expenses and obligations come due, pay them out of this fund.

ESTIMATE OF OUR FIXED EXPENSES AND OBLIGATIONS

	JAN.	FEB.	MAR.	APRIL	MAY	JUNE	JULY	AUG.	SEPT.	OCT.	NOV.	DEC.	Total 12 Months
FAMILY HOUSING													
Rent, Mortgage Payt.													
Major Fuel Bills													
Other													
FAMILY PROTECTION													
Life Insurance													
Health Insurance													
Other Insurance													
FAMILY IN COMMUNITY													
Donations													
Church													
DEBTS OBLIGATIONS													
Installments													
Other Debts													
TAXES AND LICENSES													
Taxes													
Licenses													
OTHER MAJOR ITEMS													

This is the Money We Shall Put in a Special Fund Every Week to Meet Future Expenses and Obligations. Enter it on the "Family Balance Sheet" _____

Total for the Year _____   OUR WEEKLY SET ASIDE (Divide by 52) _____

Step 3: EMERGENCY FUND

If your Money Manager is to work smoothly, you will need an emergency fund. An emergency fund provides for two things: for long-range projects — the children's education, a new house, or a good vacation; and for unexpected emergencies or for purchases you must make but haven't provided for. An emergency fund should never be allowed to grow too big. When it reaches two or three months' income, put the extra money into your regular savings.

ESTIMATE OF OUR EMERGENCY FUND

To meet unexpected expenses we shall put aside each payday $_____

This fund will be allowed to accumulate until it reaches $_____, after which we shall pay into it merely enough to keep it at that level.

Step 4: WEEKLY LIVING ALLOWANCES

In this chart living expenses are divided into six sections — how much Mother needs to run the house, how much Father needs for work, and so on. But there are extra lines in the chart to use if you want to divide things in another way. Add all your estimates to determine your total expenditures. When you subtract these from your total income, have you anything left? If so, this amount may be placed in your regular savings account.

ESTIMATE OF OUR WEEKLY LIVING ALLOWANCE

MOTHER'S EXPENDITURES	HOW MUCH A WEEK?
Food	_____
Household Operation	_____
Laundry	_____
_____	_____
TOTAL (Enter Here:)	_____

FATHER'S EXPENDITURES	
Car Operation	_____
Lunches	_____
_____	_____
TOTAL (Enter Here:)	_____

FAMILY EXPENSES	
Clothing	_____
Recreation	_____
Ordinary Medical and Drug Store	_____
_____	_____
_____	_____
TOTAL (Enter Here:)	_____

PERSONAL ALLOWANCES,	HOW MUCH A WEEK?
Minor Articles of Clothing, Personal Care, Ice Cream Cones, Etc.	
Father	_____
Mother	_____
Others in Family	_____
_____	_____
TOTAL (Enter Here:)	_____

OTHER ITEMS AND MISCELLANEOUS	
_____	_____
_____	_____
_____	_____
_____	_____
TOTAL (Enter Here:)	_____

OUR WEEKLY ESTIMATE FOR LIVING EXPENSES _____

This is the amount we shall pay ourselves every week and try to make last until the next week begins. Enter it on the "Balance Sheet."

OUR FAMILY "BALANCE SHEET"

OUR WEEKLY INCOME IS	(Step 1)	_____
OUR WEEKLY SET-ASIDES AMOUNT TO	(Step 2)	_____
OUR EMERGENCY FUND	(Step 3)	_____
OUR WEEKLY LIVING ALLOWANCE IS	(Step 4)	_____
AND THIS IS WHAT'S LEFT FOR REGULAR SAVINGS		_____

Reproduced through the courtesy of the Institute of Life Insurance.

other families. Such study also reveals what expenditures are usually incorporated into an overall plan. In this way a standard budget serves as a reminder to families of expenses they may have overlooked and that they will want to include if their budgets are going to work for them.

To adopt a ready-made budget, however, and to try to fit your own family into it seldom meets with success. Because many differences exist among individual families, including differences in goals and values, a budget is useful only when it reflects a particular family's way of living. For example, one family may prefer to spend more money for a car than the people next door, who are more interested in their ham radio outfit. The family across the street has to make provision for two riding horses, and another family in the block is supporting grandparents. In each case a unique situation exists that makes it impossible for these families to live according to a ready-made budget, even though the families may receive identical incomes and are each of the same size.

Budgets, like families, are unique.   There are different styles in budget-making, as can be observed from the financial plans that follow on pages 119 and 120. Although the two families are similar in income, size, age, and where they live, their budgets are very different in style and form. Yet each plan works well for its particular family.

The Conrad Claytons and the Joseph Krolls live on the same street in suburban Cleveland. Mr. Clayton and Mr. Kroll both work for the same manufacturing company, and each receives approximately the same take-home pay each week. Each family has three children, all in junior and senior high school. Both wives are employed, Mrs. Clayton at the public library and Mrs. Kroll as a receptionist in a doctor's office. Let us see how the Claytons and the Krolls have designed their financial lives.

In the tables that follow, you will note that the Kroll's monthly budget is not as detailed as the Clayton's. The Krolls know how much money is coming in and who has charge of it; they recognize that some expenses are fixed, and those are considered the responsibility of Mr. Kroll. The flexible expenses belong to Mrs. Kroll; it is up to her to feed and clothe the family, run the house, and pay for the dentist, doctor, hairdresser, and all those other items that eat up family money. She makes her own rules as well as her own decisions; her only limit is that she cannot spend more than $497.

Mr. and Mrs. Conrad Clayton and Family

Total Annual Income, after deductions	$10,348.00
Total Monthly Income (divide annual by 12)	862.33*

ALLOCATION OF INCOME

Fixed Expenses, per month:

Mortgage payment, including taxes	$ 79.00	
Life insurance premiums	26.00	
Bank loan	37.73	
Car payment and auto insurance	66.00	
Church	55.00	
Total		$ 263.73

Flexible Expenses, per month:

Food		225.00	
Household operations, utilities		40.60	
Clothing		46.00	
Medical and dental, routine		30.00	
Transportation		26.00	
Education		16.00	
Recreation		18.00	
Allowances:			
Mr. Clayton	$40		
Mrs. Clayton	30		
Connie	15		
Clay	12		
Jill	5		
		102.00	
Total			$ 503.60

Savings, deposits per month:

Emergency fund	$ 30.00	
College fund	50.00	
Vacation fund	15.00	
Total		$ 95.00

Total Allocations per month:	$ 862.33*

Mr. and Mrs. Joseph Kroll and Family

Total Annual Income, after deductions	$10,500.00
Total Monthly Income (divide annual by 12)	875.00*

ALLOCATION OF INCOME

Fixed Expenses, paid by Mr. Kroll every month:	288.00
Flexible Expenses, managed by Mrs. Kroll, no more than:	497.00
Savings, managed by Mr. Kroll as a fixed expense:	90.00
Total Allocations per month:	875.00*

There is nothing remarkable about either of these plans. Each one serves its own family and will do only what is asked of it. The Claytons are more comfortable and confident with a monthly plan that is detailed. It is easier for them to make decisions when they can see the details. The Krolls, too, are satisfied with their system. They have divided the financial responsibilities, and as long as each person knows what he must take care of and the amount of money he can use, they are comfortable. The important thing about a plan is not its style but whether it fits the family's needs. Only then will it work.

FOR DISCUSSION

1. Why is a ready-made budget impractical? Could you and your best friend use the same budget? Give the reason for your answer.
2. Why does a realistic budget make spending more effective?
3. Can you suggest some possible differences between the Claytons and the Krolls?

A SUCCESSFUL PLAN IS BASED ON REALISTIC FACTS AND FIGURES

A budget is useful at any time. A question that financial advisers are frequently asked is, "Who should keep a budget?" The answer, of course, is that everyone who has any responsibility for managing money should do so with the help of a budget of some kind. A budget is as important for families with very limited incomes as it is for families of means and for the people in between. A budget, regardless of how simple or complex, is the best guarantee for getting satisfaction from one's financial resources over a long period of time. It is of particular importance to young families that are still gaining experience in money management and financial know-how.

Other questions that are asked from time to time are, "When should we start a budget? Should we wait until we get out of debt? Should we wait until our earnings are more stable? Should we wait until my wife stops working and our income is reduced?" Often a person will say, "We don't need a budget; we are getting along fine and have no problems." But the time to start budgeting is *now*—problems or not.

The purpose of a budget is to help keep a family or individual out of financial trouble, and it also is the operating plan that will lead to family goals—in spite of trouble. A budget is a useful guide for any individual or family regardless of their present economic status.

Budget-making follows a carefully prescribed procedure.   Although a budget is intended as an aid to decision-making, it cannot be set up until several decisions already have been made. Before allocating any funds, the budgeter needs to gather together several facts and figures, and must have a clear idea of what he is going to do.

1. Individual or family goals identified.   What are our goals? What goals are to be given priority? These questions must be answered before any decisions about money can be made. One thing that experience has taught countless families is that budgets work best when they lead to the achievement of family wants.

2. Available resources assessed.   What funds are available now? What funds will be available over the next several months? It is necessary, as indicated in the *Family Money Manager*, to know how much income will be received, when it will be paid, and for how long a time it must serve—a week, two weeks, a month, a season?

3. Current use of money estimated.   Before further planning can be done, *financial records* of some kind may be needed; sheer guesswork is usually not a very satisfactory basis for serious planning. If no records are available, it will be helpful to keep an account of daily expenditures for a month or two. This record will then give the "planning board" in the family an idea of what funds are necessary for day-to-day living and of where expenditures might be curtailed. The records you keep need not be accurate to the last penny, but they must be honest, otherwise you are only fooling yourself. If you are treating yourself to a 65¢ sundae every afternoon, put it down. See for once what your sundaes are costing, and then decide if this is what you really want.

Chapter 12 presents some suggestions for record-keeping. You may wish to refer to it for ideas on keeping simple accounts. These accounts, which need not be complicated or detailed, will be invaluable when it comes to financial planning and decision-making. From your records you should be able to tell what your fixed expenses are, when these payments are due, and how much money you need for day-to-day living.

4. Income is allocated.   You are now ready to allocate your income. You are ready to decide how much money you will spend for food, how much for clothing, for recreation, for personal upkeep, for allowances, for operating expenses, and for all other necessary expenses. There is no formula or recipe that you can apply; each of these allocations will depend entirely on your particular family situation. Your values and goals come into sharp focus at this point and help to determine how funds will be used.

Like Tom and Lila, this couple can have their stereo if they make it a part of their financial design.

In making allocations for your fixed and flexible expenses, another rule should be observed: *save something*. Even a dollar a week or only 50¢ will add up by the end of the year. Although it appears meager to start with, in time it will amount to something. This savings account will serve as a cushion, easing you over those periods that might normally wreck the budget and cause serious financial problems.

A budget may need to be revised or even replaced.   The first budget you design may not work. In fact, it would be surprising if it did. You may be attempting too much; you may find that you are trying to reach a goal too quickly and, as a result, haven't provided enough money for food or have failed to provide anything for recreation. The happy thing about a budget, however, is that it can be torn up and another one can be developed to take its place. It may be necessary to experiment with two or three before one is finally developed that works. When a workable budget is created, it will be easy to live with, and living within it will become a habit.

Although a budget may be successful for a time, it may not continue to be successful indefinitely. Budgets need tending. They must be kept up to date. Recall the earlier discussion of how each part of a budget is related. With any change in the finances of the family or in the family itself, some attention must be given to the whole budget. As the family grows, more money will have to go for food and clothing; as income increases more may go into a savings plan toward some future goal. As the family decreases in size, other changes in the budget can be made.

FOR DISCUSSION

1. In designing a budget, what must one know about himself first?
2. What is the difference between financial records and a budget?

GOOD CONSUMER HABITS HELP MAKE A BUDGET WORK

Five rules help the budget become a useful tool for family money management. These rules relate to one's behavior as a consumer.

*Advance planning—preparing and sticking to a list—
helps the family shopper avoid extra spending at the
supermarket; and saves time, too.*

1. Develop shopping skill. Shopping centers and supermarkets are wonderfully exciting places; thousands of goods line the shelves and invite attention. It takes skill and determination to pass down the aisles and resist temptation. The skillful shopper prepares her shopping list before she goes to the market; she buys only those items she needs and can use. She has learned to read labels and to interpret them; she understands the differences among the various cuts of meat; she knows what to substitute for the higher priced items, and when. She can judge the value of the week's bargain offerings and is able to decide whether the "best buys" are best for her family. Careful shopping can save several dollars a week in the budget.

2. Curb impulse buying. Everybody is tempted now and then to go on a shopping spree and to buy something on impulse: a new kitchen gadget, or a new blouse or handbag, or a steak for Thursday's dinner. To give in to these impulses once in a while may be a healthy response to one's mood or to a special occasion. But when impulse buying is a habit, when it takes place on every trip to the supermarket or department store, then it can do real damage to even the best of budgets and financial plans. It is even worse if something bought on impulse has no use after it is taken home.

3. Use installment credit sparingly. In the chapter that follows, consumer credit will be discussed in detail. For now, it is enough to recognize that any installment purchase or loan means one more fixed expense in the budget. Although credit of this kind is readily available, and many items can be obtained on credit, it is best to be wary of the "dollar-down-and-dollar-a-month" offers. There will be times when installment purchases are unavoidable, but this kind of spending, if excessive, can become a costly way of providing for family needs or for achieving family goals.

4. Take care of the goods you already possess. Clothes last longer and remain better looking if they are kept clean and pressed. Food lasts longer when it is properly stored. Equipment lasts longer and gives better service when used according to the manufacturer's instructions. It makes sense to prolong the use of one's possessions by taking care of them; the longer we can use an article, the more we are getting for our money.

5. Learn to use other resources in place of money. It is very easy to rely entirely on financial resources for all of the goods one wants and needs. But this kind of thinking and living places a very heavy burden on the family income and often postpones the day when a goal can be achieved. By developing skills among family members, however, and by substituting for money one's time, energy, and skill, many services can be provided at home without dipping into the family funds. This kind of planning and achieving often provides far greater satisfaction, too, than does the routine of shopping and buying.

Spending money to get the most out of it is something you will have to work at, just as you will work to earn it in the first place. You have already picked up some ideas on spending money—test yourself and see how you rate as a spender:

- Do you put first things first when you make purchases, buying what you need or want the most before you buy something else?

- Do you shop in more than one store to compare the price and quality of a particular item you want?
- Do you resist the temptation to buy something just because it is on sale or just because it appeals to you at the moment, when there are other things you need more?
- Do you look for quality rather than just cost or appearance when you buy something that you can expect to last a long time?
- Do you save sales slips, guarantees, and other records of purchases so you know where to find them?
- Do you buy at stores you know are reliable?
- Do you read the labels on boxes, packages, or other purchases to determine the real quantity or quality you are getting for your money?
- Do you put money aside to save for something you want but can't afford at the moment?

All of these questions pertain to one or another of the rules for wise shopping. The more questions you can answer "yes" the higher your shopping IQ.

Whenever you spend money you will want to ask yourself two questions.

Can I really afford it? Is it worth what I'm paying for it?

Whether you can afford the purchase may be a simple matter of addition and subtraction—you have enough money or you don't. But more often it will be a matter of deciding how important this particular purchase is compared to other purchases you may want to make.

Then there are many things you'd like to have to make life easier and more fun. You are not going to deny yourself all of these—after all, life is supposed to be fun as well as work. Indeed, many things that would have been considered luxuries in past years are now considered necessities. But you are going to have to pick and choose according to whatever your particular desires are. The more limited your budget, the more picking and choosing you are going to have to do. That is a fact of life.

The next question: Is it worth what I'm paying for it? This is where spending money becomes a real skill. Worth or value is often hard to determine. Value in this case means the quality of the product itself; it also means the usefulness of the product for your particular purposes. You have to think about both. In determining value, price alone can be misleading. The lowest price may be the best value for your money, but then it may not be. The highest price doesn't necessarily mean the best value either. Usually, you will find the best value somewhere in between.

Generally, when you are buying a product where length of service and performance are important, quality—how well it is made, how well it functions, how long it will last—is the first consideration. Price is, within budget limits, a second consideration. Appearance may or may not be a consideration. If it's a suit or dress, yes; if it's an electric drill, not so much.

If you were buying a product where length of service is not so important—soap or paper napkins, for instance—the lower price is usually the better value for your purposes. Quality is not as important, as long as what you buy does the job to your satisfaction.

A father who uses his skill to fix his son's bicycle instead of paying someone else to make the repairs is indirectly adding to family income.

FOR DISCUSSION

1. What are five consumer skills that can make money more available in the budget?
2. List some ways you could substitute other resources for money in order to secure what you want.

Summary for Chapter 6

This chapter has been about budgets. A budget is a useful tool in decision-making, in providing a systematic and orderly method for managing money, and in providing families or individuals with the means for achieving future goals.

Any financial plan or budget consists of four parts: (1) a statement of income; (2) a statement of fixed expenses; (3) a statement of flexible expenses; and (4) a provision for emergencies and special goals. Savings should be maintained as a fixed expense.

In setting up a budget the important thing is to aim for a budget that will be useful to one's own family. It may be necessary to experiment with several trial budgets for a while before finding the one that works best for a particular family. The process of budget-making consists of identifying goals, assessing family resources, learning how money is used at the present time, and finally, allocating income to meet the needs and wants of the family.

Making a budget work will require the development of good consumer habits: (1) develop shopping skill; (2) curb impulse buying; (3) avoid installment plans; (4) take care of one's possessions, and (5) learn to use resources other than money in providing for some goods and services.

CAN YOU EXPLAIN?

1. income
2. budget
3. fixed expenses
4. flexible expenses

5. emergency fund
6. financial records
7. consumer skill

HOW WOULD YOU ANSWER?

1. Explain how a budget is useful in making financial decisions.
2. Can you explain how a budget will reflect a family's goals and values?

3. Of what use are financial records in budgeting?
4. How can a budget be protected against ruin caused by emergencies or unexpected events?
5. If you had the responsibility for managing the family food money, what could you do to make your funds go further?

OTHER THINGS TO DO

1. Keep a record of your expenditures and income for one month. Prepare a financial plan for yourself. At the end of the month evaluate the plan. Would you make any changes? If so, in what parts of the budget would you make them?
2. Refer to the OCCUPATIONAL OUTLOOK HANDBOOK and look up the beginning salary or wage for the job you expect to pursue. On the basis of this income figure, make a financial plan for yourself. Keep this plan until the end of the unit or course and evaluate the plan again. Make the necessary changes. Is the financial plan realistic? Show how this plan could be adjusted to meet changing needs, such as an operation, unemployment, or an injury making a person physically handicapped.
3. Conduct a survey among classmates not taking this course to see what they think of first when the word "budget" is mentioned. Then ask each person to react to the term "financial plan." Did you observe any difference in response to the two terms? If you did, how do you account for it? Which term, if any, produced a more favorable reaction? Why?
4. Discuss with your friends or classmates the problem of children's allowances. At what age do they think children should be given an allowance? How much? How often? On what basis should the amount be determined? What should the allowance be used for? What guidance should the child be given in using his allowance?
5. Work in groups of two or four and develop a financial plan for a specific family. Share each plan with the class. In what ways are these plans different? Do the plans reflect values and goals? Give examples. What do these plans tell you about the families each group created?
6. Play the game "Financing a New Partnership" (J. C. Penney Company) to become aware of the costs involved in establishing a first home. See how values and goals are reflected in a spending plan.
7. Listen to "I Can't Do the Sum" from *Babes in Toyland* and see how this person was able to balance her budget. Can you think of other songs that refer to money? Discuss the role of money in our lives.
8. Read "One Family's Spending, The First Ten Years" in *Changing Times* (January, 1970) to see how this family chose to spend their money. Discuss this article in terms of the family's values, standards, and goals. How did they use their resources to achieve their goals? How did they make decisions?
9. Find a quotation that relates to another person's philosophy of money

management. Write a short paragraph that expresses your own philosophy and compare it to the statement in the quotation.

10. Interview a case worker or someone who works with families to learn what problems families have in money management, and what services are available to help families plan their spending. What help is provided when families can't live within their income?

11. Select two case studies, (see SPENDER SYNDROME, published by the University of Wisconsin) to see two different family situations in relation to their spending patterns. Discuss each family's plan as it relates to their values and goals. Analyze each plan to see if family needs are being satisfied. Make a list of their resources—those that they are using, and those that they could use. What emergencies could occur to these families? What type of planning do you suggest for them in the future?

12. Read the book MAMA'S BANK ACCOUNT, by Kathryn McLean (Harcourt) or excerpts from it to see how Mama handled the money. Discuss such questions as: Do you think Mama budgeted? Did she have short- and long-term goals? Was her budget successful in relation to her family's needs?

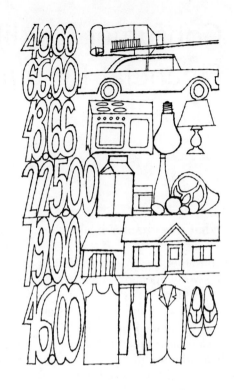

3

Financial Information to Aid in Decision-Making

7 Consumer Credit as a Financial Resource

What this chapter is about

Consumer credit is an American phenomenon. No other nation in the world operates on a credit economy to the extent that the United States does. It is one of the factors that contributes to our high standard of living; credit is as essential to the nation's economy as it is to the individual or family.

Consumer credit has made possible the purchase of automobiles, boats, home improvements, and household furnishings and equipment. It provides funds for vacations, travel, education. Almost anything that is available in the marketplace may be secured through some kind of credit arrangement.

This chapter will examine consumer credit: what it is, how it works, how it is used, and what it costs. Here are the principal ideas you will find discussed:

1. Consumer credit makes goods and services available at the time they are needed.

2. Consumer credit is available in a variety of forms, each at a price.

3. Using credit to secure goods and services adds to their cost.

CONSUMER CREDIT MAKES GOODS AND SERVICES AVAILABLE AT THE TIME THEY ARE NEEDED

Families meet needs in several ways. Families have various ways of obtaining the things they need. For example, Buddy, age 4, has a new snow suit. At least, it's new for him. Last year it belonged to Vicky, next door. Vicky's little brother Sam is wearing Buddy's old suit. By "swapping" snow suits, the two families have acquired needed garments for their boys. Exchanging articles is one way families meet needs, although it is not always convenient or feasible.

Charlie brought home a new record album. It cost him about $5; he paid cash saved out of last week's earnings. Many people meet needs or secure wants by paying cash.

Last Saturday Janet shopped for a new coat. She found just what she wanted at Gray's, and the price was within the range set by her mother. "Charge it," she said as she handed the saleslady a charge card issued by the store. "What an easy way to shop," thought Janet. She had purchased her coat on credit. This way of meeting needs is favored by many families because of its convenience.

Dave bought his "new" used car "on time." He made a down payment and agreed to pay the balance in 18 monthly installments. Elaine and Gordon decided to "finance" their automatic washing machine. They borrowed the money from the bank, agreeing to repay it in equal installments over the next twelve months. The car and the washer were purchased on credit.

What is consumer credit?   If goods and services are secured in the market, money must be paid in exchange. The money is payable either at the time of the purchase or at a later date. It is money that has already been earned or is yet to be earned in the months ahead. When we buy goods and elect to pay for them sometime in the future, we are using some form of consumer credit. Very simply, *consumer credit is the means by which we secure goods or services when we want or need them and pay for them at a later date.*

For most American families credit is an important part of their financial lives. It wasn't always this way, however. Many years ago families were reluctant to "buy now and pay later." Such a practice was the mark of a poor money manager. A good manager would avoid any kind of debt, for the burden of owing money was a fearful condition with which to live. But attitudes have changed; today families look on credit as a valuable asset, and as one of the financial resources available for meeting needs and for maintaining a satisfying level of living.

Why do families use credit?   Chances are, when you buy a car, you will use credit; seven out of every ten new cars are purchased on installment credit. Probably when you establish a home of your own, you will use credit to secure some of your household equipment. The two major purposes for which families use credit today are: (1) to finance the purchase of a car; and (2) to finance the purchase of household furnishings and major appliances such as refrigerators, stoves, freezers, washing machines, and other "big ticket" items.

Another major reason families use credit is to secure the money necessary to pay off old debts. In recent years families have been using credit to pay the costs of sending a son or daughter to college. Credit is increasingly being used for this purpose as college costs rise. Families also use credit to pay large dental and medical bills, to pay the costs of travel, and to buy major articles of clothing. In short, almost everything a family needs or wants is now available on some kind of credit plan.

FOR DISCUSSION

1. Have you had occasion to use credit? Did you feel it was a worthwhile method for securing what you wanted? Why?
2. How would you define consumer credit?
3. How does consumer credit contribute to the family's standard of living?
4. For what purposes is credit most often used by families? For what purposes do students in your high school use credit?

CONSUMER CREDIT IS AVAILABLE IN A VARIETY OF FORMS, EACH AT A PRICE

Credit is readily available. Often families use credit without realizing it. What is more, they may be totally ignorant of the cost of credit. Credit for consumers comes in many forms. Practically every family desiring to use it will find some credit arrangements available to them, provided they are willing to pay the price. Some forms of credit cost more than others. In fact, some plans may turn out to be very expensive.

"Easy credit" is advertised in the newspapers, in store windows, on the radio and television, and through the mail. "A-dollar-down-and-a-dollar-a-week" plans tempt families to acquire the television set, washer, fur coat, sewing machine, food freezer, watch, diamond ring—and all the other goods associated with a "better life." Families living in low-income neighborhoods are easy victims for such schemes. The door-to-door salesman often offers them poor quality merchandise on a costly credit plan, extending payments over many months and even years. In spite of such abuses, credit is not something sinister. When understood and used with discretion, it is an asset that families can count on to help them meet needs and emergencies and to achieve important goals.

In order to understand how credit works and to be able to evaluate credit plans, it is necessary to know something about "interest." In the last chapter we mentioned interest in relation to savings accounts. We pointed out that interest is the money that money earns. We can say also that interest is the fee one pays for using someone else's money.

Banks often advertise that they will pay $4\frac{1}{2}$ or 5 per cent interest on money in savings accounts; or they offer to loan money for home improvements or some other purpose at a given rate of interest. In the first instance if you have $100 in a bank that pays $4\frac{1}{2}$ per cent interest, your money will earn $4.50 at the end of the year, assuming that interest is payable only once a year. (Many banks now figure interest on savings accounts on a quarterly or monthly basis, however.) The bank, therefore, paid you $4.50 for the use of your money. In the same way, if you borrowed $100 at 6 per cent interest, and repaid the loan in a single payment at the end of one year, you would repay the bank $100 plus $6. You paid $6 for the use of the bank's money. These examples of *simple interest* serve to illustrate what interest means.

Any credit arrangement calling for payments over a span of several months or years includes some kind of interest charge. The rate of interest will vary, depending on the nature of the loan or the institution with whom one is dealing. But because a credit plan consists of using somebody else's money, whether it is a bank's money or a store's money, interest will be charged. In addition to an interest charge, there may also be a service charge of some kind, often referred to as a finance charge, which pays the cost of putting the customer on the books, billing him monthly, paying insurance costs if required, and any other fees. It is interest and finance charges that constitute the dollar cost of most credit plans. In evaluating any credit plan, these are the charges you will need to identify. As we examine the credit arrangements most often used, you will observe how these charges appear.

Credit arrangements may be classified into three major groups. Service credit, sales credit, and cash loans are the three major types of credit available to the consumer.

The convenience provided by the telephone is made possible by service credit.

1. Service credit. When you flip on the light switch, or call your friends on the phone, or turn on the flame under the coffee pot, you are using services made available through credit. You use the electricity, telephone, and gas, and then pay for these utilities at the end of the month. It is possible, of course, to use a pay phone and to have a coin box attached to each appliance. But arrangements of this kind would be awkward and inconvenient in homes. Therefore, utility companies provide their services on a credit basis. This form of credit is called *service credit.* Service credit is extended also by doctors and dentists who bill their patients at the end of the month, after treatment has been completed.

Unlike any other form of credit, service credit includes no additional costs. It is used every day and is simply taken for granted. Most people do not realize that many of the services they use involve some form of credit. However, without this functional and practical method of securing essential services, families would be severely handicapped in operating their homes and maintaining their families.

2. Sales credit.   Sometimes called retail credit, sales credit is made available by department stores, appliance dealers, auto dealers, and other sellers of consumer goods. This form of credit enables the customer to obtain what he needs or wants and to pay for it while he is using it. With sales credit the financial transaction is between the customer and the seller. The customer is actually securing goods with the seller's money.

The four most common types of sales credit are: (a) charge accounts; (b) revolving charge accounts; (c) credit card accounts; (d) installment sales accounts.

A *charge account,* such as Janet used when she bought her coat, is favored by many families because of its convenience, whether they are shopping by phone, mail, or in person. A charge account represents an agreement or an understanding between the seller and the customer. In return for the convenience of the account, the customer agrees to pay for his merchandise within a certain number of days following billing (usually 30). A charge account permits a customer to make several purchases at one time; it simplifies exchanging merchandise that may be unsatisfactory; and it provides the customer with a monthly statement that, in turn, is valuable in keeping financial records.

A variation of the 30-day charge account is the 90-day account. This plan permits the customer to pay for an article in three equal monthly payments. No service or interest charge is added to the bill. A 90-day account makes it possible to take advantage of sales or to make a large purchase at a time when cash may be short. For example, the Lawrences used such a plan to purchase a television set that was on sale for $121.95. Mr. Lawrence used a 90-day account to pay for the set. His monthly payments for three months were $40.65 each, exactly one-third of the sales price. No extra charge was made.

Although there is no apparent cost for credit provided through charge accounts, stores that offer this service may charge somewhat higher prices for the merchandise, and they seldom feature discounts except at sale time. In addition to quality merchandise, however, they often offer their customers extra services, such as deliveries and gift wrapping, without charge.

A *revolving charge account* allows the customer to charge only a limited amount, determined in advance by the store and the customer. The limit is based on one's income and credit rating. The customer pays a certain amount on his account each month and is charged interest on the unpaid balance. Sylvia and her husband opened a revolving account shortly after they were married. The limit they were permitted to charge was $300. Once that amount was reached, they could make no further charges. As payments were made, credit became available again, but not in excess of the $300 maximum.

Purchases made on a revolving account will cost more than the price tag indicates. Added to the original price is a finance charge on the unpaid balance each month. Usually this charge is quoted as being 1 or $1\frac{1}{2}$ per cent monthly. Over a year's time, however, the interest rate paid on the account turns out to be 12 or 18 per cent. Thus, $100 worth of merchandise, payable in twelve monthly payments, will actually cost $112 to $118.

A *credit card account,* like the regular 30-day charge account, is a convenience. Like a charge customer, the credit card holder is expected to pay his bill when it is received. But a credit card account has the added advantage of allowing the customer to choose where he will do his business. For example, an oil company credit card makes it possible to buy gas and oil at any of the company's filling stations throughout the country. A telephone credit card permits one to make long distance calls from whatever phone is at hand. These credit card plans are like the department store charge account: the transaction is between the customer and the oil company, or the telephone company. No additional fees are charged if payments are made at the time the bill is received.

An all-purpose credit card, such as those issued by American Express or by Diner's Club, allows one to charge restaurant meals, hotel and motel rooms, car rentals, gas and oil, air and rail tickets, clothes, and many other goods and services. In this case, the credit agreement is between the credit card holder and the issuing agency, and the billing is from the agency. But membership in one of these credit card plans requires an annual fee of $10 or $15.

All-purpose credit cards are issued also by many banks, or groups of banks. The card holder does not have to pay an annual membership fee; to obtain a card one must apply to a bank offering this service. Charges for goods and services are sent to the bank, and the bank in turn bills the card holder. He may pay his account in full each month

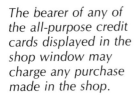

The bearer of any of the all-purpose credit cards displayed in the shop window may charge any purchase made in the shop.

and avoid any extra costs, or he may pay on a monthly plan, for which he would be charged interest on the unpaid balance. Bank credit card plans are similar in operation and cost to cash loans. These will be discussed later.

Installment sales accounts are used for buying big items—a car, new furniture, carpeting, a refrigerator, or an air conditioner. The transaction is between the dealer and the customer, but a financial agency may re-finance the sale, thus relieving the dealer of the debt.

Dave bought his car on an installment sales plan. He made a down payment, signed a contract with the dealer agreeing to make monthly payments for the next 18 months. His payments would include not only the cost of the car, but also the finance and interest charges on the unpaid balance. As it worked out, Dave bought a car on sale for $595. He made a down payment of $195, leaving a balance of $400 to be financed. Dave's monthly payments were $27.80, which fitted well into his monthly budget. However, Dave failed to figure out the total cost of what he was paying to finance his car.

Here are the details of Dave's transaction:

18 monthly payments of $27.80 each	$500.40
Down payment	195.00
Total cost of the car	$695.40
Sale price of car	595.00
Cost of financing on installment plan	$100.40

In spite of the high cost of installment sales accounts, many people use this method of "buying now and paying later." Like Dave, people welcome the convenience of financing their purchase through the dealer. They may think, too, that they receive better service on their equipment as long as they believe they are in debt to the firm from which they bought it. Often, however, the customer is unaware that his debt is actually with a financial agency.

3. *Cash loans.* The credit arrangements discussed so far are agreements between the seller and the buyer, with the exception of all-purpose credit card plans. Another widely used credit plan omits

The wise shopper first learns how much extra he must pay to buy on an installment contract.

the dealer and consists of an agreement between the individual or family and a lending institution. Instead of securing merchandise or equipment on credit, the buyer secures money. Money obtained on credit represents a cash loan.

Earlier we mentioned the couple who borrowed money from the bank to buy a new washer. To be sure, the dealer would have willingly "financed" the sale, but a cash loan gave the couple the freedom to shop around and to take advantage of price discounts that are often given only to cash customers. The kind of loan they obtained was an *installment loan,* so called because it is repaid in equal monthly payments called installments.

Also available are *single payment loans*, payable in one lump sum, plus interest, on a given date. For example, a borrower needs a $300 loan. His bank gives him the money with the understanding that it will be repaid as a single payment in 12 months. The bank charged 6 per cent interest. The cost of the loan was $18 ($300 x 6 per cent interest = $18). This kind of loan is the least expensive cash loan, but it has one big disadvantage. It is difficult for most people to save up the necessary funds for repayment. For this reason most families find installment loans easier to manage.

Where can one get a cash loan?　Cash loans are available from banks, savings and loan companies, finance companies, credit unions, life insurance companies, pawnbrokers, and sometimes from friends and relatives. The advantage of borrowing from a bona fide lending institution rather than from friends or relatives is that the entire transaction is on a business basis. There is no chance for either the borrower or the lender to be offended, nor will the borrower be obligated for anything other than what has been specified in the loan agreement or contract. Furthermore, there is every chance that the loan will be repaid on time, whereas it often happens that people postpone repaying a friend, parent, or a kind uncle.

Banks and savings and loan companies.　Banks and savings and loan companies lend money to persons who can meet their credit requirements. They may grant loans "on signature," which means that a person's signature on the contract is his pledge to repay the loan. Or the bank may ask for "collateral," which is property of monetary value put up to secure the loan. The collateral may be a car or money in a savings account. If the loan is not repaid, the bank will take the car or the savings account funds. *Collateral loans* are usually available at a lower rate of interest than are *signature loans*.

Banks offer a variety of personal loan plans. In addition to single payment and collateral loans, the installment loan is available in convenient forms. One plan that is currently advertised is similar to the revolving charge account. It is called by various names; revolving credit, check credit, and instant credit are typical examples. Such plans permit the borrower to write checks on the bank up to a specified amount. As the borrower makes his monthly payments, his checking account is credited with funds so that he may continue to draw on it as he needs. Interest is charged only on the amount outstanding.

Finance companies. Finance companies specialize in installment loans, most of which are small or modest in size, $100 to $l,000. They serve the person who may not have established a record as a sound credit risk, possibly because he is new in the community or is just starting on a job for the first time. Finance companies take greater risks than banks, and they have more expenses to meet in operating their businesses, because the money they lend is money they have had to borrow from another lending institution. Therefore, finance companies are permitted by state law to charge somewhat higher interest rates. The method of figuring interest charges will be the same as the method used by the banks.

Credit unions. Credit unions lend money only to their own members, who may be the employees of a company, members of a labor union, members of a church, or some other identifiable group. The credit union within an organization is operated by its own members and for the benefit of its members. Expenses are at a minimum, since the credit union seldom has paid employees nor does it have to pay for office space. Therefore, credit unions can make loans at a low cost; if the borrower has a savings account with the credit union, he can obtain a loan for even less.

Life insurance companies. Life insurance companies make personal loans only to policyholders. A person may borrow no more than the cash value of his insurance policy. For example, if your $1,000 life insurance policy has a cash value of $200, the company will lend you any amount up to $200. The company will charge you a simple rate of interest, which is stated in your policy. This rate varies from $4\frac{1}{2}$ to 6 per cent per year. For your $200 loan, therefore, at 6 per cent interest you will pay $12 a year. The loan may be repaid at any time. If it is not repaid, the $200 will be deducted from the proceeds of your policy whenever it becomes payable to your beneficiary or to you. Life insurance loans are the least expensive of all cash loans, but of course

By leaving an article of value at a pawnshop, one is able
to obtain a loan, usually at a high rate of interest.

the amount of money one may secure is limited by the cash value available in his policy.

Pawnbrokers. Pawnbrokers, on the other hand, offer the most expensive of all loans. They charge a very high rate of interest. In order to secure a loan, the borrower must leave something of value—a typewriter, camera, watch, furs, jewelry, musical instrument. The amount of the loan depends on the value of the article one leaves, although the loan will be for less than the value of that article. For instance, if the pawnbroker evaluates your watch at $50, he will lend you about $35, or about 60 per cent of the watch's value. To regain possession of your watch, you will have to repay the $35 plus interest. If you do not repay the loan within a certain length of time, the pawnbroker will sell the watch. Because money is available from other sources at less expense, few people now use pawnbrokers. In spite of their high interest rates, however, they still serve a need. For some people the pawnbroker may be the only source for a legitimate on-the-spot loan.

Loan sharks. These are money lenders to be avoided at all costs. They operate outside the law and, in effect, are bootlegging money at exorbitant rates. Loan sharks operate without state supervision or regulation; thus, there is no control over their practices. Their aim is to keep the borrower in debt for as long as possible, often making it virtually impossible for him to pay off his loan, preferring instead to collect the interest payments indefinitely.

FOR DISCUSSION

1. How does the rate of interest paid for credit make a difference in the cost of the goods or services purchased on credit?
2. What are the three major classes of credit? Which one of these forms has no extra charges or hidden costs attached to it?
3. What is the difference between a charge account and a revolving charge account? Between a credit card account and a charge account?
4. Explain how an installment sales plan works. What happens to the cost of merchandise obtained on this plan?
5. What are the advantages of securing a cash loan from a lending institution rather than using the installment plan offered by the dealer? Which plan would you choose? Why?
6. In your community what are the sources for cash loans? What is the rate of interest these agencies charge?

USING CREDIT TO SECURE GOODS AND SERVICES ADDS TO THEIR COST

Credit costs money. It is reasonable that credit should cost money because lenders and merchants are in business to make money. Most people who use a credit plan recognize that they are paying for the privilege, but few people actually know how much. As long as they can make the monthly payments, they are satisfied that credit is enabling them to have some of the things they want or need.

Before deciding to use a monthly payment plan or before assuming a debt that will extend over a period of time, it is wise to know how much of one's future earnings are being committed. During a period of time when monthly payments are being made, there will be that much less income to spend. When spendable income is just enough to meet living expenses, serious hardship may result if additional monthly payments are incurred. The decision to use a credit plan, therefore, must be based not only on need or desire for an item. It is necessary to consider also the extent to which one can deny himself or his family the use of monthly income that he now proposes to pledge to a creditor.

Know the cost of credit before you buy.   Knowing the cost of credit is an important aid in deciding whether to buy now and pay later. For most people, interest rates are confusing and misleading. In a study by the Survey Research Center, University of Michigan, it was learned that no matter how knowledgeable people might be about other things, most of us are unable to translate the interest charges on outstanding debts into meaningful dollars-and-cents form.[1] Figuring the dollar cost of credit furnishes more understandable information about a plan. The following guide, prepared by the Division of Home Economics, Federal Extension Service, U.S. Department of Agriculture, shows how to figure the dollar cost of credit:

(1) Add all costs. From the total
(2) subtract the cash price of what is purchased, or the money actually received from the lender.
(3) The difference equals the dollar cost of credit.

Example: Stan Norton bought a food freezer priced at $310. He made a down payment of $35 and agreed to pay the balance in 18 monthly payments of $17.50 each.

Down payment	$ 35.00
$17.50 × 18 months	315.00
Total cost	350.00
Cash price of freezer	310.00
Dollar cost of credit	$ 40.00

In this case, Stan Norton's freezer cost him $40 extra because he bought it on a monthly payment plan. He paid $40 for the use of credit.

Credit charges are calculated in several ways.   Lenders each have their own system for determining the charges they will make. Because these vary, it has been confusing for the consumer to shop intelligently for a loan or for an installment purchase. The plans most commonly used are calculated by one of the following four systems:

[1] George Katona, *The Mass Consumption Society* (New York: McGraw-Hill Book Company, 1964).

Simple interest.   Interest on a loan to be paid back in a single pay-ment is termed simple interest. In the illustration on page 135 the in-terest on the single-payment loan is 6 per cent. This means the bor-rower will pay $6 for each $100 borrowed, per year.

Interest on the unpaid balance.   A monthly rate of interest may be charged on the unpaid balance of a loan. For example, on a loan of $100 to be paid in twelve equal monthly payments, 1 per cent in-terest may be charged per month on the unpaid balance. Therefore, at the end of the first month the borrower pays $8.33 (1/12th of $100) plus $1.00 interest (1 per cent on $100). The second month he will pay $8.33 plus 92¢, which is the interest on $91.66, the unpaid balance re-maining after the first payment ($100 less $8.33). Each month, because the balance is decreasing, the interest charges will be less, but for the entire 12-month period the interest rate actually amounts to 12 per cent. Monthly interest rates of 1, $1\frac{1}{2}$, 2, or $3\frac{1}{2}$ per cent sound very low, but these rates are only for one month. The annual rate of interest, ob-tained by multiplying by 12, actually amounts to 12, 18, 24, and 42 per cent per year.

Add-on interest.   Interest added to a loan is termed add-on interest. For instance, $100 is borrowed and the interest charged is $6. This amount is added to the amount borrowed, making the total loan $106, payable in 12 equal installments. With each payment, the debt is decreased, so that at the end of six months the debt amounts to about $53. But the borrower is paying interest on the full $100, although he had the use of it for only one month.

Discounted interest.   Here the interest is deducted from the loan in advance. If interest charges are quoted as being $6 on a $100 loan, the borrower will receive $94 in cash, because the interest is first de-ducted. But he will have to repay the full $100, even though he had the use of only $94.

To eliminate some of the borrower's confusion, and to relieve him of what might be complicated arithmetic, Congress in 1969 passed the Full Disclosure Act—commonly known as the Truth-in-Lending Law. Under this act, the lender must provide the true cost of credit, in writing, to the customer. Furthermore, he must state the cost—the finance charge—in dollars and cents. He must state it as an annual percentage rate also. Let's take an example. Suppose you are buying a tape recorder priced at $110 cash. The dealer offers you a financing plan whereby you can pay for the recorder in 12 monthly installments of $10.50 each. The dealer will show you, in writing, that the dollars and cents amount to $126 ($10.50 × 12). He will then show you the finance charge, in this case $16 ($126 − $110). Finally, he will translate the dollar cost into an annual percentage rate, in this case 11.4 per cent. Knowing this, you, the customer, are in a better position to shop around and compare costs.

The cost of credit varies.   The cost of credit is determined by *whom* one borrows from, the *amount* borrowed, and the *length of time* for which the loan is made. Consideration is also given to the person's ability to repay, his reputation for paying bills, and the collateral he may offer as security. The greater the risk for the lender, the more costly the credit for the borrower.

But the cost of credit must be examined in another way. We suggested earlier that when one makes a commitment to pay so much a month over a period of several months or years, he is decreasing his spendable income during that time. He will have so many dollars less for other things. For example, Larry bought an engagement ring for Sue on the installment plan. He agreed to pay the jeweler $20 a month for the next 18 months. As a result of that decision, for 18 months Larry had $20 less to spend on his car and on dates with Sue. Therefore, he had to reduce his savings deposits, which meant that he would have less money for furnishing their apartment after they were married. In figuring the cost of credit, Larry had to measure it in terms of what he had to give up.

A good credit rating is a valuable asset.   A good credit rating is like "money in the bank." If your credit rating shows that you are responsible about paying your bills and that you have a good employment record, you can always count on being able to borrow money when you need it. A credit rating is an evaluation of a person's financial record as merchants and bankers know it. It is based on the person's earnings, on his reputation for meeting financial obligations, and on evidence of his integrity and good conduct in the community. His past use of credit will be a clue to what kind of a credit risk he is. If he buys only what he can pay for and makes his payments promptly, his credit rating will be favorable.

A person establishes a credit rating the first time he uses credit in any form. When you open a charge account in a department store you have established a credit rating. Whether your rating will be good,

Opening a charge account is the first step; careful management then follows.

fair, or poor depends on how well you handle your obligations to the store. Your performance forms the record on which additional credit may be secured. Your record with one department store also becomes available to other stores or to lending institutions. Each new credit account becomes part of the record.

In all major cities, and in every state, there are bureaus or associations maintaining credit histories of people who have used some form of credit in the city or state. If you wish to obtain a bank loan or open a charge account, the bank or merchant can learn what kind of a credit risk you are by calling the local credit bureau. If you have never used credit, and therefore have no rating, the bureau will conduct an investigation to find out if what you have stated in your credit application is true. This report is then made available to the store where you have applied for credit.

A good credit rating is a valuable asset for any individual or family. It is worth taking care of, because one never knows when he will need it. Many families believe that a good credit rating is one of their most valuable assets.

THE FOUR C'S FOR CREDIT

Character: your personal traits of honesty, sense of responsibility, signs of good judgment; your reputation in the community.

Capacity: your ability to repay.

Capital: your financial resources that may serve as collateral.

Common sense: your ability to use credit wisely.

FOR DISCUSSION

1. Why does credit cost money?
2. Explain what is meant by the dollar cost of credit. How do you compute it?
3. Explain the difference between "add-on interest" and "discounted interest."
4. What is the basis on which credit is established?
5. Explain what each of the four C's for credit means.

Summary for Chapter 7

Credit, when carefully used, permits a family to raise its level of living. By using credit a family can obtain goods and services that add comfort and convenience and that enrich the quality of life for the family members. When misused, however, credit may also cause severe financial problems and hardships.

Credit costs money. It is reasonable that it should because in using credit we are using somebody else's money. It is the responsibility of the person using credit to decide if his purpose for it warrants the cost he pays for the privilege. He has the further responsibility for selecting the credit arrangement that best serves his need at the most economical price.

The cost of credit must be considered in another way. When a family assumes a series of monthly payments that are to continue for a period of many months, it means that the family gives up the use of a portion of its spendable income during that time. In calculating the costs of credit, therefore, some attention must be given to what the family will have to forego during the period when monthly installment payments are being made.

The value of establishing and maintaining a good credit rating cannot be overemphasized. No one can foresee when he may need to obtain a particular item or service essential to family welfare. If one's credit rating is favorable, he will have no problem providing for his family's special needs. On the other hand, a poor rating may stand in the way of the best interests of his family. Credit, therefore, is a financial asset—an important financial resource intended to serve families and individuals in meeting needs and in achieving goals.

CAN YOU EXPLAIN?

1. service credit
2. simple interest
3. charge account
4. installment plan
5. collateral
6. signature loan
7. credit union
8. asset

HOW WOULD YOU ANSWER?

1. Considering how much it costs, why is consumer credit a valuable financial resource for families?
2. Why is credit an important factor in the national economy?
3. What is the difference between installment sales and installment loans?
4. What are some of the things a family must consider before buying on the installment plan?
5. In figuring the cost of credit, what must be considered in addition to the dollar cost or interest rate?

OTHER THINGS TO DO

1. Interview your grandparents or some elderly residents in your community to learn about the credit practices of families forty or fifty years ago. Was credit readily available at that time? What forms of credit were commonly used? What were people's attitudes in those days about going into debt?
2. Find out what the sources of credit are in your community. What are the rates of interest charged in each instance? On what basis do each of these agencies extend credit?
3. Make a list of the questions you would want the interviewer of a lending institution to answer before you entered into a credit agreement with the institution.
4. Find out if credit is available to teenagers in your community. If so, on what basis is it available? Is the amount of credit limited? Must parents enter into the credit arrangement also?

5. Obtain some credit applications from department stores and lending institutions. What kind of information is requested? Why is this information necessary in determining whether credit will be given?
6. Relate what the consequences may be if one fails to live up to his credit obligations. What does it mean if one's wages are garnisheed? What does repossession mean? What is bankruptcy?
7. List four things for which you would be willing to use installment credit. Give your reasons. List four things for which you would not use credit. Why? What do your lists suggest to you about your values?
8. Find as many advertisements as you can on credit and bring them to class to determine how extensively credit is advertised. Are you surprised at the large volume of credit advertising? Why? To what emotions and concerns of people does this advertising appeal? Do the advertisements give sufficient information to make rational decisions? If not, what other information is needed? What reasonable alternative to using credit can you suggest?
9. Make a chart of the four C's for credit and list under each one several words that you think describe it well.
10. Look through the yellow pages of a telephone book to find the many different types of lending agencies. Select one type and investigate the various lenders. For example, find out to whom they extend credit and what it costs. Compile a table showing the different lenders and how they differ.
11. Interview a resource person from a credit agency to find out what happens when an individual cannot meet his credit obligations. Find out what kind of help is available when a family or an individual is in a financial crisis. Find out the problems that face someone who is trying to improve a poor credit rating. Secure specific information.
12. See the film "The Owl Who Gave A Hoot" (OEO) to discover the problems of consumers in low income areas. What are some of the problems low income families face in obtaining credit from legitimate sources? How and where can low income families obtain credit?
13. Review some recent state and federal legislation related to the use of credit. Consider the advantages and disadvantages to the consumer, to the creditor, and to the economy.
14. See the filmstrip "Truth in Lending" (Federal Reserve Bank) to identify federal efforts to protect the consumer.
15. Visit several stores to find out what types of credit are available to the consumer. Contrast a regular charge account with a revolving account, and contrast a revolving account with an installment plan. List the advantages and disadvantages of each type. What is cycle billing? Why have some stores adopted this procedure? What factors determine one's ability to open a charge account? What is a credit card? What are the types of credit cards available? What are the advantages and disadvantages of using credit cards? What happens when you lose one?

8 Meeting Family Needs for Shelter

What this chapter is about

Among the many problems families must solve, the problem of housing is one of the most pressing. It is a problem that is seldom settled once and for all because housing needs change over time. Families change their minds about where they want to live, or conditions arise that cause them to move. The problem is further complicated by its costs. Thus, finding suitable shelter becomes a time- and money-consuming concern. This chapter will examine this problem and will isolate those factors a family might consider in making housing decisions. These are the major points to be discussed:

1. Housing varies among families and within the lifetime of a single family.

2. Both renting and buying have advantages and disadvantages.

3. Buying a home is a major financial undertaking.

4. Important additional costs of home ownership are insurance and taxes.

HOUSING VARIES AMONG FAMILIES AND WITHIN THE LIFETIME OF A SINGLE FAMILY

Although shelter is a need common to all families, it comes in many forms, shapes, and sizes. What is home to one family may well stagger the imagination of another. American families live in split-level, ranch, and Cape Cod houses, as shown in magazines and movies. They also live in many other kinds of housing.

A survey of housing in the United States would show that people live in adobe huts, high-rise apartments, row houses, mobile homes, and garden apartments. There are families living in converted barns, railroad flats, plantation mansions, hotel kitchenettes, rambling frame houses of the Victorian era, and converted streetcars. Houses for America's families are as varied as the people living in them.

From such a list, it would be difficult to generalize about housing in the United States. It could be said, as a general rule, that farm families live in houses and families in large cities live in apartments, or more accurately, that *some* city families live in houses but many other families live in apartments. The most that the list would tell is that housing in the United States varies in kind and quality.

It might also be assumed that there is housing for everybody, but unfortunately such an assumption would be misleading. In spite of the variety of housing, much of it is inadequate; 22 million people were

A house is in the making and a family dream comes true.

living in congested slums in the early 1960's. These slums are to be found in both city and country in all parts of the United States.

In 1970, about 64 per cent of American families lived in houses that they owned or, at least, on which they were making mortgage payments. Home ownership is part of the American Dream. Regardless of how inadequate the house may be, we may prefer to own it ourselves. To own a home is one of the major goals of most young families.

Housing is the largest item in the budget for most families. When a comparison is made between total family income and the expenditures for housing, the proportion of income devoted to shelter turns out to be, on the average, anywhere from 20 to 30 per cent. This fact is true of families who own their houses, of those who rent, those who live in public housing, or those who live in slums or suburbs. Low-income families pay a larger proportion of their income for housing than do high-income families, although in dollar amount the opposite is true.

Despite the fact that a large portion of family money must go for housing, most families have had to make compromises between what they want in housing and what they can afford. Seldom can a family afford its "dream house." Instead, families look for the house or apartment that comes as near to meeting their needs and their desires as their pocketbook will allow.

Housing needs change as family needs and wants change. The solution to the problem of housing is seldom final. Not often does a family live through its lifetime in the same house in which it started. The family homestead is no longer home for several generations of a family, as it was in an earlier era. Today American families are typically mobile, and as a result they make many changes in their housing arrangements.

Take, for example, Ann Kuchel. She grew up in New York City in an old established German neighborhood. The buildings were old and many of them were becoming dilapidated and run-down. Before Ann had finished high school, the building in which she and her family lived had to be vacated to make way for a re-development project. The Kuchels moved to another apartment house in the same neighborhood.

After finishing high school, Ann went to work as a typist for a large bank. There she made several friends, including Sue and Clara, who had just rented a furnished apartment. They were looking for a third

A young couple's first home may be a small apartment,
but it gives them the space they need for the time being.

girl to share the apartment with them in order to reduce expenses.
Ann moved in with Sue and Clara and lived there for a year, at which
time she and George were married. They found themselves a two and a
half room apartment that consisted of a living room, bedroom, kitchen-
ette, and bath. The rent included gas and electricity. Although there
wasn't much room in which to move around, they were pleased with
their apartment. It was home to Ann and George for three years. Even
after the baby was born, they were able to manage in spite of the

small space, although they were beginning to feel somewhat crowded. As long as the baby was too young to crawl or walk, two and a half rooms could hold the three of them.

They knew the day was coming, however, when they would have to find more space. They finally found and bought a two-bedroom house with living room, kitchen and bath, plus a carport and a few feet of lawn. Here they lived for the next seven years. By then their family numbered five. The two little girls shared the large bedroom, the son had the little bedroom, and Ann and George slept in the living room.

Eventually they needed more space. By now Ann was beginning to feel like a gypsy because she had moved so often. This time the family bought a new house in a development nearby, with three bedrooms, a family room, a living room, two bathrooms, a kitchen and a garage, plus a larger yard in which the children could play. It seemed like a lot of house at first. By the time the children were in high school, however, Ann felt as crowded as she had in the two and a half room apartment. She knew it wouldn't be this way long; in a few years the children would be leaving for jobs and establishing families of their own. When that day came, the three bedrooms, the family room, and all the other rooms were more living space than Ann and George needed or wanted. Once more they moved, back to a two-bedroom apartment not far from George's job. The housing cycle was complete; apartment to little house to bigger house to apartment. From renting to owning to renting.

Mobility of this sort is not unusual for families in the United States today. According to the U. S. Census Bureau, between 1948 and 1970 about 19 per cent of the population has changed residence every year. The move may only be from one block to another, or from one neighborhood to another; it is equally common for families to cross state lines or to move from one part of the country to another.

This mobility typical of American families can be attributed to several factors: (1) people seek better housing as their income improves; (2) housing needs change as the family changes; (3) job responsibilities cause families to be transferred from one plant or business center to another; (4) families seek better working and living conditions; (5) neighborhoods deteriorate so families choose to leave.

FOR DISCUSSION

1. What kind of housing is prevalent in your community? Do most families live in houses or in apartments? Are there slums located

near you? Would you say that housing is adequate for families in your neighborhood?
2. Considering the United States as a whole, do the majority of families appear to rent or to own their houses?
3. What portion of the family budget, on the average, is spent for housing?
4. What changes occurred in Ann's life that caused her to move so often?
5. What are the reasons why families move?
6. How many members in your class have lived in the same house all their lives? Of those who have not lived in the same house, how many times have they moved? For what reasons? Do these reasons agree with the reasons listed in this chapter?

BOTH RENTING AND BUYING HAVE ADVANTAGES AND DISADVANTAGES

The story of Ann and George illustrates another fact about how families meet their housing needs. At certain times they rent housing and at other times they own it. American families either rent the space in which they live or they buy it. There are some exceptions, to be sure. Families of clergymen often live in rectories or parsonages that are furnished by their congregations; military families may live in housing furnished by the government; some families live in housing that is provided by their employers—building superintendents, for example. Other than these exceptions, however, most families have to pay for their housing either in rent or as mortgage payments.

No one kind of housing is best for all families. Often the question is asked, "Which is better, to rent or to buy?" This question has no answer that will serve all families at all stages in their lives, however. For one thing, some families have no choice but to rent whatever space they can find, regardless of how inadequate. Other families prefer to rent rather than to own, as a matter of personal taste. Other families live in areas where the availability of rental property is so limited they have no choice but to buy. So the answer to the question of which is better becomes complex.

If the answer were based on what most families in the United States *do*, then one might conclude that owning a home is considered the better way. As we pointed out earlier, about 64 per cent of all families buy rather than rent. On examination, however, we might discover that for many of these homeowners, the better way would be to rent. With a house, problems of upkeep may be burdensome, or the location may not be convenient or satisfactory, or the monthly payments combined with the operating costs may be taking too large a portion of the family income.

Nor can the answer be based on the costs of owning as compared to renting. First of all, such a comparison is difficult to make. For one thing, comparable spaces are seldom being compared; rather, comparisons are made between a house and a lot, and an apartment. Furthermore, some of the costs related to both methods of paying for housing may be omitted, and if only the monthly rent versus the monthly mortgage loan payments are considered, owning may seem to be less costly. The true picture will not be obtained until added to the mortgage loan payments are the annual taxes on the property, the painting and repairs needed from time to time, and the other expenses that may be necessary for homeowners in a given community. Such costs may be for garbage removal, special street paving, or other civic improvements. With all of these extra costs added in, renting might appear to be more economical. But there is a tax advantage that exists for families who own their own homes. They are permitted to deduct from their income tax all property taxes and all the interest they pay on their mortgage loan. So the answer to the question of which is the better way, renting or owning, must necessarily be determined by something other than dollars and cents.

The question may have a more meaningful answer if housing needs are related to the stages in the family life cycle. For the single adult, newly married couple, or older people, renting is often more suitable for several reasons. These people have less need for space. Young marrieds often cannot afford to buy and at the same time to furnish a house. Renting also gives a couple an opportunity to look over a community to see if they want to live there permanently and in what neighborhood they want to locate. For older people an apartment often represents considerably less work and less responsibility.

There are advantages both to renting and to buying, as well as disadvantages, and the question must be answered by each individual family on the basis of its preferences, tastes, needs, interests, and most important, its values. There are people who could never be lured into buying a house, and there are others who could never be convinced that renting has advantages. Each family has to make the decision for itself.

*An older couple, whose children have grown, free them-
selves of the chores of home ownership by moving to a
comfortable apartment.*

What is involved in renting?   To rent a house or an apartment means
living in property owned by someone else—a landlord. You are responsible for paying a certain amount of money to him each month in
exchange for the housing. You probably will be expected to sign a *lease*
at the time you rent the dwelling. A lease is a contract between you
and your landlord specifying the amount of money you must pay, what
your responsibilities and obligations are as renter, and what the landlord's obligations and responsibilities are. The lease may cover one,
two, or three years.

Your rent, as stated in the lease, may include gas and electricity. Certain appliances such as a stove and a refrigerator may be included as part of the place you are renting. It is also possible to rent completely furnished houses and apartments.

Renting a place to live has definite advantages.

1. The renter is free to move. If he is transferred to another place of work or if he and his family choose to change residences, they may do so without the added problem of selling a house. Moving simply means packing one's personal belongings and departing. The renter, too, is often more free to come and go for extended periods of time without having to consider the maintenance of his dwelling. The apartment renter in particular is not responsible for the general upkeep of the property.

2. The renter has no maintenance bills. If a pipe bursts, or if the roof leaks, or if a stair step is loose, the bills are the landlord's, not the tenant's. In most cases the renter only notifies the landlord that repairs are necessary, and it is the landlord's responsibility to see that they are tended to.

3. The renter enjoys an ease of living, particularly if he is an apartment dweller. In the summer he doesn't have to push the lawn mower every week. In the winter he doesn't have to shovel snow.

Renting has its disadvantages.

1. Available rental property may be limited or of poor quality. In many communities the number of houses or apartments for rent are few because there is little demand for such housing. What is available may be in poor condition or in an undesirable location.

2. Renters must often put up with the whims of the landlord. If the landlord says "no pets," the family will have to get along without a dog or other animal. Or the landlord may be slow about fixing things in need of repair, thereby inconveniencing the family.

3. Renters are seldom allowed to make alterations in a house or apartment. In a rented dwelling it is usually a matter of accepting the space as it is, even though removing a wall might improve its livability and provide better utilization of space.

4. Renters of apartments may have to endure the annoyance of neighbors' radios, parties, quarreling, and the other loud noises that penetrate thin walls.

5. Renters of apartments often feel crowded. Not only is the space

within an apartment limited, but often there is little space outside the apartment building other than the public sidewalk or street.

What is involved in owning?   Becoming a homeowner is a complex process, involving much time, as well as money, and requiring many decisions. For that reason it is important to know in your own mind that this is what you want to do. As with renting, owning a home has its advantages and disadvantages; these must be weighed in light of the family's goals and needs.

Owning a home has certain advantages.

1. Homes occupied by owners are usually in the better areas of a city or town. The neighbors are all homeowners, too, and usually take good care of their property, which helps to maintain the appearance of the area.

2. Buying a home represents an investment. The monthly payments on the mortgage loan build an *equity* in the house. Equity is the money value of property on which no debts are owed. Owning property is therefore a form of savings. Should the family wish at some time to sell the property, they will recover the money paid on the loan and possibly more if real estate values have risen. A renter can never recover any of his monthly payments.

3. Owning a home represents a tax advantage. The home owner is allowed to deduct from his income tax each year the property taxes on the house and also the interest on the mortgage loan. These deductions represent a major tax saving for most families.

4. The homeowner usually has more space and more privacy than the apartment dweller. Furthermore, it is his space; he can use it as he and his family wish.

Home ownership also has some disadvantages.

1. Owning a home can be expensive. Maintenance and repairs on a home cost money. Property taxes, insurance, and sometimes special assessments may come to several hundred dollars each year.

2. The homeowner may have to sell his house at a loss. If he is transferred to another community because of his job, for instance, he may have to dispose of his house hastily and at a time when real estate values are down.

3. Homeowners can become slaves to their property. Taking care of a house and yard is time-consuming and sometimes back-breaking.

Along with the advantages of owning a home go certain disadvantages—like the time and expense needed for upkeep and repairs.

The care of a lawn can use up one's weekend and interfere with golfing, fishing, picnicking, and trips. Cleaning, washing windows, polishing floors, refinishing a room, or meeting emergencies such as a leaky roof or a failure in the heating system—these can be tedious chores, as well as plain hard work.

FOR DISCUSSION

1. What are the advantages of renting a place to live? What are the disadvantages?
2. In your community would it be desirable to rent?

3. What advantages does owning a home offer? What are the disadvantages?
4. What factors need to be considered when deciding whether to rent or to buy?

BUYING A HOME IS A MAJOR FINANCIAL UNDERTAKING

Whether a family can afford it or not, the urge to own a house is strong and forceful. Once the house is purchased and the family has moved in, a major goal has been achieved. Probably a home represents the most important investment a family will ever make. The commitment extends over many years and may greatly influence the use of money for other family expenditures and savings plans. Buying a home, therefore, needs consideration on levels other than sentiment and emotion.

Know what you can spend.   The first question to answer in the process of becoming a homeowner is, "How much can we afford to pay for a house?" No one can answer this question for you, but some general rules have been suggested.

One rule that may serve as a guide is that a family should not spend more than 25 per cent of its income, after taxes, on housing. In other words, if a family's take-home pay amounts to $400 per month, the most the family should plan to spend on housing is $100 each month. This amount should include not only the monthly payments, but the costs for utilities, insurance, taxes, and maintenance as well.

Another rule that may be of help is that a family should not purchase a house that costs more than two and a half times their annual income. Thus, if its income per year amounts to $10,000, a family can afford a $25,000 house ($10,000 x 2½). This rule provides a clue to the price range that is reasonable.

Rules can only be guides, however. What a family decides it can spend for housing will depend on what assets it already has, what debts are outstanding, what plans the family has for the future, the stability of its income and expectations for an increase, and the kind of life the family members want to live. Real estate specialists and people who handle home loans for banks, savings and loan associations, and insurance companies agree that the biggest danger in owning a home and enjoying it is that of taking on a greater financial obligation than one can afford.

After a family has decided how much it can spend each month for housing and what it can safely make as a down payment, the family is ready to determine what price house will fit its budget. The Osbornes went about estimating the price they could afford to spend for a house in just this way. Fred and Mollie Osborne had a monthly income of $575 after taxes. They had accumulated $3000 in savings and planned to use $2000 as a down payment on the house they would eventually buy. They studied their monthly expenditures and knew that the most they could pay for a house would be $125 a month. From their banker they learned that a monthly payment of $125 would secure a twenty-year loan at $7\frac{1}{2}$ per cent interest, in the amount of $15,520. Adding the $2000 down payment, they could afford and were in a position to buy a $17,520 house. The Osborne's banker used a table similar to the one below, which shows twenty-year loans.

Maximum Loans for Twenty Years Determined By Size of Monthly Payment

Monthly Payment	7 Per Cent Interest	$7\frac{1}{2}$ Per Cent Interest	8 Per Cent Interest
$ 50	$ 6,450	$ 6,210	$ 5,980
80	10,320	9,930	9,560
100	12,900	12,410	11,960
125	16,120	15,520	14,940
150	19,350	18,620	17,930

What to look for in a house.   Once they knew what they could afford to spend safely, Fred and Mollie shopped for houses in the $17,000 to $18,000 range. Price was only one consideration, however. There were several other factors that had to be considered, each of which influenced where they would look and what house they could buy.

   1. The neighborhood.   There needed to be an elementary school within walking distance from home; they wanted a conveniently located shopping center, nearby recreational facilities, and a church. They were hopeful, too, that they would find neighbors with whom they could feel "at home."

2. The community facilities. Public transportation was necessary within a short walk from the house; there needed to be water, sewers, fire and police protection, good street lighting, and garbage collection.

3. The space. The Osbornes wanted a house having a minimum of two bedrooms, with an opportunity for conveniently adding a room later on. The yard had to be large enough for a garden and play space for two children; a garage and storage facilities were needed for a car, bikes, wagons, a lawnmower, storm windows, ladders, and an outboard motor.

In choosing a location, a family must consider the availability of schools and transportation.

The Osbornes might also have studied the Checklists on the following pages to help them determine the housing features that were most important to them. Then when they were house hunting, they could make a point of looking for those features.

In addition to all of these considerations, the Osbornes might also have thought about these questions, each of which is important to the home buyer:

Is the property likely to increase in value?
What are the zoning regulations in the neighborhood?
What additional furniture and equipment need to be purchased in order to adequately furnish the house?

If the house is not a new one, crucial questions relating to the condition of the structure should be considered:

What will it cost to get the house in shape for our family?
In what condition are the wiring, plumbing, heating, roof, and floors?
Does the house need repainting?

The Osbornes had to look for many months before they found a house they could afford and that met their other specifications as well. Once the house was found, the steps toward ownership began.

Buying a house involves some important transactions. Becoming a homeowner involves transactions that may take several weeks or months to complete. We can outline the process as follows:

1. Securing a lawyer. The process of buying a home is as legal as it is financial. The home buyer will need the help of a qualified lawyer at several points along the way. No papers should be signed without first having them examined by the family lawyer.

2. Signing the sales agreement or contract of purchase. Once he has decided on a house, the buyer signs an agreement of his intention to purchase the house. It is accompanied by a cash deposit called *earnest money,* which signifies that he has every intention of going through with the deal provided he can obtain financing. If for any other reason he changes his mind about buying, he will lose the deposit. This sales agreement is one of the first papers he will sign, and it should be carefully reviewed by his lawyer.

3. Arranging for the financing. Since most home buyers can not afford to pay for a house all at once, financing usually consists of a *down payment* and a *mortgage loan.* The down payment is the cash a buyer is able to offer as part of the payment for the house. For most buyers the down payment is modest, amounting to possibly 20 or 25

The purchaser of a house will want to discuss with a lawyer the legal aspects of such a transaction.

per cent of the price and sometimes even less. Down payments should be as large as possible but should not use up total savings—there are other costs coming up. The mortgage loan is the loan from a financial institution covering the balance due after the down payment has been made. The larger the down payment, the smaller will be the amount of the loan. Most mortgage loans today are *amortized loans*, which means the borrower makes a fixed monthly payment that includes the interest on the loan and a portion of the principal, thus reducing the debt month by month.

4. *Preparing financially for the closing.* The final settlement takes place on the day the buyer takes possession of the property, after the financing has been arranged. It is another day for signing papers, so it is necessary to have one's lawyer present. To be signed is the *note*

Checklist for Houses

Outside House and Yard

_____ attractive, well-designed house

_____ suited to natural surroundings

_____ compatible with houses in the area

_____ good drainage of rain and moisture

_____ dry firm soil around the house

_____ mature, healthy trees—placed to give shade in summer

_____ convenient, well-kept driveway, walks, patio, porch

_____ suitable use of building materials

_____ lot of the right size and shape for house and garage

_____ enclosed yard for children

_____ parking convenience—garage, carport or street

_____ distance between houses for privacy

_____ sheltered entry—well-lighted and large enough for several to enter the house together

_____ attractive landscaping and yard

_____ convenient service entrance

Outside Construction

_____ durable siding materials—in good condition

_____ solid brick and masonry—free of cracks

_____ solid foundation walls—six inches above ground level—eight inches thick

_____ weather stripped windows and doors

_____ non-corrosive gutters and downspouts, connected to storm sewer or splash block to carry water away from house

_____ copper or aluminum flashing used over doors, windows and joints on the roof

_____ screens and storm windows

Inside Construction

_____ well-done carpentry work with properly fitted joints and moldings

_____ sound, smooth walls with invisible nails and taping on dry walls; without hollows or large cracks in plaster walls

_____ properly fitted, easy-to-operate windows

_____ level wood floors with smooth finish and no high edges, wide gaps or squeaks

_____ well-fitted tile floors—no cracked or damaged tiles—no visible adhesive

_____ good possibilities for improvements, remodeling, expanding

_____ properly fitted and easy-to-work doors and drawers in built-in cabinets

_____ dry basement floor with hard smooth surface

_____ adequate basement drain

_____ dry, well-ventilated attic

_____ sturdy stairways with railings, adequate head room—not too steep

_____ leakproof roof—in good condition

_____ adequate insulation for warmth and soundproofing

Living Space

_____ convenient floor plan and paths from room to room

_____ convenient entry with foyer and closet

_____ work areas (kitchen, laundry, workshop) with adequate drawers, cabinets, lighting, work space, electric power

_____ private areas (bedrooms and bathrooms) located far enough from other parts of the house for privacy and quiet

_____ social areas (living and dining rooms, play space, yard) convenient, comfortable, large enough for family and guests

_____ rooms conveniently related to each other —entry to living room, dining room to kitchen, bedrooms to baths

_____ adequate storage—closets, cabinets, shelves—in attic, basement, garage

_____ suitable wall space and room size for your furnishings

_____ outdoor space convenient to indoor space

_____ windows located to provide enough air, light and ventilation

_____ agreeable type, size and placement of windows

_____ usable attic and/or basement space

_____ possibilities for enlarging the house if and as necessary

_____ attractive decorating and fixtures

_____ extras—fireplace, air conditioning, porches, new kitchens and baths, built-in equipment, decorating you like

Checklist for Apartments

Building and Grounds

_____ attractive, well-constructed building

_____ good maintenance and upkeep

_____ clean, well-lighted and uncluttered halls, entrances, stairs

_____ reliable building management and supervision

_____ attractive landscaping with adequate outdoor space for tenants

_____ locked entrances, protected from outsiders

_____ clean, attractive lobby

Services and Facilities

_____ laundry equipment

_____ parking space (indoor or outdoor)

_____ receiving room for packages

_____ convenient trash collection and disposal

_____ adequate fire escapes

_____ storage lockers

_____ locked mail boxes

_____ elevators

_____ engineer on call for emergency repairs

_____ extras—window washing, decorating, maid service, shops, doorman

Living Space in the Apartment

_____ adequate size

_____ convenient floor plan

_____ suitable wall spaces and room sizes for your furniture

_____ adequate daylight

_____ pleasant views

_____ soundproof. Listen for talking, plumbing, footsteps, equipment from other apartments or hallways.

_____ attractive decorating and fixtures

_____ agreeable size, type and placement of windows

_____ windows with screens and storms, blinds or shades

_____ good ventilation

_____ easy cleaning and maintenance

_____ attractive, easy-to-clean floors or carpets

_____ furnished appliances in good condition

_____ clean, effective heating

_____ individual heat controls

_____ up-to-date wiring

_____ conveniently placed electric outlets

_____ well-fitted doors, casings, cabinets and built-ins

_____ extras—air conditioning, carpeting, dishwasher, disposal, fireplace, balcony

Reproduced from Money Management, _Your Housing Dollar_, copyright by Household Finance Corporation for the loan, which is a promise to make payments as agreed upon. Another paper for signature is the *mortgage,* which is the legal agreement pledging the house as security for the payment of the loan and outlining what will happen to the property if the borrower fails to make payments. The mortgage is recorded with the county clerk and remains on record until the loan is paid up.

At the closing, the new homeowner receives a title insurance policy to protect him from any loss resulting from a defective *title*. The insurance company has searched all records concerning the property and finds that no other person has any claim on the house or lot. Finally, the new owner will receive a *survey* of the property showing its exact boundaries.

The buyer will pay closing costs, including legal fees, fees for the title search and the survey, for recording the mortgage, and other charges that may have to be included in the bill. These costs usually come to several hundred dollars, depending upon the price of the house and its location.

It pays to shop carefully for a mortgage loan.   Home loans may be secured from savings and loan associations, savings banks, commercial banks, life insurance companies, and private lenders.

Three types of mortgage loans are available: conventional loans, Federal Housing Administration (FHA) insured loans, and Veterans Administration (VA) guaranteed loans. With a conventional loan the home buyer deals only with the lender and pledges his house as security for the loan. Most mortgage loans granted today are of this type. In the case of FHA and VA mortgage loans, the lending institution takes a smaller risk. With an FHA loan, the Federal Housing Administration insures the lender against loss in case of default. For this insurance the borrower pays a small monthly premium. With a VA loan the Veterans Administration guarantees a large portion of the loan, made to a qualified veteran, for no extra charge.

When a prospective home buyer applies for an FHA or a VA loan, the Federal Housing Administration or the Veterans Administration appraises the house to determine a reasonable price and must also approve the lending institution and the terms of the loan. Because of the added security that FHA and VA loans provide, the home buyer is able to obtain a larger loan, with a longer time to pay, and usually at a lower interest rate. On the other hand, such loans take longer to process and may delay the completion of the purchase. Also, the lending institution is not permitted to be as flexible in the negotiation as when the loan agreement is made simply between the lender and the borrower, as in the case of a conventional loan.

The home buyer should make it his business to shop around for his loan in order to find the lender who can offer him money on the most favorable terms. The preferred mortgage loan will be one bearing a low rate of interest.

Interest charges will be included as part of each monthly payment on the principal; the amount of interest adds up to a substantial sum by the time the house is finally paid for. Therefore, three things should be kept in mind when planning the financing of a home: (1) the size of the down payment should be as large as possible in order to keep the amount borrowed to a minimum; (2) the length of time for which the loan is made should be as short as the family can manage; and (3) the lowest possible interest rate should be obtained. The reason for these rules becomes clear when we examine the table that follows.

Monthly Payments on an Amortized Mortgage of $10,000

Term of loan	Interest Rates				
	6%	6½%	7%	7½%	8%
10 years (120 months)	$111.00	$113.50	$116.10	$118.70	$121.30
20 years (240 months)	71.60	74.60	77.50	80.60	83.60
25 years (300 months)	64.40	67.50	70.70	73.90	77.20
30 years (360 months)	60.00	63.20	66.50	69.90	73.40

From the table, note that the longer the term of the loan the smaller the monthly payments. Note, too, that the size of the payments increases as the rate of interest increases. But see in the following table what is actually paid by the end of the loan period.

Sum of Monthly Payments Necessary to Pay Off An Amortized Mortgage of $10,000

Term of Loan	Interest Rates				
	6%	6½%	7%	7½%	8%
10 years (120 months)	$13,320	$13,620	$13,000	$14,240	$14,560
20 years (240 months)	17,180	17,904	18,600	19,340	20,060
25 years (300 months)	19,320	21,250	21,210	22,170	23,160
30 years (360 months)	21,600	22,750	23,940	25,160	26,420

What does this table tell us? It shows clearly why a shorter loan at low interest is a less costly method of financing a mortgage. Keep in mind that the loan is for a total of $10,000. Assuming this loan can be secured at 6 per cent interest, the lender will receive a total of $13,320; the thirty-year loan at 6 per cent, although the monthly payments are less, will pay the lender $21,600. But 6 per cent loans are rare; most lenders charge at least 7 or $7\frac{1}{2}$ per cent interest. From the table, note the difference one would pay for the loan at 6 per cent for ten years, and for thirty years. What happens to the $10,000 loan at 6 per cent for thirty years? Yes, one pays more in interest than was actually borrowed.

It must be pointed out again, however, that all interest charges on a mortgage loan are tax deductible. For home owners this becomes one of their most important deductions, reducing the annual income tax considerably.

FOR DISCUSSION

1. How can one estimate how much he can afford to spend for a home?
2. What should one look for when shopping for a home?
3. What are the steps in the process of buying a home?
4. Explain what is meant by "earnest money." When is this money paid?
5. What three factors should be considered in financing a home?

IMPORTANT ADDITIONAL COSTS OF HOME OWNERSHIP ARE INSURANCE AND TAXES

Insurance may be required to cover the mortgage. Even after the house is "signed, sealed, and delivered," there are other costs to consider. The lender with whom the loan was arranged may insist that the borrower take out some kind of life insurance in the amount of the loan so that the loan will be paid off if he should die. The homeowner, too, may want the same protection for his family. The lender may therefore arrange for such a policy and include the cost of it in the monthly payments. Or the buyer may reserve the right to secure this protection from his own insurance agent.

The insurance agent may very possibly suggest a *mortgage protection policy*. This policy, which is actually a special term insurance policy designed to cover the period of the loan, decreases in value as the amount of the loan decreases. Thus, if a loan is for $10,000 for twenty years, the policy covering it will be for a term of twenty years. At the start it will have a face value of $10,000, but as the loan is repaid, the face value of the policy will decline. Should the policyholder die at any time during the twenty-year period, the proceeds will be sufficient to pay whatever remains due on the loan, and the family will have no further responsibilities as far as paying for the house in concerned.

Like all life insurance policies, the cost of this protection depends on the age of the policyholder at the time he buys the insurance and on the size of the policy. However, it is the kind of protection home-owners feel they must have, and so do the people responsible for lending the money.

Property insurance is required.   The house is now yours—you have just closed the sale. All the papers are signed. You are moving in to-morrow. What if the place burns down? What if there is a bad storm and the roof is seriously damaged? What if it is attacked by vandals? What if someone is seriously injured while on your property? When you stop to think about the things that can happen, the list is alarming. Your lawyer and the lender tell you that what you need now is some kind of property insurance. As a matter of fact, the lender may insist on it. Few families today feel that they can afford to get along without some kind of protection against losses to their property.

One way of providing this protection is through a series of insurance policies: a fire policy, a burglary and theft policy, a policy against storm damages, and a liability policy. In recent years the insurance companies have developed a *homeowners policy*, which covers a variety of risks. This policy is probably the best buy for most families. With one policy the family house and property are protected against losses from fire, storm, accidents, theft, vandalism, and many other hazards. In addition, the policy provides liability coverage in the event that someone other than a member of your family is injured or his possessions are damaged on your property. For example, a caller may trip over a loose brick in your sidewalk and break his leg. Your liability coverage would cover such an accident. Further, the same coverage is your protection in the event that you or a family member cause damage elsewhere. For instance, a child may throw a ball through the neighbor's picture window, or your dog may bite the mailman.

If the homeowner's property is covered by insurance, a fire will not be a total economic disaster.

The cost of a homeowner's policy will vary according to where one lives, whether protection services such as fire and police departments are conveniently available, and the kind of building and the value of the property that is being insured. The annual cost for this policy may range from $50 to $150, depending on these factors. The policy is usually written for a three-year period, but with premiums payable annually.

Another annual expenditure is the tax on the property. Property taxes are levied by the local government and may be included in the monthly payments on the mortgage, in which case the lender assumes the tax payments. This method of paying taxes will increase the size of the homeowner's monthly payments, as would be expected.

The amount of the tax bill will depend entirely on where one lives and on the community services that the tax money provides. If, for instance, the school system is growing rapidly, more tax money will be needed to finance school expansion and increased costs of education. Property taxes are used to pay for police and fire protection, schools, streets, the public library, public parks and recreation areas, and many other services provided for residents in the community. These services are expensive and are becoming more so; for that reason families are increasingly aware of the rising cost of owning property.

FOR DISCUSSION

1. What are the insurance needs for a homeowner? Why is it a good idea to own a mortgage protection policy?
2. Does a renter have any need for property insurance?
3. What are property taxes used for?

Summary for Chapter 8

Meeting the need for adequate housing is not a simple matter. A person is limited by his financial resources in the choice of housing. These limitations usually conflict with the aspirations and values of the family in relation to the house they want and desire. Even with careful planning, the family will most likely have to make compromises with their wants, and still spend a larger portion of income for shelter than for any other item in the budget.

The cost of housing consists of more than the monthly payments for rent or for the mortgage. Operating costs—electricity, gas, and telephone—must be considered; taxes, insurance, maintenance, and repairs add further to the annual housing bill. What a family can afford for shelter, therefore, must be calculated with these necessary extras in mind.

Money spent on housing is seldom resented; the exception to this statement will be those low-income families who are forced by circumstances beyond their control to pay high rents for extremely inadequate housing. The majority of families, however, willingly pay the money designated for housing. It is not mere shelter that is being paid for, but a *home*. Housing, after all, is but the setting in which a home is created.

CAN YOU EXPLAIN?

1. lease
2. equity
3. earnest money
4. down payment
5. mortgage loan
6. amortized loan
7. note
8. title
9. closing costs
10. mortgage protection policy
11. homeowners policy
12. property tax

HOW WOULD YOU ANSWER?

1. What factors need to be considered when deciding whether to rent or to buy?
2. List the factors that you would consider when deciding how much you could spend for housing.
3. Why is a short-term loan usually less expensive that a long-term loan?
4. If you decided to buy a house, for what new expenses would you allocate money in the budget?
5. In figuring the cost of housing, what other expenditures must be considered in addition to the monthly payments for rent or mortgage?
6. Assume you are going to buy a house for a family of four. What are the factors, other than price, that will influence your selection? What things do you consider essential and what are you willing to give up or compromise on? Give reasons for your answer.

OTHER THINGS TO DO

1. Discuss the relationship of the family life cycle to the type of housing needed for the family. Using the family life cycle, chart the housing needs a family might anticipate during its life span.
2. Contact a realtor and learn what it costs to rent or to buy three similar dwellings that he may have available. Which would you select for your family and why? List the factors that you would consider in deciding how much to spend for housing.
3. List the factors that would influence your family's choice of a new home, assuming they were going to move.
4. Read the advertisements in your local newspaper of houses for sale. Make a list of the prices asked for homes of different sizes. Note the different selling features and the locations. Estimate the total cost of one of the houses if purchased with a mortgage loan of $7\frac{1}{2}$ per cent for twenty years.
5. Study the interest rates on housing offered by various lending agencies in your community. What interest rate does each charge for mortgage loans? What are the arrangements for repayment of the loan? What lending agencies grant FHA or VA loans?

6. Find out what the tax rate is on private houses in your community. Has this been increasing over the past ten years? How is the tax computed or assessed?
7. Work in small groups and collect floor plans and pictures of houses that appeal to you. Analyze your pictures to decide what values have been given major emphasis. Also identify the stages in the family life cycle for which each house would be appropriate. Give reasons for you opinions.
8. Ask an attorney about the legal aspects of buying or building a home. Have him explain a mortgage agreement, contract of purchase, title protection, deed, and other legal terms and procedures a buyer must cope with in making property transactions.
9. Invite a banker, FHA representative, and a savings and loan association representative to discuss the types of loans available, sources of loans, the amount one can borrow from each source, down payment requirements, interest rates, and length of loans and special features or characteristics of each type of loan.
10. Collect and study several legal contracts related to housing, such as a lease and a contract to purchase a home. What are the common features on both contracts? What are the features unique to particular documents?
11. Refer to THE 1971 YEARBOOK OF AGRICULTURE, A GOOD LIFE FOR MORE PEOPLE, for information on how space for living will help provide a better living environment.
12. Use the kit entitled "The Home: An Environment for Human Growth" (J. C. Penney Company) to see how homes attempt to fulfill man's social, physical, and psychological needs.

9 Paying the Costs of Transportation

What this chapter is about

The automobile industry is one of the largest in the United States, and the automobile represents one of the major possessions of American families. Transportation costs rank with those for food and shelter as a budget item. This chapter explores the costs of automobile ownership and operation. These are the major ideas:

1. People are dependent on transportation.

2. The costs of operating a car are a significant budget item.

3. The purchase of an automobile is a major investment.

4. Adequate insurance coverage is expected of all car owners.

5. Renting or leasing a car is an alternative to owning one.

PEOPLE ARE DEPENDENT ON TRANSPORTATION

Suppose for a moment that all forms of transportation were stopped for a week. No buses could operate, no trains, planes, subways, taxis, trucks, or private automobiles. City streets and country highways would be quiet, parking lots would be empty, airports would be idle, bus and train stations deserted. Nothing could move. What would it be like for people? What problems would such a transit stoppage create for families?

Possibly you live in an area so conveniently located you can walk to the various places you must go: school, job, shopping center, church, doctor and dentist, and all the other places you go regularly.

Even if you do live within walking distance, the chances are that you don't always get there on foot. One characteristic of Americans frequently noted by foreign visitors is that we seem to prefer riding to walking, even though walking might be better for us. Children ride to school, adults ride to their jobs, families ride to church. They ride to the store, to the medical center or doctor's office, to the park; young people ride to the movies, or to the bowling alley, or to their favorite hangout. It is hard to imagine getting along without some kind of transportation. Indeed, individually and as a society we are dependent on wheels.

For most families in the United States transportation means the family car. In 1970 about 80 per cent of all American families owned a car. Although the United States contains only 5.7 per cent of the world's population, Americans own over 48 per cent of all the passenger cars in the world according to the Automobile Manufacturers Association. Whether we live in very large metropolitan areas or in rural farming communities, a car appears to have a rightful place in the family regardless of the size of the income.

In 1970 cars were owned by 25 per cent of all households earning less than $1,000. As income increased, car ownership did also: 50 per cent of all families earning $2,000 to $3,000 owned cars; 70 per cent of all households earning $4,000 to $5,000 owned cars; 75 per cent of the households earning $5,000 to $6,000 and 92 per cent of all families earning between $7,500 and $10,000 owned cars. Two or more cars were owned by one out of every four car-owner families, or 29 per cent of all the households in the United States.[1] With automobile ownership so prevalent among American families, it is clear that the family car is part of our way of life. To own a car is the aspiration of almost every young person of driving age.

FOR DISCUSSION

1. Why is it said that Americans are dependent on wheels?
2. Who owns cars in the United States? Is car ownership confined only to affluent families?

---

[1] Statistics used in this and the preceding paragraphs are from *Automobile Facts and Figures, 1971,* Automobile Manufacturers Association, Detroit, Michigan.

THE COSTS OF OPERATING A CAR ARE A SIGNIFICANT BUDGET ITEM

For families who have always owned an automobile, the costs of ownership are taken for granted in much the same way as are the costs of food, clothing, and shelter. It is assumed that the cost of living includes the costs of a car, together with the expenses that normally go with such ownership. These expenses amount to a sizable sum of money over a year's time. In terms of actual dollars and cents, it might be cheaper to use some other kind of transportation, assuming, of course, that another kind of transportation is available. However, each automobile owner values the car in the driveway for a variety of reasons—for the freedom it gives him, for its convenience, for the recreational activities it makes possible, and for the satisfaction of having a car of his own.

Because the costs involved in car ownership are sizable and include far more than the purchase price, they represent a significant factor in family money management. Money spent on a car means less money for other things. Knowing what these costs amount to will help the family decide if automobile ownership is something they can afford.

The costs of operating a car total about $1,400 a year. Before its engine will start, a car needs gas, oil, lubrication, and water; only the water is free. Before the car can legally be taken out of the driveway, it must have license plates and the driver must have an operator's license. Before it is economically safe to drive down the street or out on the highway, the owner must have proof that he can financially cover any accident involving injury to other persons or their property; most car owners provide this proof with insurance. Already, without even going any place, the car owner has spent several hundred dollars. Added to these expenses are the costs for repairs and maintenance during the course of the year and, finally, the cost of *depreciation*. With all of these *operating costs* plus depreciation, the car owner who drives at least 10,000 miles will spend over a thousand dollars a year. These costs are itemized in the table on page 182. Notice how costs vary according to where one lives. Why is this so?

One item of expense that needs further explanation is "depreciation." Depreciation is the value a car loses as it ages. Although this expense is a difficult one to determine accurately, it is estimated that a luxury car loses about 50 per cent of its original value in the first two years. If this is so, a car that cost $6,000 when new will have depreciated in value to about $3,000 by the time it is two years old, even though it may have been driven no more than a few hundred miles.

The cost of owning a car does not stop with the purchase
price; the costs of operation, expenses for maintenance
and repairs, and insurance must be included.

Another way of estimating depreciation is to subtract 20 per cent of the purchase price each year. Thus, the depreciation on a car costing $3,000 when new will be $600 per year. Since the cost of depreciation does not involve money out of the pocket as do expenses for gas, oil, and insurance, people often do not include it in their estimates of what their car is costing them. Not until they want to trade in their car for a new one do they realize that the normal wear, tear, and aging have been costing them money. The $3,000 sedan is now, after three or four years of driving, worth only about $1,000, assuming that the car is in good condition.

Additional costs include parking fees and tolls. A car is usually kept in a garage, carport, driveway, or space in a parking lot. Although parking expenses are not relevant to all families, for large-city car owners the costs of parking and housing a car are high. The cost of garaging a car in New York City, for example, will range from $25 to $85 per month; space in an outdoor parking lot will run about $25 a month. For many people, too, there is the cost of daily parking at their place of work. An automobile owner who drives to his job may have to pay $5 or more a week to park his car in a parking lot. The employer may provide parking space for employees, but to use it the driver might be charged a nominal fee, possibly $25 to $75 a year.

Another expense to be reckoned with is the matter of tolls and fees. In some areas, tolls are charged for driving on expressways, through tunnels, and over bridges. In such localities, those fees become a part of the daily transportation expense.

Costs of Family Car Operation for First Year

(A Small U.S. Car Purchased at $2,800)

COSTS	NEW YORK, NEW YORK	JACKSON, MISSISSIPPI	GRAND ISLAND, NEBRASKA
Insurance (no teen drivers)*			
Bodily injury and liability (10/20/5)	$ 229.00	$ 78.00	$ 45.00
Medical Payment ($2,000)	19.00	13.00	8.00
Comprehensive	156.00	67.00	45.00
Collision ($50 deductible)	234.00	107.00	90.00
	$ 638.00	$ 265.00	$ 188.00
Taxes			
Sales and local taxes	$ 196.00	$ 84.00	$ 142.00
Registration (license)	22.50	90.00**	15.50
Driver's license	5.50	5.00	1.50
	$ 224.00	$ 179.00	$ 159.00
Depreciation (20 per cent of the purchase price per year)	$ 560.00	$ 560.00	$ 560.00
Maintenance	$ 100.00	$ 100.00	$ 100.00
Operating costs (figured on the basis of driving 10,000 miles at 2¢ per mile)	$ 200.00	$ 200.00	$ 200.00
TOTAL COSTS	$1,722.00	$1,304.00	$1,207.00

 * Auto insurance rates from Insurance Services Offices, New York, New York.
 ** Includes additional taxes.

In estimating automobile costs, some people figure the total operating and ownership costs at about 10¢ a mile, assuming the average miles driven per year are about 10,000. With service charges, taxes, and other costs going up, 10¢ is probably too low. Thus, this method of estimating automobile costs is rough, but it can be a guide to a potential car owner who wants a general idea of how much to budget for automobile transportation.

FOR DISCUSSION

1. What items should be included when figuring the costs of operating a car?
2. What is meant by depreciation? How do you calculate this cost?
3. Is there a rule of thumb that can be used to determine the costs of car operation per year?

THE PURCHASE OF AN AUTOMOBILE IS A BIG INVESTMENT

So far, the discussion has concerned only the day-to-day costs of operating a car. Consider now the cost of buying a car. For a family making monthly payments on the purchase of a car, the portion of income spent on automobile ownership becomes one of the most sizable items in the budget. Prices for new cars range from about $2,000 to $7,500 or more. The price for a used car can be as low as $50 and as high as $4,000 or $5,000, depending on the make, model, and condition. The cost of a car, therefore, can be "big money."

Families replace their cars frequently. Unlike other major purchases such as washers, ranges, and refrigerators, the purchase of a car is made with the expectation of replacing it before it has worn out. In fact, it is not uncommon for a car to be replaced before it has been completely paid for. One study, in 1965, showed that nearly 40 per cent of the new car buyers in 1964–1965 owned their previous cars less than three years.[2] It is estimated that the average car owner replaces his

---

[2] Alfred Politz Research, Inc., "National Automobile and Tire Survey, 1965," in *Automobile Facts and Figures, 1967*; Automobile Manufacturers Association, Detroit, Michigan.

car every three or four years, making an expenditure each time of $1,000 to $3,000. Assuming that expense is typical, if a family buys a car every four years at a cost each time of $2,000, then over a forty-year period the family will have owned ten automobiles, with a cash outlay for the cars amounting to $20,000. Add to this sum the costs of operation and maintenance estimated at $1,000 per year. In forty years, therefore, the family will possibly spend $60,000 for automobile transportation ($20,000 for ten cars, plus $40,000 for operation and maintenance). If a family replaces its cars frequently, the cost of car ownership may possibly exceed the cost of housing over the lifetime of the family.

Like all major purchases, car buying requires careful consideration. Seldom can a family afford to purchase a car casually or on the spur-of-the-moment. The wise buyer determines his transportation needs in advance and chooses a car that most nearly meets those needs at a price he can manage.

A salesman, for example, who uses a car on his job wants a car with low operating costs and one that will not accumulate repair bills. Therefore, he may buy a new sedan each year, with only a radio and heater as extra equipment. A family of seven living in a mountain area has need for a large car and a rugged one. They select a moderately-priced station wagon. A retired couple needs a car that will haul their house trailer from Michigan to Florida each winter and also furnish them with transportation for the whole year. Each of these families has different needs for a car and different considerations that influence their decisions.

The purchase of a car, whether new or used, represents a major expense and should be preceded by a series of questions:
- What will the car be used for—business, recreation, long trips, local transportation?
- How much can we afford to pay for a car? What can we afford to spend on it per month?
- What body style will best meet our needs—a station wagon, a sedan, a two-door, or a pick-up truck?
- What extra equipment do we need—a radio, a heater, power steering, power brakes, white sidewalls, air conditioning?
- Will a used car serve our needs, or will we be better off to buy a new car that will probably have lower maintenance costs?
- How will we finance the purchase—by paying cash out of savings, by borrowing, or on the installment plan available through the dealer?

The kind of car that an individual or a family finally selects will also be a reflection of their values. Often people select their cars on the basis of the pleasure they derive from driving a particular kind, possibly a convertible or a foreign sports model or a large luxury auto with a variety of gadgets. Although it is no longer a novelty to own a car, its purchase still represents something more than mere transportation for a great many families.

There are two ways to pay for a car.   Families obtain their cars (1) by paying cash saved in advance, or (2) by using credit. Far more families buy their cars "on time" than families who pay cash. Despite the fact that credit charges add to the cost of the car, American families generally prefer to ride now and pay as they are riding. The largest single use of credit in the United States is for the purchase of automobiles.

When a family or an individual is ready to buy a new or used car on the installment plan, they have their choice of two methods of financing: (1) they may borrow the necessary cash from a financial institution, the most commonly used being commercial banks, insurance

Choose a car in terms of how it will be used. This family logically chose a station wagon.

*Financing their new car with a bank loan allows a couple
to shop around for the make and model they want.*

companies, and credit unions; or (2) they may finance the car through
their automobile dealer. Life insurance loans are only available to
policyholders and are limited in amount by the cash value of their
policies; credit union loans are available only to members. Therefore,
most auto financing is done through banks or through dealers. Of
these two sources, most people prefer bank-financed loans; these are
usually, although not always, less expensive than dealer-financed
plans.

Many banks today offer auto loans at a lower rate of interest than are
available on personal loans because the auto is accepted as collateral.
You will recall from Chapter 7 that a collateral loan is one for which
something of monetary value is put up as security for the loan. In the
case of auto loans, it is the car that becomes the security. In addition
to being more economical, a bank loan also permits the buyer to "shop
around" and to buy his car where he can get the best deal or where he
finds the make and model that he prefers. In other words, he can be
more independent as a buyer and is in a better position to bargain with
the dealer.

The advantage of financing through the dealer is that it permits one-
stop shopping; that is, all arrangements for the purchase can be taken

care of at one time and in one place. Some people believe that they get better maintenance on their cars as long as the dealer has an interest, in the form of a loan, on the car. These people might be surprised to know, however, that it is common practice for dealers today to sell the installment contracts they make with buyers to banks or sales finance companies, thus relieving themselves of any financial interest in the cars they have sold.

Auto loans, like any loan or installment purchase, cost money. The price of a car, listed by the dealer at $2,500, is the price when cash is paid; if the car is purchased on credit, add to this price the interest charges on the loan to learn the actual price you pay for the car. Here is how it worked out for one couple. After looking around they finally decided to buy a new sedan listed by the dealer at $2,775, complete with radio, heater, automatic transmission, and power steering. The dealer gave them a trade-in allowance of $850 on their old car, leaving a balance due of $1,925. They borrowed this amount from the bank; their loan was payable at $92 per month for twenty-four months, and by the time the loan was paid off, they had paid the bank $2,208. Financing their car had cost them $283 ($2,208 less $1,925); therefore the car actually cost them $3,058 ($2,775 plus $283).

Dealer's price for new car, including extras and taxes		$2,775.00
Trade-in allowance on old car		850.00
Balance to be financed		$1,925.00
Amount of monthly payments	$92.00	
Number of monthly payments	24	
Total amount of monthly payments ($92 × 24)		$2,208.00
Dollar cost of credit ($2,208 − $1,925)		$ 283.00
Total cost of new car ($2,775 + $283)		$3,058.00

FOR DISCUSSION

1. How is it possible that the cost of car ownership may exceed the cost of housing?
2. What are some of the questions that should be considered at the time a car is purchased?
3. What are the two ways in which families pay for cars?

ADEQUATE INSURANCE COVERAGE IS
EXPECTED OF ALL CAR OWNERS

When Grace O'Toole bought her first car, she was stunned to learn what the insurance would cost. She protested to her father, but he shook his head and said, "Grace, if you can't afford the insurance, you can't afford the car." What he was saying was that no responsible car owner can afford to be on public highways and streets unless he is insured.

No matter how careful a driver may be, accidents do happen, causing millions of dollars worth of damage each year, to say nothing of the lives that are lost and the injuries that are caused. In 1970, over 52,000 people were killed in automobile accidents and over five million people were injured. Here's something for young adults to think about: almost 35 per cent of all fatal accidents in 1970 involved drivers under age twenty-five, although this age group represents only about 22 per cent of all licensed drivers in the United States.[3] This alarming statistic indicates the reason why most insurance companies now charge higher rates for insurance on autos driven by young men under age twenty-five.

Most states today require automobile owners to show evidence that they can be financially responsible for any damages they cause to other people or their property. These damages can be very costly, running to several thousands of dollars. Most families or individuals do not have adequate resources to cover such costs themselves. Therefore, they buy automobile insurance.

Automobile insurance usually consists of four separate coverages. Unfortunately, many automobile owners do not know what their insurance coverage provides. As a result, they have no idea what protection they have or do not have. As long as they are accident-free, their ignorance causes no heartbreak, but when a claim is filed, they are often disappointed and upset.

Automobile insurance is not usually a single kind of insurance, but rather a "package" made up of several different coverages; two kinds of *liability insurance, medical payment insurance,* insurance covering *comprehensive physical damage* to one's automobile, and *collision insurance* are the common kinds of protection included in an auto in-

[3] The Travelers Insurance Companies, Hartford, Connecticut.

Because so many fatal accidents involve drivers under age twenty-five, most auto insurance companies charge higher rates for young men in this age group.

surance policy. The automobile insurance buyer can reduce the cost of his insurance by eliminating some of these, but before making such a decision he should fully understand what he is eliminating. Let us see what each of these coverages provides.

1. *Bodily injury and property damage liability coverage.* Liability insurance is the most essential insurance in the package. It protects the auto owner, members of his family who may drive, or other persons who have permission to use his car against losses involved in injuring or killing another person or persons and against damages caused to other people's property. Without such protection a car owner could be financially ruined for life if he were involved in a serious accident.

Nan and Barry were proud of their first new car the afternoon they picked it up from their dealer. They planned to call their insurance agent as soon as they reached home. On the way from the dealer to their residence, less than a mile, they struck a car entering the highway from a side road. One person was killed and two more were permanently disabled. In the law suit that followed, Nan and Barry were held responsible for the accident. They will spend the rest of their lives paying for the damages set by the court.

Liability insurance is often referred to as 10/20 or 10/20/5 (or $100,000/$300,000/$25,000). These figures indicate what the insurance company promises to pay: up to $10,000 for injuries to any one person, up to $20,000 for all the injuries involved in any one accident, and up to $5,000 for damages to other people's property; or up to $100,000 for injuries to one person, up to $300,000 for all injuries involved in an accident, and up to $25,000 for damages to other people's property. Most states require a minimum of 10/20/5, but many drivers today feel that this coverage does not provide enough protection because the courts have been awarding higher settlements in accident cases.

2. Medical payment insurance. Medical payment insurance covers the insured and his family, as well as any passengers or guests, should they be involved in an auto accident that results in the need for medical care.

3. Comprehensive physical damage. Insurance for comprehensive physical damage covers losses to the policyholder's car that are caused by vandalism, theft, storm damage, hail, falling objects, and other catastrophes named in the policy. It excludes damages caused by collisions.

4. Collision insurance. Collision insurance protects the owner against damages to his own car as a result of a collision with another car, or a telephone pole, or a brick wall, or whatever he may happen to hit. This coverage is usually sold with a *deductible* of $50 or $100, which means that the policyholder pays the first $50 or $100 on any repairs and the insurance company pays the balance. Collision insurance is not required by law but it is usually required by the financing agency, that is, the bank or the sales finance company. Most owners of new cars buy this coverage; owners of old cars that are worth only a few hundred dollars will often not carry it.

The cost of auto insurance is determined by four factors. The amount that you will have to pay for your auto insurance depends on four factors.

1. The amount of coverage you choose. Insurance termed 10/20/5 costs less than policies with higher limits, although the difference is surprisingly low. Collision insurance with a $100 deductible is less expensive than insurance with a $50 deductible.

2. The area in which you live.   Insurance rates are higher in congested urban areas where traffic is heavy than in less crowded areas where traffic is light.

3. The age and the factory price of your car.   Insurance on new cars is usually higher than on old models because the value of the car is greater. Also, the more expensive the car, the higher the insurance rate because of the car's greater value.

4. The ages of the drivers of your car.   As already indicated, rates for insurance on cars driven by young male drivers will be higher.

The cost of auto insurance has been increasing; it is well to recognize why. As the number of accidents increases, the insurance rates go up. The cost of repairs on today's cars has increased, and the settlements in court cases have been rising. In an effort to keep insurance costs down, the insurance companies wage safe driving campaigns. But the real answer lies with the driving public; it is only the drivers themselves who can reduce the number of accidents each year. In 1970, according to the Travelers Insurance Company, 82 per cent of all fatal highway accidents were caused by careless and reckless driving. To encourage

Some insurance companies give special consideration to drivers who have successfully completed a driver education course.

safe driving, some auto insurance companies are now offering lower premium rates to policyholders who have accident-free records. Some companies also give special consideration to younger drivers who have successfully completed a driver education course.

FOR DISCUSSION

1. What is meant by the statement "if you can't afford the insurance, you can't afford the car"?
2. What are the four kinds of auto insurance coverage? Which of these is said to be the most important?
3. What factors determine the cost of auto insurance?

AN ALTERNATIVE TO OWNING
A CAR IS TO RENT ONE

Many people have discovered that they do not have to buy a car in order to enjoy the mobility and freedom that owning a car provides. These people, who must be licensed drivers, rent or lease a car for the period they want or need it. Car rental agencies have become "big business" and may be found in every city in the country and even in some small communities. Renting a car for the weekend, or for a vacation period, or for occasional short daily trips relieves a person of the costs of caring for a car, insuring it, and garaging it. For those people who only want or need a car infrequently, renting one may be their answer.

Cars may be rented by the day, week, or month. Some agencies provide long-term rentals or leases that make possible having a car for several months, or even years. Rates vary, depending on what is provided in the rental agreement and the kind of car that is rented. On a short-term basis, the agency usually offers a car at a daily rate plus a certain amount per mile. The gas and oil are furnished, as well as insurance and maintenance. For example, a renter may secure a sedan for $8 a day and about 11¢ a mile. On such a basis one could rent a car for twenty-four hours, drive it 100 miles, and pay $19. The rental agency may offer special weekend, weekly, or vacation rates also.

Some rental agencies offer cars at budget rates, but the renter buys his own gas and oil. If he is taking a long trip or using the car extensively during the rental period, he will probably save money with such a plan.

FOR DISCUSSION

1. For short-term car rentals, how are fees usually stated? What is furnished the renter by these fees?
2. For whom would you recommend renting rather than buying an automobile?

Summary for Chapter 9

No one who has ever owned a car will deny that it takes a lot of money. Despite the cost, however, the typical American willingly pays the price and continues to be proud of his possession. The price he pays for the satisfaction of having his own automobile is substantial and of course limits expenditures for other needs and wants. The prospective auto owner must decide to what extent he can curtail other expenditures and postpone achieving other wants, knowing that the car will create a continual expense.

The cost of an automobile does not end with the purchase price as do many of the other "big ticket" items we buy. The more the car is driven, the higher the operating costs. Since there is little satisfaction to be gained from possessing a car and not being able to drive it, the car is going to be a meaningful possession to the family only if plans for using it and maintaining it are considered along with the purchase price. Gas, oil, and an occasional grease job do not complete the list of extra costs. Adequate insurance protection, replacement of tires or a new battery, license plates, anti-freeze for cold-weather driving, and minor or major repairs as the case might be—all contribute to the costs of owning a car. Before purchasing a car, therefore, the buyer assumes that he can meet these costs, many of which recur regularly; his assumption is made on the basis of his needs for transportation and his other family needs and commitments as well.

CAN YOU EXPLAIN?

1. operating costs
2. depreciation
3. dealer financing
4. liability insurance
5. collision insurance
6. $100 deductible

HOW WOULD YOU ANSWER?

1. What factors would you need to consider in order to determine whether you could afford to own a car?
2. What are the satisfactions of owning a car that justify its expense? What would you be willing to give up in order to own a car?
3. Why is depreciation considered an operating expense? Do you think it is reasonable to put it in this category? Why?
4. What are two factors that contribute to the increase in auto insurance rates?
5. How does safe driving affect the cost of auto insurance?
6. Why is the cost of insurance greater for male drivers under age twenty-five? Do you believe that it is fair to charge higher rates for these drivers? Why?

OTHER THINGS TO DO

1. List the ways in which your family is dependent on some form of transportation. If your family does not own a car, what do you estimate your transportation costs are per week?
2. Visit an auto dealer and a lending institution to investigate the plans available for financing the purchase of a new car. Did you find any difference in the plans offered by the dealer and the financial institution? Which plan is preferable as far as you are concerned? Why?
3. Find out what registration fees your state charges for a new medium-priced car. What are your state regulations regarding the financial responsibility of drivers?
4. Determine what opportunities are available in your community for renting a car. What are the rates?
5. Assume you are about to buy a new automobile. It is the first automobile you have owned. You have no car to trade. You know you will have to arrange financing, and you also know you will have to make a down payment. The car is priced at approximately $3,000. How large a down payment will you offer? How will the size of your down payment affect the total cost of the car? What insurance coverage will you buy? Why? What will this coverage cost you the first year? In addition to the cost of insurance, what other expenses will you have to meet as owner of the new car? What will the depreciation be on your car the first year?
6. Think about your own transportation problems. Evaluate your real reasons for driving or riding in a car, or for wanting to own one of your own. Consider the cost of a car, either at your own expense or someone else's. In view of these costs, are your reasons for driving still valid?

7. Find articles in current periodicals on the concerns and problems of transportation to become aware that this is a major concern to individuals and families.
8. Contact a representative from the American Automobile Association (AAA) or another automobile association and find out what is actually being done to improve automobiles in terms of safety and air pollution.
9. Arrange for a banker, a car dealer, and a representative from a small loan company to speak to your class. Find out what it costs to buy a car on time and how each of these people would suggest paying for a car.
10. Work in small groups and prepare a report on what it would cost to buy a new car, a used car, a motorcycle, or to rent or lease a car. Be sure to check on factors such as: purchase cost, taxes, extras, operation cost, maintenance, license, and trade-in value.
11. Secure a copy of your state drivers' handbook to become familiar with the insurance laws and regulations in your state.
12. See the filmstrip "Automobile Insurance" (Insurance Information Institute) to secure information on bodily injury coverages, property damage coverages, and the method used to determine the cost of automobile insurance.

10 Protecting Family Income

What this chapter is about

For most families the ability to meet daily needs and to achieve long-term goals hinges on the existence of a steady income. Family health and morale, too, depend on a regular income. Therefore, one of the major problems in family finance is to provide for the economic security of the family in case income is stopped. This chapter explains how most families achieve at least a degree of economic security through life and health insurance, together with Social Security benefits. The five major concepts to be developed are:

1. Families protect income by sharing certain risks through insurance.

2. Health insurance protects against economic loss caused by illness or accident.

3. Life insurance protects against economic loss caused by death or retirement.

4. Social Security, a government-sponsored insurance program, adds to the financial security of most American families.

FAMILIES PROTECT INCOME BY SHARING CERTAIN RISKS THROUGH INSURANCE

Seldom does a day go by that the newspapers do not carry a story of an economic setback that has beset a local family: a home destroyed by fire, an automobile demolished in an accident, a neighbor critically ill in the hospital, or the death of a parent whose children attend your school. Any of these events can cause a severe financial drain on family income. From a practical point of view, few families can sustain such large financial losses. To protect themselves against such possible losses, families buy insurance.

All insurance is based on the same principle—risk-sharing. Through the purchase of insurance families share the cost of the possible economic disasters that may beset them. Previous chapters have explained the functioning of property insurance and auto insurance. You will recall why these kinds of insurance are necessary. Even more essential are two other forms of insurance protection: health insurance and life insurance.

Loss of income can be an economic disaster for a family. Because families maintain their style of living and build their futures on the dollars they earn today and expect to earn tomorrow, loss of income can have tragic results. Such a loss may occur at any time as a result of an illness, disability, or the death of the family breadwinner. Loss of earned income will also result from unemployment and retirement.

Despite the tragedy of a serious illness, disability, or death, and the disruption that comes with unemployment and retirement, the need for food, clothing, and shelter continues. These are ongoing needs that must be met regardless of one's income. In addition, any previous commitments—to make payments on a car, to pay the mortgage, or to pay off other outstanding debts—must be met in order to protect the investment they represent. Finally, any plans for the future, such as those for the children's education, may have to be reviewed and either abandoned or some new provision made to carry them out. Since all of these responsibilities depend upon family income, the possibility of a loss of income must be faced realistically and practically.

An insurance policy will not prevent the occurrence of a disaster. Although insurance cannot prevent disasters from happening, it does ease the financial strain created by such events. That is the major reason people buy insurance—to protect themselves against severe economic losses, the most serious of which is loss of income. For the majority of American families, life insurance and health insurance are the most practical means of covering the possible loss of income due to illness, disability, and death. Life insurance also serves to replace income lost when the family wage earner retires. Life and health insurance, therefore, play an important part in family financial plans because of their role in assuring the continuity of family life in case income is unexpectedly cut off or is threatened by large medical expenses.

FOR DISCUSSION

1. What is the most serious loss a family can experience? Why?
2. What kinds of insurance protect families against this loss?

HEALTH INSURANCE PROTECTS AGAINST ECONOMIC LOSS CAUSED BY ILLNESS OR ACCIDENT

Health insurance is designed to meet two important needs. Individuals and families purchase health insurance for the following reasons:

1. To help pay for hospital, surgical, or medical care needed as a result of an accident or illness.
2. To help provide an income for the family in case income is cut off because of an accident or illness.

Every minute, according to the Health Insurance Institute, 754 Americans are injured or become acutely ill. Fortunately, many of these illnesses or injuries are slight, involving no great expense or time lost from work. Such misfortunes can usually be taken in stride. What most families fear is a serious illness, perhaps running into months or years, an emergency operation, or a crippling accident. These misfortunes can run up staggering hospital and medical bills and become a heavy drain on family income, often causing drastic curtailment of other activities. According to the Health Insurance Institute, expenditures for personal health care more than doubled in the ten-year period 1960–1970: from $125 to $280 per capita. Because most families cannot sustain such heavy financial burdens, nine out of ten persons today carry some form of health insurance.

Health insurance is obtainable from three sources on a group or on an individual basis. *Group insurance* policies, as the term suggests, cover groups of people and are taken out by an employer, a union, a cooperative, or some other kind of organization. Under such plans, each member of the group receives health insurance protection for himself and usually for members of his immediate family. The employer or the organization having the master policy usually pays part or all of the premium. On an individual basis, health insurance is purchased by a person directly from an insurance company and is paid for by the policyholder.

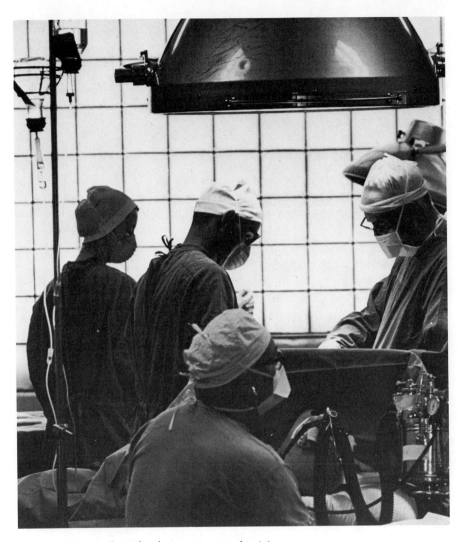

With the costs of medical care constantly rising, a
family needs health insurance protection.

The three different kinds of organizations that provide one or more types of health insurance are: (1) Blue Cross and Blue Shield, which are state or local associations providing hospitalization and surgical and medical benefits; (2) insurance companies, which provide hospitalization, surgical and medical benefits, and also loss of income protection; and (3) independent organizations sponsored by unions, fraternal orders, professional associations, or other groups offering varying plans, some providing only hospitalization benefits, and others, complete medical coverage.

The insurance companies pay cash benefits directly to the person insured, and the insured pays his bills himself or he may instruct the insurance company to make direct payments to the doctor or hospital. Blue Cross and Blue Shield and the independent groups usually provide *service benefits*, meaning that payments are made directly to the hospital and doctors.

Five kinds of health insurance policies are available. Available on either a group or individual basis are five types of health insurance:

1. *Hospital expense insurance.* Hospital expense insurance helps pay for the cost of hospital care. A specific amount is usually allowed for each day of hospitalization up to a maximum number of days. In addition, benefits are provided to meet other hospital charges, such as medications, x-rays, and the use of the operating room. Hospital insurance is the most widely used kind of health insurance.

2. *Surgical expense insurance.* Surgical expense insurance helps to pay the surgeon's fees. The amount paid for any one operation is listed in the policy. For example, the allowance for a tonsillectomy may be $80, for an appendectomy, $200. Surgical expense insurance is the second most widely used kind of health insurance. It is often bought in combination with hospital expense insurance.

3. *Regular medical insurance.* This type of insurance helps pay the cost of a doctor's care at home or hospital, or for a patient's visits to the doctor's office. The maximum number of calls allowed for each sickness or injury and the amount payable per call are specified in the policy.

4. *Major medical expense insurance.* Major medical insurance provides protection against the major costs of a serious or prolonged illness and is the fastest growing kind of health insurance in the United States. Practically every type of expense is covered, including services such as nursing care both during the critical period and during convalescence. Benefits may run as high as $15,000 or more—a sum most families could not afford to pay out of regular earnings and savings.

Major medical insurance helps pay most kinds of expenses both in and out of a hospital, when they are for treatment prescribed by the physician. These may include doctor bills, nursing care, x-ray and laboratory charges, medicines, ambulance service, a wheelchair, crutches, and other costs. Because it offers such a wide range of benefits and provides such high maximums, major medical insurance contains two features to help keep the premium within the policy-holder's means.

A *deductible* provision calls for the policyholder to pay a basic amount before the policy benefits begin, for example the first $500. Sometimes the deductible amount is covered by the benefits of a basic hospital and surgical plan.

A second feature—the *co-insurance provision*—calls for the policy-holder to share the expenses beyond the deductible amount. Most policies pay 75 or 80 per cent of expenses above the deductible amount. The policyholder pays the rest.

A major medical policy may set specific maximum benefits for certain expenses, such as hospital room and board and the cost of surgery.

5. *Disability income insurance.* This kind of policy helps replace income when a wage earner can't work because he is sick or injured. The amount of replacement income and the length of time it will be paid can be chosen to fit particular needs. The maximum benefit, however, is usually no more than 40 to 60 per cent of an individual's earnings.

Benefit periods for disability insurance policies can range up to 12 months, two years, five years, or to age 65. But most policies provide for a wait of a week, a month, two months, or 90 days before benefit payments begin. The purpose of this waiting period is to bring down the cost to fit each family's financial situation. The choice a wage earner makes depends partly on how long his company will pay him while he is not able to work. Another consideration is the family's savings or other resources. By meeting the expenses of a short illness out of their own savings and using insurance to protect against longer disability, a family can buy protection at lower cost.

Short-term policies usually pay benefits for one or two years. The purpose is to provide "readjustment" income while the family is planning what it will do if the wage earner's disability should continue. Long-term policies often pay benefits for life if the policyholder was disabled by an accident, and from 10 years up to age 65 for illness. Professional people, especially doctors, lawyers, and others who are self-employed, often purchase long-term policies. Naturally, the longer the benefit period, the higher the premium for the policy.

Measuring family needs for health insurance begins with an inventory of present protection. Almost everybody who works already has some protection against financial losses in time of ill health or injury.

Today millions of workers belong to group health insurance plans of one kind or another. Many can count on a certain amount of sick leave with pay. Most wage earners are covered by Workmen's Compensation, a form of government insurance, which gives some protection against medical costs and loss of income caused by accident or illness occurring in connection with their jobs.

In determining the kinds of individual policies and provisions to obtain for himself and his family, a person should review the health insurance protection he already has, and also consider these questions:

1. What are the important losses to insure against? An important lesson learned about health insurance over the years is that it is economical to insure against only the most serious or financially crippling losses that a family may suffer. The minor medical expenses occurring in any family can better be met as part of the regular family financial plan.

Settling the hospital account is easier when one knows first what his health insurance will provide.

2. What should one look for in a health insurance policy? A second lesson for families to learn is that it is important to know exactly what their health insurance policy provides. Often families are disappointed to find out that the protection they thought they owned is the very protection not included in their insurance policy. It is essential to know what expenses the policy covers, the members of the family that are covered, what conditions are not covered, what the maximum benefits are, what waiting periods may be required, how many days, if any, must elapse before benefits are payable, and whether maternity benefits are provided. This last point will be of special importance to new families. Most hospitalization policies do not provide maternity benefits until the policy has been in force for a certain period of time. In some cases, no provisions of any kind are made for obstetrical cases. Young couples will want to review their health insurance with this point in mind, to be sure they are prepared for the costs of having their first baby.

The cost of health insurance can only be determined on an individual basis.   Because there are so many individual and personal factors to consider and because each kind of health insurance policy has its own special requirements and provisions, health insurance costs can only be determined on an individual basis. The age of the insured, the extent of coverage, and the numbers of people covered by a policy affect the cost of health insurance protection. In addition, rates for health insurance vary considerably. It is reasonable, for example, to expect that a hospital insurance policy providing benefits for up to ninety days of hospitalization will cost more than a policy covering only twenty-one days; that a major medical policy with a $300 deductible will cost less than a policy with a $50 deductible; and that a disability income policy with a waiting period of three months will cost less than a policy with a waiting period of only one week.

An insurance agent can help a family determine its health insurance needs.   Because of the many variations among policies and because each family has a different set of health insurance requirements, the services of a health insurance agent are essential in securing protection on an individual basis. An agent will be able to answer the specific questions related to coverage and costs that pertain to one's own family and needs.

To start planning a satisfactory health insurance program for an individual family, the agent needs to know exactly what health insurance protection the family already has on a group basis and what that group coverage provides. This information can be obtained readily from the employer or union or whatever organization is responsible for the master policy. Any person so covered should make it his business to learn what protection is thus provided and what he must do to receive any benefits. When the agent knows what insurance benefits are assured through the group plan, he will then be able to suggest ways to meet additional needs for health insurance. It is most important for the family to know what health benefits they are buying so that they will know exactly what can be expected of their insurance.

FOR DISCUSSION

1. What are the two major needs for health insurance?
2. What three kinds of organizations provide health insurance?
3. There are five kinds of health insurance policies available. Describe them.
4. What are some of the factors that contribute to the cost of health insurance?

LIFE INSURANCE PROTECTS AGAINST ECONOMIC LOSS CAUSED BY DEATH OR RETIREMENT

Life insurance is designed to meet two major needs. Families purchase life insurance for the following reasons:

1. To provide income in case of the premature death of the chief wage earner.

2. To provide a fund for use in an emergency, for a special purpose, or for a retirement income in later years.

These two needs—for immediate protection and for savings—arise as the family makes its financial plans and is confronted by two major considerations: planning for the unexpected and for the future. These two basic considerations prompt families and individuals to buy life insurance; in fact, six out of every seven American families own some kind of life insurance.

Of these two needs, the most important is the family's need for income protection in case the chief wage earner dies. Life insurance provides cash to meet final expenses, taxes, and other outstanding obligations. Second, life insurance provides the family with a monthly income until other arrangements can be worked out or for as long as the children are growing up. Third, it provides a fund for emergencies. Finally, it provides funds for special goals.

The insurance money that is buying income protection in case of death is very often building up a cash value that the family can draw upon in times of emergency or for special purposes. In one family, for instance, the cash value of a life insurance policy may be used to help send a son or daughter to college, or to pay for a daughter's wedding. For another family, it might be used to make the down payment on a house. Another family may use it at the time of retirement to provide a monthly income. This feature, the *cash value*, makes life insurance different from all other forms of insurance. The cash value may be taken in the form of a low-cost loan, to be repaid later, or if protection is no longer needed, the cash may be withdrawn and the policy terminated.

Life insurance, therefore, helps to meet family needs for money both in case of death and during the policyholder's lifetime. As a rule of thumb, the growing family's major need for life insurance is to provide cash and monthly income in case the major wage earner dies. The chances, however, are that the wage earner will live, and that the life insurance he purchased for the protection of his family in its growing up years can be used for his retirement income. Many families today count on using their life insurance in this way. They depend on it to provide added income in their later years.

A family's life insurance needs are not static, however. Keep in mind the family life cycle. Visualize a curve that begins with marriage, rises as children come along and grow up, and then falls again at the point where the parents retire. Life insurance is most needed for income protection when the curve is on the rise. When the curve is declining, the family life insurance can be put to other uses. Thus, the policies originally purchased for family protection are at the same time providing the savings necessary for retirement or some other goal.

Income must be protected to provide for daily needs and for future goals. Let us examine more closely the family's major reason for obtaining insurance—to provide income protection. Families live both in the present and in the future, and they build their plans on the assumption that there is and will be an income. For instance, when a family buys a house and agrees to make payments for the next twenty or thirty years, their agreement is based on the belief that there will be a continuing income. Another family wants the children to have an opportunity for higher education and embarks on a college financing plan over a long period of time. Again, the plan depends on income. In other words, at the same time that people are managing their money for present needs, they are also committing it for future goals. To achieve these goals incomes must be protected.

But income must be protected for an even more urgent and essential reason—to meet the day-to-day living expenses for food, shelter, clothes, and the many other costs necessary to the support and health of family members. To provide for these needs is the first consideration in planning a life insurance program.

Families have different life insurance needs. No two families have the same life insurance needs. Just as no money management plan fits all families, neither will a single life insurance plan. Individual differences, goals, and needs determine what a family's life insurance program should provide.

The Crandells, for example, are supporting Mr. Crandell's mother and must consider her care in the even that Mr. Crandell should die. The Melchiors, a family of six, own several pieces of rental property from which they can expect a good income over the next fifteen or twenty years; their need for life insurance may be less than the Crandells'. Then down the street live the Stanhopes; their son Billy is physically handicapped and will probably never be able to care for himself. They will have to provide for his care as long as he lives. Their need for life insurance is quite different from that of the other families. The father of the Childress family, next door, is covered by Social Security, and his employer provides group life insurance and a group retirement plan. Their life insurance needs will not be the same as those of Charlie Preston, who is self-employed and has no company benefits to help out. Every family is unique; their needs for life insurance are therefore also unique.

Life insurance, like health insurance, may be obtained on a group or on an individual basis. Life insurance is available at a moderate cost on a group basis through one's employer, or union, or other organization in which he holds membership. It is not uncommon, as a matter of fact, for an employer to provide life insurance protection in an amount up to one or two years' salary at no cost to the employee. On an individual basis, a person negotiates directly with the life insurance

*A father's life insurance assures him that his family's
needs will be met should anything happen to him.*

company through its agent or sales representative. In this way, a life
insurance policy can be tailored to fit specific needs and can be secured in any amount that a family needs and can afford.

There are four basic types of life insurance policies. The four types of
life insurance policies form the basis for meeting specific family needs.
Let us see what each of these policies provides.

    1. *Straight life policies.* A straight life policy provides lifetime pro-
tection. It is the most widely used, most flexible, and least expensive
of all types of permanent life insurance. The premiums are lower because the cost of the insurance is spread over the lifetime of the insured. As the premiums are paid through the years, the straight life
policy accumulates a cash value that the policyholder may use as he
wishes.

2. *Limited payment policies.*   Like straight life insurance, a limited payment policy provides lifetime protection; however, premiums are paid only for a specified number of years. Because fewer premiums are paid on a limited payment policy than on the straight life policy, each premium is larger. Like straight life policies, limited payment policies also build up cash values.

3. *Endowment policies.*   More than any other life insurance policy, an endowment policy puts the emphasis on savings. Its purpose is to accumulate a definite amount of money within a certain period, while at the same time providing life insurance protection. If the policyholder lives, the whole amount of the policy is paid to him when the endowment period ends. Should he die before that time, the full amount of the policy is payable to his beneficiary. Because the emphasis is on savings, the premiums for an endowment policy are higher than for the other types of life insurance.

4. *Term insurance policies.*   A term insurance policy offers protection only for a stated number of years (or term) and usually does not have any savings element through accumulated cash values. Should the policyholder die during the term, the full amount of the policy is paid to his beneficiary. If he outlives the term, the protection stops when the term period expires. The premium is usually lower because the risk is for a shorter period of time. In many cases, the policyholder may renew the policy at the expiration of the term, but because he is several years older, the premium will be higher.

Three types of combination policies are available.   In addition to the four basic policies, there are other plans, or combination policies, that have grown out of them.

1. *Family income policies.*   The family income policy is one of the most widely used of the combination policies. It includes both straight life and term insurance and is less expensive than if each policy were purchased separately. With a family income policy, the family is assured of a regular monthly income should the policyholder die during the term, which, for example, may be twenty years. The income is paid from the time of death until the end of the term. In addition, the full amount or face value of the straight life portion is payable to the beneficiary. If the policyholder is alive at the end of the term, as is usually the case, the family is still protected for the future by the straight life portion of the policy.

2. *Family policies.*   A family policy provides insurance on the lives of every member of the family. The largest amount of insurance is on

the father and is the permanent, straight life type. In addition, there are lesser amounts of term insurance on the lives of the wife and children.

3. *Retirement income policies.* A retirement income policy offers financial protection for the family during the period when the owner is building savings in the policy to provide a retirement income for life.

An insurance agent can help a family determine its life insurance needs and costs. Life insurance is purchased on the basis of family needs which, in turn, are determined by family assets and income. Here the need for a specialist becomes apparent. A life insurance agent can be helpful in reviewing with the family its total financial picture and can help in planning an effective program of protection. He will recommend the kind of life insurance policies suited to the family's needs and pocketbook. He will also recommend methods of paying for the insurance and for using it in the years ahead.

A qualified life insurance agent helps a family measure its needs for protection and build a program to meet those needs.

The costs of life insurance depend on the age of the person when he takes out a policy. The younger a person is, the less will be the *premium*—the amount he pays each year for his life insurance. Life insurance premiums are payable annually, semi-annually, or quarterly. Premiums may be paid on a monthly basis also, and in some cases even weekly.

Life insurance policies are usually purchased in units of $1,000. For example, one buys a policy worth $1,000, $2,000, $5,000, and so on; this amount represents the total benefits that will be paid by the life insurance company. This amount is called the *face value* of the policy.

The table on page 211 showing some typical premium rates helps to demonstrate what is involved in estimating life insurance costs. As you look at the table you will immediately observe two things: (1) the rates for each kind of policy are different; and (2) the older a person is, the more he pays in premiums. Can you explain why the rates are different and why one's age affects the rate?

Every policy has certain specific provisions, each of which affects the premium rate. Term insurance, you recall, provides protection only and is intended to cover only a limited time period. Therefore, the premium rate is less. Endowment policies provide savings as well as protection, thus the premium rate is much greater than for term insurance. A large portion of each premium goes into the savings portion of the policy. Premiums for straight life insurance are less than for limited payment life because the cost of the policy is spread over the lifetime of the insured instead of being confined to a limited number of years. As with everything else, so with buying life insurance—one gets just what he pays for.

It is understandable that the policyholder's age should affect his premium rates. The older a person is, the greater the risk of death. In other words, a person who is twenty years old is likely to have more time to pay for his insurance than a person who is forty years old.

Refer again to the same table. Can you calculate the cost of $5,000 worth of straight life insurance purchased at age eighteen? Notice that the premium rate is $14.90 for a $1,000 policy. For a $5,000 policy the annual premium would be $74.50. Thus, the person buying that policy would pay $74.50 every year for as long as the policy remained in force. What would the premium be for a $5,000 five-year term policy? How long would that policy be in effect?

Perhaps no other major investment deserves more time and thoughtful attention than the planning of a life insurance program, simply

Approximate Annual Premium Rates for Men*
for $1,000 of Life Insurance

Bought at Age	Straight Life	Limited Payment (20-Year)	Endowment (20-Year)	Term 5-Year Renewable
18	$14.90	$23.00	$46.50	$8.95
20	15.55	23.85	46.55	9.30
25	17.35	26.00	46.70	9.35
30	19.65	28.75	47.00	9.40
40	26.55	35.80	48.75	11.60

* Rates for women will be somewhat lower.

because everything about it is geared to the uncertain future. In buying life insurance the family is buying future income, an income that may be called upon next year, or in ten years, or not for forty years.

FOR DISCUSSION

1. What are the two major needs for life insurance?
2. What funds does a family need in the event that the major wage earner dies?
3. What are the four basic types of policies? Which of these furnishes protection only? Which provides a substantial savings fund?
4. Why are premium rates less for younger people?

SOCIAL SECURITY, A GOVERNMENT-SPONSORED INSURANCE PROGRAM, ADDS TO THE FINANCIAL SECURITY OF MOST FAMILIES

Fortunately, most families today already have a start toward creating a program of financial security. Thanks to the provisions of the nation's Social Security legislation, they can count on a monthly income in the event that the family wage earner dies or is disabled. At retirement time the family can count on a monthly income plus health insurance benefits. These provisions represent, for most families, one of their most important financial assets.

Congress reviews and revises the Social Security program about every other year, bringing the benefits in line with the cost of living. The

Retired couples depend on Social Security for a significant portion of their retirement income.

figures given below can therefore be considered as examples to illustrate how the program works.

Social Security provides three types of benefits. Actually Social Security is the abbreviated and popular name given to an insurance program that came into being through federal legislation and which is administered by the federal government. It provides for three types of monthly payments potentially worth many thousands of dollars to a family.

1. *Survivors' benefits.* In the event of death of a person covered by Social Security, his spouse will receive a monthly income if there are dependent children under eighteen years of age (twenty-two years of age if a child is in school). Thus, a wife whose husband is covered by Social Security will receive a regular monthly income until the youngest child is eighteen or twenty-two, should her husband die. Regular monthly payments will be resumed when she reaches age sixty. In addition, she will receive a single payment to a maximum of $255 at the time of her husband's death.

2. *Disability benefits.*   Social Security provides a monthly income for a person who is so disabled that he cannot work and whose prospects for returning to work in the near future are not promising.

3. *Retirement benefits.*   A monthly income is provided under this legislation for retired workers, beginning at age sixty-two at a reduced rate. If a person works to age 65, he will receive full benefits.

In addition, Social Security provides hospital and medical benefits for persons age sixty-five and older. This portion of the program is known as *Medicare.* Benefits are provided automatically to help pay hospital and nursing home charges. Also, for a special monthly payment to the government, benefits are available to help pay for physicians' services.

Social Security is paid for by employer and employee.   Although Social Security is administered by the government, it is paid for by individuals and their employers. Like income tax deductions, a deduction designated for one's Social Security payment is withheld from each paycheck. This amount is matched by the employer. The amount withheld depends on one's salary or wages. For example, John Greenwold, age thirty, is employed by the supermarket on Main Street. His annual earnings are $7,800 a year, or $650 a month. In 1971, 5.2 per cent of his monthly salary was deducted for Social Security. This

Employed workers pay for Social Security coverage through a payroll deduction system, with employer and employee sharing the cost.

deduction amounted to $33.80 per month and is matched by his employer.

John is married and has three children, ages two, five, and seven. If he were to die now, his wife and family would receive a monthly income of $434. As each youngster reached eighteen or twenty-two, (provided he remained in school), the income would decrease. The monthly payments would stop altogether when the last youngster reached his eighteenth or twenty-second birthday. For John's wife, benefits would resume again when she reached age sixty.

More than likely, however, John will live to retire. It is hard to predict what his average earnings will amount to in the next thirty-five years. Suppose, for example, that his income remains $7,800 and never changes—a most unlikely event. John and his wife (who is the same age as her husband) will receive a monthly retirement income of $323.00 for as long as they both live. In addition, John and his wife will be entitled to health benefits that cover hospital expenses, medical treatment, and nursing home care if needed.

If John becomes disabled before retiring and can no longer work, he can apply for disability benefits. The amount of these benefits will equal his retirement income at age sixty-five, plus additional income for each child under eighteen.

Most people qualify for Social Security. Almost everybody who works in paid employment is covered by Social Security. This coverage includes everybody employed by business or industry and by most state and local governments. It includes farmers and professional people, it includes people who are self-employed, people who work part-time, and people who work as domestics. It includes women, men, and teenagers. Among the workers not covered are those who work for the federal government, because they are covered under another program, and railroad employees, also covered under another similar program.

To be "covered" means that one is insured under the provisions of the Social Security legislation. Survivors' benefits are payable to the beneficiaries of any covered worker, regardless of how brief a time he was so insured. To qualify for retirement and health benefits, one must have been covered a certain number of *quarters*. A quarter is a period of three months; there are four quarters in a year. A young person will need to be covered for forty quarters (ten years) in order to qualify for retirement benefits when he is sixty-two or sixty-five years old.

The benefits provided by Social Security are of major importance to most families. Social Security is the foundation upon which a life insurance agent plans the life insurance program for a family. He calculates the income that will be derived from Social Security and adds to it the income that may be expected from group life insurance and from a pension plan, and other resources. He then estimates the additional income that may be required to meet family needs. To provide this income, he will recommend a particular life insurance program, made up of one or more policies.

Life and health insurance, together with Social Security benefits, can provide economic security for families. To best understand how life and health insurance, together with Social Security benefits, combine to build a plan of financial security for a family, it will be helpful to look at one family's program.

Mr. and Mrs. Mitchell live in a small city in Connecticut. They have been married for sixteen years. Ed Mitchell is forty and his wife, Betty, is four years younger. They have two children. Barbara is fourteen and Jack is ten. The family's income is just over $10,000 a year.

Like most people who work, Mr. Mitchell is covered by Social Security. He is also covered by a group health insurance plan through his employer. It is a comprehensive health plan, combining features of regular hospital-medical-surgical plans and major medical plans. Mr. Mitchell pays the first $50 of medical and hospital bills, and the policy pays 80 per cent of additional bills up to a maximum of $15,000. Mr. Mitchell's employer pays part of the cost of the policy and deducts Mr. Mitchell's share from his pay check. In addition, Mr. Mitchell has a disability income policy that will pay him a monthly income if he is disabled and cannot work. He will be entitled to disability benefits under Social Security also.

If Mr. Mitchell were to die now, some funds would be paid immediately from life insurance, plus $255 from Social Security. This cash would help clear up the family's debts. The rest of the life insurance is planned as continuing payments to fit Mrs. Mitchell's needs. Mrs. Mitchell is a graduate nurse, and although she would probably return to nursing if her husband died, the plan allows her to stay home with the three children until they finish school.

Life insurance has been fitted around Social Security to make the most of both. Social Security payments combined with life insurance would provide a monthly income that would last until Barbara and Jack finished school. At that time the Social Security payments would stop but insurance payments would add to the income Mrs. Mitchell earned and tide her over until her widow's payments from Social Security began at age sixty.

The main reason Mr. Mitchell bought life insurance was to provide an income for his wife and children if he should die. But he really expects to reach retirement age, and chances are he will. When he turns sixty-two he will face a new financial problem. This his life insurance will help solve. At retirement, Mr. Mitchell can expect about $200 a month from his company's pension plan. Added to this will be his Social Security retirement income, and the income then available by using the cash values in his life insurance policies.

The Mitchells now have a financial plan that will serve them if Mr. Mitchell should not live. But that plan will also help them in case of a more likely possibility—that they will spend many happy years of retirement together.

Women Need Life Insurance, Too!   Traditionally, life insurance has been thought of as being for men only, and that is how it was sold. The family life insurance was thought to be for the replacement of the income earned by the major wage-earner, usually the father. Times have changed.

Today, with more than half of the women contributing to household income, the loss of that income can be a major blow to the family financial resources and to the family life style. This accounts for the reason why women in large numbers are becoming owners of life insurance. Women are buying it for the same reasons as men: to protect their dependents and to supplement retirement income in later years; to provide for college educations for their children; to pay off a mortgage.

Nor is it only the working woman who is buying life insurance in this day and age. Many wives and mothers are now taking out a life insurance policy, especially if there are young children in the family.

In the event that a mother should die, the costs for household help to care for her children would be a severe burden on the family's resources. This is further evidence of the economic value of the services provided by the wife and mother. It is only in recent years that any attempt has been made to measure basic services in dollars and cents.

FOR DISCUSSION

1. What benefits are available through Social Security?
2. Who pays for these benefits? What role does the federal government play in the Social Security program?
3. What does it mean to be "covered"?

Summary for Chapter 10

Perhaps no other problem in family living is as puzzling and profound as the matter of providing for the unexpected and the unforeseen. Insurance is the only known way we have of providing for the future uncertainties that can befall a family. For this reason families own it and depend on it as the cornerstone of their plans for financial security.

No two families define security in the same way—what constitutes security for one family may not be adequate for the family across the street. On one point, however, there can be general agreement—provision must be made for the unexpected accident, illness, or death. Furthermore, retirement, which may appear a long way off, requires planning if it is to be a time of active participation in and enjoyment of community and family life. To meet these needs life and health insurance, together with Social Security, have been developed.

CAN YOU EXPLAIN?

1. risk-sharing
2. group insurance
3. service benefits
4. Blue Cross and Blue Shield
5. major medical insurance
6. cash value
7. family income policy
8. premium
9. face value
10. quarters

HOW WOULD YOU ANSWER?

1. What is the purpose of insurance? List as many kinds of insurance as you can that are needed by most families.
2. How does life insurance differ from other forms of insurance—fire, auto, and hospital, for example?

3. What kind of health insurance policy provides for daily care and treatment in a hospital? What kind helps meet the expenses of a prolonged and costly illness? What kind is designed to help a family continue to meet the expenses of daily living if income is cut off by illness?
4. Although this chapter discussed the life and health insurance needs of families, what needs might a single person have for such protection? Why?
5. Do you see any reason why members in a family other than the wage earner should be protected by life insurance?
6. Life insurance premiums are lower for young people; auto insurance rates are higher. Why is there a difference?

OTHER THINGS TO DO

1. Consult your parents and find out the kinds of insurance your family owns and for what particular purposes. How many members of your family are covered by Social Security? In reviewing your family's program for financial security, do you see any omissions for which provision might be made?
2. Interview a life insurance agent in your community, and on the basis of your interview prepare a report for your class. Here are some questions you might ask him:
   a. Should the mother of a family carry life insurance? How about the children?
   b. What provisions are there for the policyholder who can no longer pay his premiums?
   c. Are life insurance policy benefits paid in one lump sum, or are there other methods of payment? Which method is best for a growing family?
   d. What is there about his business that gives the insurance agent the greatest satisfaction?
3. Consult the hospital administrator in your community and learn what changes have occurred in hospital and medical costs over the past ten years. Develop a chart showing the trend in fees for a semi-private room; for the operating room; for the delivery room; for the anesthetist. On the basis of what you have learned, what conclusions can you make regarding the rates for health insurance?
4. Visit the Social Security office near you to find out how the program popularly called Medicare works. Medicare was organized in 1966 when the Social Security program was expanded to provide health benefits for older people. What are its advantages?
5. Examine several sample copies of different types of insurance applications. Find out what type of information is needed on the forms. Why is it important to give accurate and correct information?

6. Ask a life insurance agent to explain what he thinks is the minimum coverage a person or family needs at the various stages of the life cycle.

7. See the filmstrip "Consumers in Action" (Institute of Life Insurance) and evaluate the goals of the young couple in relation to the future. What place did insurance play in their decision making? What other factors influenced their decision? What changes may this couple decide to make in their present insurance program? What factors will influence their decisions?

8. Use the decision-making process and select the types and kinds of insurance the couple might need in the filmstrip, "Marriage and Money" (Institute of Life Insurance).

9. Choose one of the couples from the kit "Financing a New Partnership" (J. C. Penney Co.) and design a suitable insurance program for them.

10. Look in the yellow pages of the telephone book to see how many insurance firms are listed. What types of insurance are represented? How would an individual or family go about selecting an insurance agent? Check the Consumer's Guide to see if it contains useful information about insurance companies. Make a list of the insurance companies that advertise on television. Would such television advertising be a factor in influencing your choice of company? Why or why not?

11. Brainstorm on the major hazards an individual or family faces. Then identify how insurance can help provide security to these families.

12. Prepare some review questions on insurance and play a game such as Quiz Bowl, Jeopardy, or academic baseball to see if you understand the basic principles of insurance.

13. Use the multi-media kit entitled "Priorities, Decisions, Security: The Role of Life Insurance in a Young Life Style" (Institute of Life Insurance) to become acquainted with basic life insurance concepts and the role life insurance plays in personal and family life.

14. Consult your parents and find out the kinds of insurance your family owns and for what particular purposes. How many members of your family are covered by Social Security? In reviewing your family's program for financial security, do you see any omissions for which provision might be made?

11 Savings and Thrift in Family Life

What this chapter is about

Like the weather, saving money is something everyone talks about, but unlike the weather, we can do something about it. Most people will agree that saving is as much a part of money management as is spending. But many people find it much harder to save money than to spend it.

Is there any compelling reason why families should save money? If there is a reason, how should a savings program be carried out? These are the questions to be discussed in this chapter. The discussion will develop four main ideas:

1. Thrift adds mileage to family money.

2. Successful savings programs result when goals are definite.

3. Savings programs are successful when they are systematically tended.

4. Saving, by the way of investing, is effective for achieving long-term goals.

THRIFT ADDS MILEAGE TO FAMILY MONEY

Every now and then the newspapers report the death of an old man or woman who lived as a recluse or a derelict. When the police or civil authorities investigate the place in which the deceased lived, they find thousands of dollars tucked away in boxes, drawers, bags, and other unlikely places. Would you say such a person was thrifty and a saver? It all depends on how you define saving, doesn't it? More accurately, such people would be called hoarders. They amass secret stores or money over the years but never put their money to any use.

Savings does not suggest that a resource is not used. In areas where there is a serious water shortage, for example, people save water; that is, they use it carefully and only for their most important needs. They do not waste it but they do use it. They practice conservation. So it is with people who are thrifty and save money. They use their money, but they also conserve it by avoiding waste.

Anyone who cares about making his money go further can find ways of saving. In talking about thrift and saving we are talking about two closely related ideas: (1) the conservation of the resources we won, and (2) a program of systematically setting aside a portion of our income for use at a later time. As we learn to be good conservationists we are helped to become good "set-asiders" because we find we have more to set aside.

Thrift may be defined as the *economical use of resources*. The thrifty person is one who is concerned with getting his money's worth out of whatever he owns, as well as making the most of his money. He is conserving his resources. He takes care of his clothes in order to get more wear out of them; he uses the leftovers from last night's dinner; he keeps his equipment in good repair. He has learned that if he takes good care of what he owns, he does not have to spend money on replacements as frequently. And if he isn't spending money on replacements, he has money for other things. Conservation and thrift, therefore, mean avoiding waste; taking care and keeping up; and saving what we already have.

Habits of thrift make it easier for us to take the next step: to save a portion of our income on a regular basis. This practice is simply an extension of the thrift concept. What we are doing in a savings program is putting money to work for us in order to extend or prolong its usefulness.

FOR DISCUSSION

1. What is the difference between hoarding and saving?
2. How does thriftiness help one to save money?

It's easy to put money aside in a savings fund when it is for a special goal—a wedding, for instance.

SUCCESSFUL SAVINGS PROGRAMS RESULT
WHEN OBJECTIVES ARE CLEAR

Generally speaking, people save money in order to make use of it at a later time. In other words, they are deferring satisfaction from their income. The things for which people save are as varied as people themselves. There are two broad categories of reasons, however, for which people save money: (1) for a particular goal or goals; and (2) to meet emergencies.

When one has a clearly defined objective in mind, saving money for it is no problem. Jan is saving for her wedding; the Prestons are saving for retirement; Sally, age nine, is saving for a pair of skates; Dick is saving for a car; Betty and her parents are saving for college; and the Whites are saving for a vacation. Each of these people is saving for a purpose. Each has a goal and it's the goal that is important.

The other reason that motivates people to save is to be able to meet emergencies. The Carlsons recall the unexpected expense when the hot water tank sprung a leak two years ago. Stella remembers what it was like last year when she lost her job and had no funds to fall back on.

An *emergency fund* can be more difficult to accumulate and maintain than a fund for "fun." It's human nature to want to avoid thinking about crises or disasters, and so we forget to make plans for meeting them. But not all emergencies are disasters. They can be, and very often are, opportunities. With that idea in mind—of being ready to take advantage of opportunities when they come along—an emergency fund is much easier to maintain. Opportunities may be dramatic events, or they may be so insignificant that they almost pass unnoticed. A special sale of sheets and blankets can be an opportunity for the family who needs sheets and blankets. So can the offer of a new job in another community be an opportunity, although it means moving and all that goes with it, including extra expenses. Whatever the opportunity, big or little, a savings fund will help one take advantage of it.

People often ask the question, "How large should an emergency fund be?" The answer is again a matter of individual and family choice. Financial advisers suggest, however, that as a general rule an emergency fund should equal about two or three months' income. Therefore, if the family income is $400 a month, a safe emergency fund should amount to $800 to $1,200. Once that level is reached, extra money can be added to other savings funds or used in some other way. When any of the emergency money has been used, it should be replaced again by regular deposits.

Saving for a particular goal is not difficult for most people, especially if the goal is not too far off and if it is something of real value and importance to them. The girl who is saving for her wedding finds it easy to put her weekly deposits in the bank; her goal is firmly fixed. Little Sally is having a more difficult time. She wants the skates, to be sure, but she wants so many other things, too. Her goal is not firmly set. Although she is only nine, she is not unlike adults in this respect. No matter how old they may be, most people find that it is not easy to save money on a regular basis unless they are saving for something they are sure they want.

Most families and individuals have more than one goal for which they save. The Whites, who are saving for a vacation, also are saving

A furniture sale may be just the opportunity a family has been waiting for—and they can take advantage of it if they have money set aside in an emergency fund.

for a new house. The Prestons are saving for a new washer as well as for retirement. The Carlsons, too, are planning for retirement. These families have short-term and long-term goals. Because people have a variety of goals for which they are saving, they choose a variety of means for saving.

FOR DISCUSSION

1. What factors motivate people to save?
2. What is an emergency fund? Should everyone have such a fund?
3. Why is it important for most people to have a savings goal?

SAVINGS PROGRAMS ARE SUCCESSFUL WHEN
THEY ARE SYSTEMATICALLY TENDED

Even though they know the answer, people often ask the question, "When is the right time to start a savings program?" For any person, young or old, who has no plan or system for saving but who does have an income for which he is responsible, the time to begin saving is now. The sooner one begins, the sooner he will achieve his objectives. Sometimes we hear a person say that his income is so small there really is no sense in starting a savings account because it wouldn't amount to anything. Yet if he saved only 50¢ a week, he would have $26 at the end of a year, plus some interest. This amount would be money he wouldn't otherwise have, possibly, because 50¢ a week is so easily dribbled away with nothing to show for it.

Most people who are starting out on a savings venture find much satisfaction in seeing their nest egg grow. Some folks, as a matter of fact, find such satisfaction in watching their savings fund accumulate that they need no further incentive to keep up the savings habit. And habit is the key to success in a savings program. More than the amount set aside each week, or each month, it is the regularity with which it is done that creates a sizable savings account.

There is another key to success as well: Pay your savings fund first. In other words, set aside your savings on payday. Often amateur savers start out planning to save everything left over at the end of the week or the month. To their surprise, nothing is left over. So it is a good habit to pay yourself first.

The secret to savings growth is compound interest. At the beginning of this chapter it was suggested that there is a difference between hoarding money and systematically saving it. It is quite possible to be a systematic hoarder as well as a saver; the factor that makes the difference between hoarding and saving is *compound interest*.

Earlier in this book the subject of interest came up. It was defined, you recall, as money that money earns. Money saved in the teapot on the shelf does not earn interest; money saved in a savings account does. A savings plan extends the use of our money by increasing it—through interest. Compound interest is interest that is paid on all the accumulated interest earned in the preceding period, as well as on the amount deposited by the saver. This principal is at work in any savings program, whether it be in a bank, a savings and loan association, credit union, or life insurance. (Government bonds and other securities increase in value somewhat differently.)

Let us see how compound interest works. Suppose you deposit $100 in a savings account on the first of January. Interest is compounded semi-annually at 4 per cent per year. On June 31, your account would be credited with $2 [$100 × 4 per cent ÷ 2 (six months)]. Now your savings amount to $102. On December 31 your account would be credited with $2.04 ($102 × 4 per cent ÷ 2), and would total $104.04. The table below shows how a savings account grows at 4 per cent interest compounded semi-annually. Can you see the value of a systematic plan for savings? How much will your account total at the end of five years? How much greater is this than the amount you deposited?

Benjamin Franklin in his *Poor Richard's Almanack* stated it this way:

> Money makes money
> And the money
> That money makes
> Makes more money.

How Money Grows At 4 Per Cent Interest Compounded Semi-Annually
(Savings Deposits of $10 on the First of Each Month)

Year	Amount Deposited	Interest Earned	Year-End Value of Account
1	$ 120	$ 2.61	$ 122.61
2	240	10.18	250.18
3	360	22.90	382.90
4	480	40.98	520.98
5	600	64.95	664.65

Where to save depends on one's savings goals.   Because most families and individuals have several goals in mind, some short-term and others long-term, they often use more than one kind of savings plan. There are several commonly used savings outlets, that is, places or institutions in which savings funds may be deposited: banks, savings and loan associations, credit unions, government bonds, and investments (stocks and bonds, mutual funds). Life insurance, as pointed out in the previous chapter, is a means for saving also.

Each of these sources has its own distinctive features; the one chosen will depend on what the person plans to do with his money and how soon he wants it. Short-term goals may best be achieved by using a bank, credit union, or savings and loan association; one's funds are easily and quickly available with these organizations. Long-term goals may best be achieved by using one or more of the other plans— government bonds, life insurance, or investments.

In general, there are three things to consider before selecting a savings outlet:

1. How safe will my money be? Is the institution and its management reliable so I need not worry that it will fail and my total savings be lost? What risk is there that my savings fund will shrink in amount and I will not get back my original deposits?

Each deposit and withdrawal is recorded in a savings bank passbook, as well as the amount of compound interest earned on the balance in the account.

	DATE	WITHDRAWAL	DEPOSIT	INTEREST	BALANCE	TELLER
1	8-06-71		***60.83		**531.95	DEP 06A
2	8-10-71	INTEREST		****2.11	***534.06	
3	9-09-71		***60.83		**594.89	DEP 06A
4	9-10-71	INTEREST		****2.40	***597.29	
5	10-04-71	***23.69			**573.60	WD 06A
6	10-10-71	INTEREST		****2.56	***576.16	
7	10-18-71		***60.83		**636.99	DEP 06A
8	11-08-71		***60.83		**697.82	DEP 06A
9	11-10-71	INTEREST		****2.79	***700.61	
10	12-06-71		***60.83		**761.44	DEP 06A
11	12-10-71	INTEREST		****3.06	***764.50	
12	1-07-72		***60.83		**825.33	DEP 06A
13	1-10-72	INTEREST		****3.44	***828.77	
14	2-07-72		***60.83		**889.60	DEP 05B
15	2-10-72	INTEREST		****3.73	**893.33	
16	3-03-72	**875.00			***18.33	WD 04B
17	3-10-72	INTEREST		****2.85	****21.18	

DEPOSITOR'S NAME ON PAGE ONE

2. How easily and quickly can I get my money when I want it? Some savings funds may take several days to withdraw, thus you may need a savings account with immediate withdrawals.

3. What rate of return will I receive on my money? In other words, how much money will my savings fund earn in interest?

Now that you are aware of some of the points to consider in choosing a savings plan, let us see what the available plans are and how they differ?

Bank accounts.   For convenience and ease in starting and maintaining a savings plan, there is nothing like a bank. Most commercial banks offer customers two kinds of accounts: checking and savings. Mutual savings banks, operating in eighteen states, specialize in savings accounts only. Checking accounts, which are not intended to serve as savings outlets, will be discussed in the next chapter.

Savings accounts have three distinct advantages for families and individuals:

1. The bank accepts small deposits. An account may be opened with as little as $1. At the time the account is opened the depositor receives a *passbook* in which is recorded the amount of the deposit. Each time he adds to his account, or makes a withdrawal, the transaction is recorded; interest earnings are recorded as they become due. Thus the passbook contains an up-to-date record of one's savings plan.

2. One's money is readily available for withdrawal. Any time the depositor wishes to withdraw funds from his account, he may readily do so by presenting his passbook at the bank. He may receive the money in cash or as a check payable to himself or to a creditor. There is no charge for withdrawals. In fact, the depositor is not charged any fees for the normal services provided by a savings account.

3. Interest is paid on the funds in the account. You have probably seen statements such as "interest paid from day of deposit" and "interest paid quarterly" in bank windows or in bank advertisements in the newspapers. The kind of interest being referred to is compound interest; this is an important feature of savings accounts. Interest rates vary, but most banks today are paying from 4 to 5 per cent compounded semi-annually or quarterly.

Savings and loan associations.   An account in a savings and loan association is much the same as a savings account in a bank. Small deposits are accepted; compound interest is earned on one's money; and withdrawals usually may be made at any time.

Savings and loan associations, sometimes called building and loan associations, perform two services: they serve as savings institutions and they specialize in lending money for the purchase of homes. In

American families and individuals have a good record as savers—they know it pays to defer satisfaction from a portion of their money.

addition to offering customers a regular savings account, they also offer investment accounts that require deposits of $100 or multiples of $100. A favorable interest rate is paid on either kind of account, reaching over 5 per cent compounded quarterly in some cases.

Savings and loan associations are popular among families as places for savings, but because these institutions are far less numerous than banks, many families cannot be as conveniently served by them.

Credit unions. Credit unions serve the same saving and lending functions as banks, but on a private basis. A credit union is often organized for the employees of a large company; some labor unions have established credit unions for their members; some churches, too, have set up credit unions for the members of their congregations.

A credit union is a cooperative organization whose members share in its management and control. Since a credit union serves a particular clientele and is housed on the premises of the company or organization whose employees or members are served, there is no cost for office space. The necessary book work is done by members, so there is little or no cost for operation. Earnings can therefore be shared by all the depositors because there are no expenses or salaries to pay. As a result, the rate of interest paid is high—4 to 6 per cent is not unusual. Also, members of credit unions may borrow from the union at low interest rates.

For people who qualify, membership in a credit union is a profitable savings outlet, offering convenience, good earnings, safety, and prompt payment of withdrawals.

Government bonds.   A government bond is a certificate issued by the U.S. Department of the Treasury promising to pay the owner a stated sum of money on the date the bond matures (the date when the bond reaches its full value). Because of the safety and the convenience they provide, U.S. government bonds are a popular form of saving, particularly for long-term goals. Bonds may be purchased from most banks and from all post offices. A favorite way of buying them is through the payroll savings plan; an employee may request his employer to withhold a certain amount from his salary each payday for the purchase of bonds. Using this method one can maintain a savings plan on a regular basis.

The government bond preferred by most people, especially those who can only save small amounts at a time, is the *Series E bond.* These are issued in units of $25, $50, $100, $500, and $1,000, at a purchase price set at three-fourths of the full value of the bond. Thus, a $25 bond may be purchased for $18.75; a $50 bond costs $37.50, and so on. A bond reaches its full value five years and ten months after the date of purchase. In other words, $18.75 saved in January, 1972 becomes $25 by October, 1977.

Bonds, however, may be redeemed (cashed in) at any time after the first two months following purchase. They begin to increase in amount after six months, although the rate of increase is low during the first few years. People are thereby encouraged to hold their bonds until maturity. Bonds need not be cashed in at the time they mature; a ten-month extension is allowed. The bonds then continue to earn interest at the rate of $5\frac{1}{2}$ per cent compounded semi-annually.

FOR DISCUSSION

1. What are two keys to success in a savings program?
2. How does compound interest contribute to one's saving account?
3. What should one look for in selecting a place to save?

4. What advantages does a savings account in a bank offer?
5. Describe other available savings outlets.

SAVING BY WAY OF INVESTING IS EFFECTIVE
FOR ACHIEVING LONG-TERM GOALS

The savings plans discussed so far are for the accumulation of known amounts of money. The saver takes little or no chance that he will not get his money back. He knows, too, that his funds will increase at an exact rate. Each of the plans is a sure, safe, and conservative way of providing funds for later use.

Investing in stocks involves some risk. There is another method of accumulating funds in which one's money stands a chance of substantially increasing in value. The money may decrease in value too. We are talking about an investment program in which one buys *securities* from which he expects to receive an income; he also expects his original investment to increase in value. Securities are shares of ownership—*stocks* and *bonds*—in American business enterprises. Stocks represent ownership; bonds represent loans to business and industry and are usually of interest only to large investors.

By owning stock families or individuals share in the ownership of such industries as General Motors, IBM, Standard Oil, Westinghouse, RCA, General Electric, American Airlines, and several hundred other large and small companies that sell shares of their businesses on the stock market. In the business pages of the daily newspapers one finds the current price of all the stocks offered to the public. The prices may rise or fall each day, depending on business conditions.

The purchase of stock works in the following way. Suppose you wanted to buy some shares of Jet Airlines, Inc. The price, on the day you buy, is $18 per share. You have enough money to buy ten shares. You go to a broker, a person who specializes in selling securities, and ask him to buy ten shares of Jet; for his service you will pay a small fee or commission. For about $185 you become an owner of ten shares of Jet. You selected this stock because you expect that during the next several years it will increase in value. Instead of being worth $18 a share, you expect that in five or ten years your stock will be worth $50 or $60 a share, and possibly more. You also expect that the annual earnings of the company will be high and that the company will therefore pay regular dividends to its shareholders every year. A dividend is one's share of the company's profits.

There is no way of guaranteeing what a company's dividends will be, nor can you know for sure that the stock will increase in value. It is possible that in ten years your stock will still be worth $18 per share. There is a chance, too, that it will have decreased in value and be worth much less. So there is a risk involved in this kind of investment plan. The record of American business and industry is remarkably good, however. The careful investor can be reasonably sure that his money will bring a good return. But to be an investor, one should know what he

Long-term family goals may often be achieved by investing in stocks and bonds.

wants his investment program to do and then select the securities that will help him accomplish his purpose.

An investment program is developed with one of two purposes in mind: (1) to add to one's present income, in which case the investor will look for a stock showing a long record of annual dividend payments that give a favorable return on one's investment; or (2) to increase one's capital in the future, in which case the investor will look for a growth stock; that is, stock in a company that shows promise of future growth.

Because the average family cannot afford to take chances with its investment program, it would be folly for them to "go it alone" in the stock market unless they were extremely knowledgeable about it. Knowing how to select stocks and when to buy requires a knowledge of the market that most of us do not have. Successful investors seek the counsel and guidance of specialists—brokers representing qualified firms that are members of the major stock exchanges. If a would-be investor is not acquainted with a reputable broker or firm, he is well advised to consult his banker.

Mutual funds are another type of investment program. Many families want to share in business prosperity but are reluctant to assume the responsibility for selecting and managing stocks themselves. These people may purchase mutual funds, thereby investing in an investment company. An investment company gathers together the savings of many people, forming a fund with which to purchase a wide variety of stocks and bonds. Income from these investments is shared by all the people in the group. Mutual funds appeal to people as a form of forced saving, because in most cases the investor agrees to make payments to the fund on a regular basis over a certain number of years.

An investment program is not recommended as a family's first savings plan. Experts in the financial field advise people to have the following three assets before they start to invest:

1. An emergency fund of ample amount so that the family will have a cash reserve sufficient to meet obligations and to provide for short term goals.

2. A life insurance program that will guarantee an adequate monthly income for the family.

3. The purchase of a home, if home ownership is one of the family's goals.

FOR DISCUSSION

1. As a means of saving, how do investments differ from a bank account?
2. What does stock ownership mean?
3. What risk is there in an investment program?
4. Before starting to invest in stocks what other assets should a family own?

Summary for Chapter 11

It's a funny thing about saving—some people find it easy and can manage to set aside something out of even a very small income; others have a hard time making ends meet on $15,000 or more a year. Yet everybody agrees that saving is a good idea; those who don't save feel guilty for their failure, and those who do save wonder if they save enough.

But as a whole, American families do well as savers. One out of every four families owns government bonds; nearly two-thirds of all families have savings accounts; and six out of seven families own life insurance. In addition, 64 per cent of all families own their homes, which can be considered a form of investment.

Although the importance of saving something on a regular basis has been emphasized, it is true that there are some families whose incomes are so small they cannot afford to save. Other families, also living on small incomes, manage to save—but not very much. Low-income families can demonstrate their thrift by how saving they are with what they have and how well they can substitute other resources for money, thus freeing their limited funds to meet other needs or wants. By making a child's dress instead of buying it for $4.95, a mother may release as much as $3 or more for other needs. By learning to shop wisely, it may be possible to save as much as $1 a week on food, and that means a dollar for use elsewhere. This kind of saving is as important as saving in a bank.

Because many people find it hard to postpone their wants, they have a hard time maintaining a savings program. Here are some suggestions that might help one get established in a savings pattern:

1. *Have something to save for.* Maybe it will be a new coat, or a typewriter, or a trip, or a Christmas fund. Working towards a goal is

Thriftiness means taking care of the equipment we already own, as well as setting aside money in a savings fund.

much easier than simply saving for the sake of saving, and there is much satisfaction in accomplishing a goal on one's own.

2. *Pay yourself first.* Include yourself among the obligations you must meet on payday. This method will also help you save on a regular and consistent basis.

3. *Find a "painless" method of setting aside money.* If you are one of those people who finds that saving requires more self-discipline than you can manage, find a savings method you can't feel. A payroll savings plan may be the answer, for your savings will be deducted

from your paycheck before you receive it, and you will be spared the temptation to put off saving on your own.

4. *Save long enough to see your money grow.* Seeing the result of compound interest as it adds to your savings account will provide incentive and even a thrill. It's like finding new money, and it's all yours without working for it.

5. *If nothing else works, commit yourself to a forced savings plan.* Sign on the dotted line, and agree that you'll make regular payments as called for in the contract. It might be an agreement with the bank that you'll join a Christmas Club, although these plans seldom pay interest. Or you may take out a life insurance policy, which means that you agree to pay premiums on a regular basis. It is also possible to buy mutual funds on a contractual basis or to invest in securities on a monthly payment plan.

The future belongs to those who prepare for it. Preparation may consist of many things, but one thing is sure: money in a savings plan will help with whatever plans you make.

CAN YOU EXPLAIN?

1. emergency fund
2. compound interest
3. passbook
4. credit union

5. Series E bonds
6. securities
7. stocks and bonds
8. mutual funds

HOW WOULD YOU ANSWER?

1. How are the terms hoarding, thrift, and saving similar? How do they differ?
2. How would you go about selecting a place for your savings account? What are the factors you would consider?
3. Why do financial advisors urge families to maintain an emergency fund? Where should such a fund be kept? Why?
4. Assume that you had to explain to a stranger in this country how it is possible to make money grow. What would you tell him?
5. At what stage in the family life cycle would you expect a family to begin an investment program? Give the reasons for your answer.
6. This chapter has emphasized the desirability of having goals for saving. Why not encourage people to save just for the sake of saving? Wouldn't this be just as effective?

OTHER THINGS TO DO

1. Investigate the interest rates paid on savings accounts by the banks and savings and loan associations in your community. When is interest payable? Determine which institution will be the more profitable for you to use as a savings outlet.
2. List your personal goals for saving. Work out a savings program that you could start now and that would lead to your first goal.
3. Determine what savings goals might be expected at each stage of the family life cycle. How would you recommend that these goals be achieved?
4. Choose a stock on the New York Stock Exchange. Watch its performance by making a line graph showing the daily closing price for three weeks. Look at the financial page of the newspaper or use current magazines to find all the information you can about the stock. If you had the money to invest, would you invest in this stock? Why or why not?
5. Find several quotations that refer to savings and thrift. Select one and write a short paper on what that particular quotation means to you and how it applies to everyday life.
6. Brainstorm on the ways of saving to see how many methods for saving you can think of. Did you save only the resource *money* or did you include *other* resources? Why do you suppose people save things? Make a list of things that people save.
7. Read the book MAMA'S BANK ACCOUNT by Kathryn McLean (Harcourt) to see how Mama saved for her family. Was her saving haphazard or systematic? Was she hoarding or was it a form of savings? Justify your answer. What, exactly, *was* Mama's bank account?
8. Find a cartoon that illustrates one of the ways people save or are thrifty with their resources. Share your ideas with other classmates. Does this reflect your philosophy of saving? Justify your answer.
9. Read the book HOW TO BUY STOCKS by Louis Engel (Little, Brown) to find out how to deal with brokers and how the stock exchange operates.
10. Interview a representative from a mutual fund and prepare a report that will explain what a beginning investor should know about mutual funds.
11. Read the book UNDERSTANDING THE STOCK MARKET: A GUIDE FOR YOUNG INVESTORS by Janet Low (Little, Brown) to gain some basic and practical information about the stock market.

12 Using Business Methods to Simplify Money Matters

What this chapter is about

Personal and family living are made up of many activities, events, and responsibilities. Among them is the matter of keeping track of family money as it comes in and goes out. These financial affairs are of sufficient importance to deserve systematic and orderly handling. In this chapter we will look at some businesslike procedures for conducting financial affairs. The way a family chooses to keep its financial records and to manage its income has a direct relationship to the family's financial planning, to the control of expenditures, and to the practical matter of preparing income tax returns. These are the major ideas that will be developed:

1. Controlling family funds starts with a checking account.

2. Financial records are a picture of the past and a guide for the future.

3. A file of financial information can be a tool in decision-making.

CONTROLLING FAMILY FUNDS STARTS WITH A CHECKING ACCOUNT

One thing about family living—it isn't all moonlight and roses. And it isn't only a matter of making big decisions and dealing with big issues. There are the everyday chores to be done—washing dishes, shoveling snow or mowing the lawn, washing diapers, planning and preparing three meals a day, washing clothes, and cleaning the house. And once or twice a month there are bills to be paid. It's possible, of course, to attend to all these chores in a systematic manner in order to save time and effort. We each work out our own work-simplification system and manage to reduce these tasks to a routine that suits our needs and purposes. Managing the bills and handling family funds can also be routinized so that we can stay on top of things financially with the least effort and without headaches. It all can be accomplished by adopting some simple business methods suitable for home and family life.

Even before they were married, Millie and Ed decided that money matters would be managed in a business-like manner. Millie had been a private secretary to an executive of a large corporation; among her duties had been to keep his personal and family accounts, to take care of his financial papers and records, and to see that his family bills were paid and the checkbook balanced. She could see the value of keeping family financial matters on a business-like basis, and Ed was in full agreement. "Business-like basis," as far as Millie and Ed were concerned, meant setting aside one drawer in the kitchen for a kind of office from which they could conveniently conduct their financial affairs. It meant opening a checking account so they would have the convenience of such an account; it meant they would maintain a record-keeping system that would help them at income tax time and also be a valuable aid for future financial planning and decision-making. Because of Millie's business experience, they agreed that she would be the financial secretary for the family. Her first task was to open a checking account.

Checking accounts serve three important functions.   The first function of a checking account is to provide a convenient method for paying bills. It saves time and it is a safe way to transmit money. Second, a checking account, if accurately and carefully handled, is a simple bookkeeping system that provides a monthly accounting of the flow of family income. Finally, a checking account provides a handy record-keeping system. One's cancelled checks serve as legal proof that a bill has been paid, and are accepted as evidence for income tax deductions at any time a tax return is challenged.

How does a checking account work?   Checking accounts are offered by all commercial banks, and by some savings banks and some savings and loan institutions. There are two kinds of checking accounts: *special* and *regular*.

When you have a special checking account, you pay a fee for each check you write. Usually this fee is 10¢ per check. You may also be charged a small monthly service charge of about 50¢.

With a regular checking account, no fees are charged as long as the balance on deposit earns enough income to cover the service costs for the bank. Some banks may charge a monthly maintenance fee or add a service charge for any transactions (deposits and withdrawals) beyond a specified number. For example, the bank may allow you to write ten checks per month at no charge and then charge a fee for all those checks written in excess of ten.

The kind of account that is best for you depends on how many checks you write in an average month and the amount of money you keep on deposit in your account. If you have to write only a few checks per month, a special checking account is usually cheaper. However, if you write ten or more checks a month, you may find a regular checking

A bank official looks on as a girl fills out the application form and signs the signature cards to open her checking account.

account to your advantage. Since charges vary from bank to bank and from community to community, you will want to investigate several banks to see which offers you the best arrangements.

To open either kind of account you must fill out an application form, furnished by the bank. The application asks for information about one's age, address, and place of employment. At this time you must be ready to make a deposit. A deposit is made by filling out a deposit slip, just as you will do each time you put money in your account. You will be asked also to sign a signature card in order to show how you will sign your name each time you write a check. The bank teller will take the deposit slip and money for deposit and will in turn give you a checkbook and a duplicate copy of the deposit slip.

Writing checks.   A check used in payment of a bill is the same as money, for it represents one's instructions to the bank to pay from one's account to whomever is named on the check the amount of money indicated on the check. Because a check is money, it must be made out carefully and correctly. Each check should be written in ink; it should be accurately dated; the "pay to the order of" line should be legibly written and any name correctly spelled; the amount of the check should appear in clear numbers and be placed as near the dollar sign as possible so that no one can write in another figure. On the line below, the amount of the check should be written out in words, starting at the very edge of the line, again so that no other word can be inserted. The signature should be written exactly as it was on the signature card, which was filled out when the account was opened. At the same time that the check is written, the *check stub* should be completely filled out with: the number of the check; the date; to whom the check is issued and for what purpose; and the amount of the check. The check stub also provides space for subtracting the amount of the check from the balance as indicated on the preceding check stub. The check writer thus has a running account of his bank balance, as well as a record of his expenditures.

Balancing the checkbook.   At the end of each month, the bank sends a statement of the account, together with all of the month's cancelled checks, to the owner. The *bank statement* shows each deposit and lists each check written against the account that has cleared through the bank. It often happens that some checks are issued but do not get cashed immediately, so these are said not to have cleared through the bank. Since these checks have not been cancelled, the bank statement shows no record of them.

```
No. _157_        BAY CITY NATIONAL BANK        6-30
                                                 81

            BAY CITY, MICH., August 25 19 72

PAY TO THE
ORDER OF ——— Richard H. Kimball ——— $ 10 00⁄100

——— Ten and 00⁄100 ——————————— DOLLARS


                    Harlan P. Rogers
```

*The lines drawn on the check protect the writer of the
check from any attempt to alter the name or amount.*

When the bank statement arrives, the careful manager proceeds to
balance her checkbook. That is, she checks the record of her deposits
and checks, as shown on her checkbook stubs, against the bank statement to be sure she hasn't made any mistakes and to be certain that
the bank has not made an error. Here is how Millie balanced her
checkbook:

1. She counted the cancelled checks to see if she received all of
   the checks charged to her account on the bank statement, and
   then she arranged them by number or by date of issue.
2. She reduced her bank balance on her check stub by the amount
   she was charged for service fees by the bank. Ten checks at 10
   cents each plus the monthly service charge of 50 cents came to
   $1.50. Her check stub showed a balance of $98.25. The adjusted
   balance is: $ 96.75
3. The bank statement showed a balance of: $114.70
4. She checked all her cancelled checks against the check stubs and
   listed all the checks written but not cleared:

Telephone Company	$ 7.95
Dr. White, dentist	10.00

Total	$17.95

5. She subtracted item 4 from item 3 $96.75

Millie and the bank agree. The bank serves Millie as an auditor of
her banking business through the monthly statement it provides. This
helps Millie keep her records straight and accurate.

FOR DISCUSSION

1. What three functions are accomplished by a checking account?
2. What is the difference between a regular and a special checking account?
3. Why should checks be carefully made out?
4. What is the purpose in balancing a checkbook?

FINANCIAL RECORDS ARE A PICTURE OF THE PAST AND A GUIDE FOR THE FUTURE

Most people want their record-keeping to be simple. They want a system that takes as little time as possible to attend to; they want their records to provide all of the information they need at income tax time; and they hope their records indicate how they are doing financially.

There are several kinds of records and ways of keeping them.   Fred keeps a ledger with columns of carefully entered figures, systematically telling the story of his monthly income and what he has done with it. Phil uses a shorthand notebook in which he enters his fixed expenses per month and allows room to note any item useful in preparing his income tax return. Ed uses his cancelled checks as his record, together with his bank statements; Sharon keeps a series of envelopes in which she files receipted bills and paycheck stubs. Henry uses his cancelled checks, his bankbook, and a file folder containing receipted bills.

From such an array of records it appears difficult to know just what records are. They seem to be anything from a complete bookkeeping system to a rather casual collection of bills, checks, and receipts. The most important function of a record-keeping system, however, is its usefulness to the family keeping it. Whether the system is formal or informal, records should serve as tools to help individuals and families do better the jobs that have to be done anyway. We have to file income tax returns, and we have to make plans and decisions as to how we will use our financial resources. When one knows fairly well what he needs his records for, he can more readily decide the kind of record-keeping system to set up.

Records are necessary for income tax purposes.   Federal income taxes and in some cases the state tax as well, are withheld from the salaries or wages of most employed citizens. This "pay-as-you-go" plan means that a certain portion of one's salary is deducted from each paycheck by the employer; the money deducted in this way is used for paying one's income tax. The amount deducted, however, is not necessarily the exact amount of taxes owed the government. The withheld portion may be too much or it may not be enough. Therefore, it is required by law for every person, regardless of his age, to file an income tax return if his annual income totals a certain amount. For example, in 1971 all single persons whose total earnings amounted to $1,700 or more, had to file. Tax returns are due on April 15 each year.

The Federal Income Tax Return represents a full accounting of one's income minus certain deductible exemptions and expenses. In order to compute his tax accurately and fairly, the taxpayer relies on his personal records of income and expenditures. The more accurate his records, the more likely it is that he can keep his tax to a minimum. Although it is not our purpose here to explain how to calculate income taxes or how to fill out an income tax form, it will be our purpose to examine the tax form to learn what records a family or individual should keep in order to prepare the income tax return each year.

Income. The first portion of the tax return consists of a statement of income. All income received during the year must be reported. For those people whose only source of income is salary or wages, this portion of the tax form presents no problem. Their employers will provide them with an official statement (W-2 form) showing their earnings and the amount of tax withheld. They will attach this statement to their tax return.

Many families receive income other than what is earned on the job, however. Interest earned on money in savings accounts is income and must be reported, as must the interest earned on savings bonds that have been cashed during the year. All rents received during the year are counted as income. Prize money won in contests must be reported; if the prize is in the form of merchandise, the cash value of the prize is given as income. For example, if you were to win a trip or a new television set, your income tax return would state the value of the prize in dollars and cents.

The income tax law states that people who regularly receive tips on their jobs must declare, as part of their income, the amount of money they receive in this way. This group of people includes, for instance, waiters and waitresses, taxicab drivers, porters, and hairdressers.

The instructions accompanying the Federal Income Tax form lists the various kinds of income that must be reported, as well as the kinds of income that are exempt. Examples of exempt income are scholar-

A Peace Corps volunteer teaches Peruvian children in a
small school that he built. Not his salary, but his living
and travel allowance, are tax exempt.

ships to students, proceeds of a life insurance policy paid on the death
of the policyholder, proceeds from a health insurance policy, Social
Security payments, public welfare payments, and living and travel
allowances paid to Peace Corps volunteers. Families frequently receive
both kinds of income—taxable and exempt.

Having accurately stated his total income, the taxpayer is ready to
take the next step in preparing his tax return.

Exemptions and deductions. Every taxpayer is allowed to claim as
tax-free a portion of his total income. In other words, a certain amount
of money is exempt from taxes. The portion that is non-taxable is
based on the numbers of people who are dependent on him for their
support. For each such dependent the taxpayer is allowed an exemption; he is permitted to count himself as a dependent also. In 1971,

for example, each exemption amounted to a tax-free amount of $675; in 1972 the personal exemption is $750.

The Jack Roberts family includes the parents and two children. Jack' claims four exemptions. Thus his exempt, or tax-free, income in 1971 amounted to $2,700 ($675 × 4 family members). Dorothy Singer, a nurse at the Elmsford Clinic, is unmarried and has no other person dependent on her salary. Her exemption is $675. Larry Comstock, also single, supports his widowed mother and fifteen-year-old sister. He has three exemptions; his exempt income amounted to $2,025.

In computing his income tax, the taxpayer is allowed to make certain *deductions*. The kinds of deductions permitted are specified in the income tax instructions from the Bureau of Internal Revenue. If he claims any of thesē, the taxpayer must be able to verify each item he deducts. Therefore, financial records are necessary.

Deductions are permitted for any expenses one has in connection with his job. If a person has to buy his own uniforms, for example, as is required of policemen, laboratory technicians, nurses, or beauty operators, he is permitted to deduct the cost of these from his income. Also deductible are special tools or equipment purchased for one's job. Dues for professional or business organizations are deductible; expenses for business trips away from home are also permissible deductions. For example, Virginia Anders, a hairdresser at the Beauty Box, bought six uniforms, each costing her $10.95. She was allowed to deduct $65.70 ($10.95 × 6) from her income. In addition, she was a delegate to the state convention of hairdressers and paid her own expenses. The two-day meeting cost her a total of $67.45 for travel, hotel, meals, and miscellaneous expenses. When Virginia filed her income tax return, she claimed a total deduction of $133.15 for business expenses.

Deductions are permitted within certain limits for medical and dental expenses. Deductible expenses include fees paid to doctors and dentists, the cost of drugs and medicines, hospital and clinic charges, ambulance costs, premiums paid on health insurance policies, the costs of eyeglasses, hearing aids, dentures, wheel chairs, crutches, and other identifiable charges resulting from medical treatment. The limitations on how much one may deduct for medical and dental purposes are defined in the instructions accompanying the tax form. Only those expenses that exceed the limitations are deductible. But in order to know if one qualifies for this deduction, he must know what his total expenditures for medical and dental care have been. Therefore, it is a good procedure to keep a full record of such costs. Clarence Buxton's records for medical and dental care showed expenditures for the year as follows:

Dr. Kendall, dentist, for Buddy's braces	$600
Dr. Schwab, dentist, for self and wife	40
Dr. Custer, M.D.	
Physical check-up for self	75
Treating wife, bronchial pneumonia	50
Flu shots for Buddy	10
Dr. Forster, eye examinations for wife	15
Allied Optical Service, glasses for wife	32
Majestic Health Insurance Co., premiums	88
Community drug store, prescriptions and medicine	64
	$974

When Clarence figured his tax, he found that his medical and dental expenses came to $974, most of which was deductible.

Deductions are permitted for contributions to one's church, to any charitable organization, and to educational institutions and organizations. Again, one needs to know what his annual gifts amount to and, in order to accurately claim these deductions, must be able to show evidence for each donation listed. Doris Groves deducted $341 for contributions. Her itemized list showed $260 to Prince of Peace Church ($5 each week); she had cancelled checks as proof. Her other contributions were listed as follows (in each case she had a receipt):

Community Red Feather Appeal	$10.00
Fairmount Hospital Association	7.00
Girl Scouts	5.00
Camp Swannee for Underprivileged Children	25.00
New Library Fund Drive	15.00
County Tuberculosis Association	3.00
Desk and lamp donated to Salvation Army	
(assessed value)	9.00
Red Cross	2.50
Cancer Society	2.50
School for the Blind	2.50

Deductions are permitted for interest paid on loans, mortgages, and installment-plan purchases. On loans and installment purchases, the interest is the only deductible item; no service charges or other costs can be added. If the loan agreement does not specifically state the interest being charged, the tax instructions explain how to compute the interest.

A laboratory technician who must buy his own uniforms for work can deduct this expense from his taxable income.

Deductions are permitted for the other taxes one must pay. These include state and local income taxes, sales taxes, gasoline taxes, real estate and personal property taxes, and school taxes. Tax receipts on annual tax payments to state and local governments are an important aid in computing this deduction. In the case of sales taxes and gasoline taxes, receipts are not usually available; therefore, some record of those purchases on which taxes are charged is helpful. Irv Swanson bought his first car out of his earnings as an after-school employee at the Busy Bee Supermarket. The sales tax on his car amounted to $18;

interest on the loan amounted to $70; taxes on the gas, figured at 6¢ per gallon in his state, came to $15 for 250 gallons purchased during the year. All told, Irv's deductions, as a result of his car purchase, came to $103.

Dollars can be saved on taxes by keeping records of deductible items. A family has no way of knowing at the beginning of the year what event may occur that can be claimed as a substantial deduction, but without records to prove it, there will be no way to justify the deduction on the tax return. Very possibly it will turn out that taking the standard deduction will be to the family's advantage; on the other hand, if deductions can be itemized they may amount to more than the standard deductions and constitute a savings on the total tax bill. A useful system for maintaining records of deductible items is to keep a simple file of large envelopes labeled Contributions, Other Taxes, Medical and Dental, Business Expenses, and Interest on Loans. During the year place in the envelopes the receipts and cancelled checks relating to each classification.

Records are an aid in future decision-making. Millie and Ed, mentioned earlier in this chapter, took seriously something Millie's former boss had told them just before they were married. They were discussing with him some of their financial concerns and ambitions. He reminded them that they were starting a new household and that each of them was bringing to the household his individual attitudes about money as well as his individual practices in handling it. He pointed out that probably it would take a few months before they would have their individual differences woven together.

"During those first few months," he said, "why don't you keep an account of your expenditures, week by week, or even day by day? In order to know where you're going, you have to know where you are." He went on to explain that if they took a good look at what they were doing with their income, it would be much easier to make plans for its use in the future. "As a matter of fact, it is a good idea for everybody to take a picture of themselves in this way, but for a new family it is a must."

And so in the kitchen "office," Millie kept an account book in which she recorded the weekly cash expenditures for food, household supplies, household operating costs, clothing, drycleaning and shoe repair, cigarettes, beverages, magazines and newspapers, and recreation. While she was at it, she recorded the expenditures they made by check also: rent, utilities, car payment, contributions, and other expenses. In this way she had a complete record in a convenient form of what they were using their money for. Her bookkeeping duties, which took only a few minutes every week, turned out to be a most useful tool when it came to financial planning.

Useful categories for setting up an account book might be adapted from this list:

> Food
>> At home
>> Away from home
> Tobacco and Beverages
> Housing and Household Operation
>> Shelter
>> Utilities
>> Supplies and operation
> Household Furnishings and Equipment

A busy homemaker who takes time to keep her financial records up-to-date knows where her money is going and can more readily make plans for its future use.

Clothing and Accessories
Transportation
   Car
   Other
Medical and Dental Care
Personal Care
   Cleaners
   Laundry
   Hairdresser, barber
   Cosmetics and grooming aids
Recreation
Reading and Education
Insurance
Gifts and Contributions

After six months of marriage Millie and Ed examined their account book, and were surprised at what they learned about themselves. For two people, they were spending an unreasonable amount of money on food, compared to the food costs suggested in the spending guides they obtained from the library. They felt also that they had spent too much on recreation, a category that included expenses for records, movies, bowling, ball games, parties. On the basis of their findings about themselves and how they were using their money, Millie and Ed set up a trial budget. They put themselves on an allowance system, increased their savings by cutting down on some of their other expenses, and made arrangements for meeting some of the big expenditures they would have to face in a few months, but which they had completely forgotten. Until this time, for instance, they had given no thought to a life insurance premium coming due in another month, nor had they considered how they would pay for the car insurance. Millie and Ed are not unlike thousands of other young couples. But they caught themselves before they were in serious trouble, and admitted that they had been riding high.

Record-keeping does not have to be a burdensome chore. A simple household account book, available at a dime store or stationer, is all the equipment necessary. Some banks provide record books free of charge. It is also possible to make an account book by simply using an ordinary notebook and ruling in the necessary columns. Record-keeping takes no special skill. One doesn't need to be an accountant or a bookkeeper. But it does take willingness and attention, and complete honesty. The record will be meaningless if all expenditures are not entered. If, for instance, Millie wanted to hide some expenses from Ed by not entering them in her book, her record would be incomplete and misleading. When we say all expenditures should be entered, we also recognize that each family member should have some money that is his and his alone, and for which no accounting is necessary.

Millie and Ed continued to keep their account book up-to-date after they had their budget planned and adopted. At the end of the second month A.B. (After Budget), they reviewed their record to be sure they were managing according to their design. Some alterations were needed. They were trying to be too ambitious in their savings plan, and they had not allowed enough for clothing and upkeep or for Ed's lunches and pocket money. From their records, they were able to evaluate their financial progress. They could see how they were doing as managers. They could judge how realistic they had been in planning, and they had a way of measuring how close they were to achieving their goals. It took the guesswork out of their financial appraisal.

FOR DISCUSSION

1. What are the two major reasons families keep financial records?
2. What is the difference between exemptions and deductions?
3. List the deductions available to individual or family taxpayers.
4. How do financial records assist one in making future plans?

A FILE OF FINANCIAL INFORMATION CAN BE A TOOL IN DECISION-MAKING

Financial decision-making is serious business. It often affects the use of family funds over a long period of time. Many problems appear complicated; the alternative solutions are confusing. Most families, therefore, need all the information they can get. As a help, it is useful to build a personal or family library of financial information.

Financial advice and information is readily available: in the community, through government agencies, from national organizations and associations, and in monthly periodicals, newspapers, books, and pamphlets. Some sources of information are given here to suggest where a family may turn for advice when necessary and where free or inexpensive informational materials for a personal file may be obtained.

*The local public library may have just the information
you need to help solve a financial problem.*

Sources of financial advice are available in the community.   No
matter where one lives, he can be reasonably sure that there will be
someone not too far away who knows much about finance. A banker
can give advice on matters that relate to budgets, savings, mortgages,
loans, and taxes; a lawyer can help with problems concerning taxes,
mortgages, loans, installment sales contracts, insurance programs, and
Social Security. The nearest regional or area office of the Social Security Administration will help any family needing assistance in filing a
claim or in figuring what coverage they have. When it comes time to
file one's Federal Income Tax return, he may enlist the free counsel
of a member of the staff in the regional office of the Internal Revenue
Bureau.

The local library is a gold mine of information. Here may be found
books written for the general public that deal with family money management. The librarian will be acquainted, too, with articles of general

interest that may relate to a particular problem one may be investigating. From the librarian one can also learn of other sources of information.

Many national organizations provide financial information. There are many organizations or associations that prepare informative bulletins or pamphlets on financial topics, most of which are available free of charge or at a nominal price. Here are six organizations that provide consumer information on family finance:

For information on bank service:

American Bankers Association
815 Connecticut Avenue, N.W.
Washington, D.C. 20006

For consumer information on insurance, budgeting, credit, home ownership, and other topics of consumer interest:

Council for Better Business Bureaus
845 Third Avenue, New York, New York 10022

For money management information: booklets on The Food Dollar, The Clothing Dollar, Savings and Investment Dollar, Shelter Dollar, Automobile Dollar, and others (25¢ each):

Money Management Institute
Household Finance Corporation
Prudential Plaza, Chicago, Illinois 60601

For information on life and health insurance, budgeting, and related topics:

Institute of Life Insurance
277 Park Avenue, New York, New York 10017

For information on consumer credit:

National Consumer Finance Association
1000 Sixteenth Street, N.W., Washington, D.C. 20036

For information on stocks and bonds:

New York Stock Exchange
11 Wall Street, New York, New York 10005

For information on automobile insurance, and other casualty insurance:

Insurance Information Institute
110 Williams St., New York, New York 10038

Magazines and newspapers carry articles of financial interest. Family finance is a subject of concern to so many families today that editors of family magazines frequently include articles on money matters. Your daily newspaper may also include a column of special interest and help. Magazines that make a regular practice of providing consumer and financial information include *Better Homes and Gardens, Good Housekeeping, McCalls,* and the various publications sold in supermarkets. One magazine that specializes in family finance and consumer education is *Changing Times,* the Kiplinger Magazine. For information about products and appliances, *Consumer Reports,* published by Consumers Union, furnishes the results of their testing and ranks the items according to their overall quality.

Maintaining a file of clippings, articles, and bulletins will serve as a quick reference when one is confronted with a financial problem. Don't be discouraged if your file doesn't have the exact answer to your problem; files seldom do. But you will find that such a reference shelf will probably contain a clue to where your answer may be found, or it may open up additional alternatives that you have not considered.

FOR DISCUSSION

1. To whom would you turn in your community for financial advice? List the financial topics with which each of these sources might help you.
2. Have you been aware of articles on money management in magazines you have read regularly? What are some of the financial topics about which articles have been written?

Summary for Chapter 12

Not all aspects of personal and family living lend themselves to system and order in quite the same way as money does. There are two by-products that result from using business methods for managing financial affairs: money is more effectively managed, and time is released for other family activities.

A checking account is a convenience in making payments; it helps control some expenditures that one may be tempted to make, and it provides a valuable record of what one has done with his money.

A simple record-keeping system that provides files for all receipts and cancelled checks that might be possible income tax deductions can be a money-saver and a guide.

A simple system of keeping accounts of daily or weekly expenditures can help one evaluate his financial progress and measure how effective he is in working toward his goals.

One thing about money is that it doesn't grow on trees! No matter how much or how little of it the family has, money has to stretch a long way; systematic management, consisting of some elementary business techniques, can help to stretch it further.

CAN YOU EXPLAIN?

1. regular checking account
2. special checking account
3. check stub
4. bank balance
5. bank statement
6. exemption
7. standard deduction
8. W-2 form

HOW WOULD YOU ANSWER?

1. What are the reasons for which individuals and families use checking accounts? Why might a checking account tend to curb one's spending?
2. Does your state levy an income tax? If so, what is allowed for exemptions? What deductions are permitted?
3. What kinds of records would you advise a young couple to keep for tax purposes? The young couple might ask you why they should keep records at all. What would you tell them?
4. When you receive your monthly bank statement, why may some items not be on the statement?
5. Why should you compare the monthly bank statement with your check book balance?
6. Explain what value there is in keeping expenditure records. It is said that one can learn a great deal about a family's goals and values by reviewing its account book. Why?

OTHER THINGS TO DO

1. Obtain information from a bank of your choice about the checking accounts available to the customers. What fees are charged for each kind of account? For what purpose? What procedures must be followed in opening an account?
2. Explain the purpose of the Better Business Bureau. Describe how the bureau protects the consumer. Take their two slogans, "Before you invest, investigate" and "Read before you sign," and show how the advice suggested in these quotations can help a consumer.

3. Make a list of all the different kinds of taxes a family might pay during the year and when the payments are due. How can a family plan for these items in its financial plan?

4. Obtain a current Federal Income Tax form. Study it and then make a list of the deductible expenditures for which you should keep a record to have on hand when filling out your income tax return. List places where a person or family may secure without charge sound information regarding income tax.

5. Take a field trip to one or more banks to find out what services are available to depositors.

6. Find articles in periodicals on the concept of the "cashless, checkless society" to see what this means to the consumer. Do you favor this method of managing money? Give reasons for your answer.

7. Compile a list of organizations and periodicals that would help a consumer make a financial decision. Are you surprised at the list? Discuss the types of information available to individuals through some of these sources.

8. List all the benefits that a citizen in your community receives as a result of taxes.

9. Look at the various forms that are used to calculate local, state, and federal taxes to become familiar with the information required. Then see if you can find out how the tax dollar is distributed at these levels. Prepare a chart to show the tax dollar distribution in your country.

10. Discuss what is meant by this quotation by Oliver Wendell Holmes: "I like to pay taxes. With them I buy civilization."

Epilogue
Money Matters—
People Count

"Good grief, there's a lot to learn about family money!" Charlie Brown might say if he had been reading over your shoulder as you studied this book.

"There's a lot more you don't know, Charlie Brown!" we can hear Lucy hollering, and she is probably right. For indeed, there is a lot more to know about family money than appears between the covers of this book.

This book attempts to help students understand the role that money plays in family living. Its chief concern has been with families; its major emphasis has been on the multiple resources available to a family, with a focus on money.

Important as money is in family living today, it is not the most important factor in family life. There are values that far outweigh the monetary value of dollars and cents, values that no amount of spending or budgeting will achieve: love, friendship, and respect, for instance. No amount of money can buy the good feeling a father has as his little daughter snuggles in his arms; nor can the pleasure and satisfaction that comes with seeing a son hit his first home run be measured with a dollar sign; neither can the invigorating feeling of a hike on an autumn day as the leaves are turning red and gold.

Yes, family life is made up of many things. Money, as emphasized in previous chapters, is only a tool that helps the family realize some of these fundamental values. There is no virtue in money—only in what money can do. Nor is there any real value in money management, except what it can contribute to family relationships, individual development and growth, and personal and family achievement. As was stated earlier, family money is important for two reasons: for the needs basic to life itself that it helps to provide, and for the things it enables one to do and to become. Whatever else can be said about money and its place in the life of the family is secondary.

Does this suggest that money and what we do with it really isn't very important? Not at all. Because the end-product of family and personal money management relates intimately to people—to you, your parents, your brothers and sisters, aunts, uncles, and cousins, and all the folks up and down the street, it becomes very important. Our attention has been directed toward some of the "big issues" of family living in an effort to see how the use of financial resources can best serve the purposes of the family as they resolve these issues, or at least as they face them. It does matter, for instance, that decisions requiring the use of money be made with care; many of those decisions have to be lived with for a long time to come. It does matter how one chooses to use credit, for the cost of credit must be counted in two ways: by the price one pays for the use of someone else's money, and by the measure of those things one gives up as he pays off his debt. It does matter that family income is protected against critical economic risks, because so much of family living and planning for the future hinges on this income. It does matter that one enter into home ownership knowing that there is more to it than monthly payments. It does matter that a savings program back up financial decisions and activities so as to add further to economic security.

Thus this book draws to an end. Not long ago, on the outskirts of Atlanta, there was a large billboard. On it was displayed only a few words lettered in bright gold on a purple background:

MONEY MATTERS

BUT NOT AS MUCH AS YOU

That is what this book is about.

READING FOR A PURPOSE

ONE | The Social and Economic Setting in Which Families Live

Read one of the following biographies or another of your choice. Identify several values and analyze the sources of these values in this person's life.

ABRAHAM LINCOLN, by James Daughtery. Viking Press. A poet writes about the famous Abraham Lincoln.

THE BABE RUTH STORY, by Babe Ruth and Bob Considine. Dutton. The only authorized biography, beginning with his childhood, of the greatest baseball player of all time.

TO CATCH AN ANGEL, by Robert Russell. Vanguard. A story of how Robert Russell was able to complete his Ph.D. degree even though he was blinded at the age of five.

CHILD OF THE DARK, by Carolina Maria de Jesus. Dutton. A woman living in a Brazilian favela envisions a better life for herself and her children and, through her diary, is finally able to realize it.

CHRISTMAS WITHOUT JOHNNY, by Gladys Hasty Carroll. Popular Library Edition. A story of a young sensitive school boy who was helped by a superintendent.

THE DIARY OF A YOUNG GIRL, by Anne Frank. Doubleday. The diary of an adolescent girl describes the two years she and her family hid in a warehouse attic during the Nazi occupation of Holland.

EVERYTHING BUT MONEY, by Sam Levenson. Simon and Schuster. A humorous story about the author's earlier years in East Harlem.

HARRIET TUBMAN, CONDUCTOR ON THE UNDERGROUND RAILROAD, by Ann Petry. Crowell. The story of the woman who helped more than three hundred slaves escape from the South on the Underground Railroad.

LUTHER BURBANK: PLANT MAGICIAN, by John Y. Beaty. Messner. The principles of plant life that Burbank learned at an early age formed the basis for his later accomplishments in breeding plants.

MADAME CURIE, by Eve Curie. Doubleday. The background and private life of this famous woman scientist, revealed by her daughter.

PROFILES IN COURAGE, by John F. Kennedy. Harper. Recommended for young people in the abridged edition of this popular adult book about eight Americans who took courageous stands at crucial moments in public life.

THE ROCK AND THE WILLOW, by Mildred Lee. Lothrop. In spite of her family responsibilities and the hardships of the depression years, Enie Singleton sets her sights on a college education.

THE STORY OF MY LIFE, by Helen Keller. Doubleday. Helen Keller wrote her auto-biography when she was a college junior. The book relates her problems in learning to cope with a world of normal people—those with sight, speech, and hearing—and how she achieved success.

THE THREAD THAT RUNS SO TRUE, by Jesse Stuart. Scribner. Jesse Stuart describes the joys and frustrations of his teaching career.

WINTER WHEAT, by Mildred Walker. Harcourt. A story of a young girl whose college education was always dependent upon the success of the winter wheat crop. One year the crop was poor, so Ellen took a job teaching country school. This gave her a chance to think about the real values of her life.

THE YOUNG WINSTON CHURCHILL, by John Marsh. World Distributors, Ltd., Manchester, England. The early years of Britain's Prime Minister.

Read one of the following books or another book of your choice on families. Observe incidents that show relationships between what a family thinks is important and the family's goals.

BANNER IN THE SKY, by James Ramsey Ullman. Lippincott. Young Rudi Matt is determined to conquer the mountain that took his father's life.

THE FAMILY NOBODY WANTED, by Helen Doss. Little, Brown. A minister and his wife adopt twelve children, all of mixed racial parentage.

GIANT, by Edna Ferber. Doubleday. The story of a woman who married a man whose values were completely different from her own.

GIANTS IN THE EARTH, by O. E. Rolvaag. Harper. The story of a Norwegian couple who lived out on the prairies in Dakota and what this environment meant to each one of them.

THE GOOD EARTH, by Pearl S. Buck. World. A story of a Chinese peasant couple who accumulated land while weathering famine and drought.

IT'S LIKE THIS, CAT, by Emily Neville. Harper. A boy growing up in New York City develops in his understanding of other people—his parents, an older boy in trouble, and his first girl.

KAREN, by Marie Killilea. Prentice. Through the courage and determination of her family, a little girl born with cerebral palsy is taught to walk, talk, and write.

LITTLE BRITCHES, by Ralph Moody. Norton. A boyhood chronicle of a family's struggles against almost insurmountable odds on a Colorado ranch.

LITTLE WOMEN, by Louisa May Alcott. Cromwell. Always popular is this story of the home life of four sisters in New England.

ONION JOHN, by Joseph Krumgold. Crowell. The friendship of Onion John, a squatter, and twelve-year-old Andy is indestructible, until Andy finds himself siding with the townspeople against Onion John.

THE PEARL, by John Steinbeck. Viking. The pearl that Kino found did not bring the happiness that he thought it would.

A RAISIN IN THE SUN, by Lorraine Hansberry. Random. The tensions and explosive drama in a middle-class family are revealed in this play, set in Chicago's South Side.

SWIFTWATER, by Paul Annixter. Houghton. Bucky, who lives in the Maine woods, takes care of his ailing father's traplines and at the same time wants to have a sanctuary for wild geese.

Read one of the following books, or another of your choice, and describe how basic needs are being met for these individuals, or how they help to provide for some of the basic needs of others.

CRESS DELAHANTY, by Jessamyn West. Harcourt. Delightful short sketches of the high school years of a girl growing up on a ranch in California.

GO, TEAM, GO, by John Tunis. Morrow. This action-packed story deals with a basketball tournament in Indiana.

IN A MIRROR, by Mary Stolz. Harper. A detached and realistic self-appraisal enables a college girl to solve her problem of being over-weight.

JOHNNY TREMAIN, by Esther Forbes. Houghton. After injuring his hand, a young silversmith's apprentice finds a new role—helping to further the American Revolution.

A LOVE, OR A SEASON, by Mary Stolz. Harper. A story of the values of friendship.

MRS. MINIVER, by Jan Struther. Harcourt. The story of a woman and the delightful episodes that cover her life over a two-year span.

OUT ON A LIMB, by Louise Baker. McGraw. Although her leg was amputated when she was eight years old, the author displays determination and a sense of humor in spite of her handicap.

SEVENTEENTH SUMMER, by Maureen Daly. Dodd. A story of two seventeen-year-old girls in a small-town setting who experience their first loves.

SO BIG, by Edna Ferber. Doubleday. The mother of the household manages all the problems of running a large truck farm and rearing a family without losing her gay, indomitable spirit.

THE STORY OF ALBERT SCHWEITZER, by Jo Manton. Abelard. An engrossing biography of the famous doctor who gave up a personal career to become a medical missionary in the jungles of Africa.

Read one of the following books, or another of your choice, and describe the ethnic background that a family in this country reveals, or the cultural differences that an individual encounters in another country.

AT HOME IN INDIA, by Cynthia Bowles. Harcourt. The daughter of an ambassador to India found more similarities than she expected between herself and her new friends in India.

THE CHOSEN, by Chaim Potok. Simon and Schuster. The story of two teenager Jewish boys who grew up in a section of Brooklyn but lived in entirely different worlds. It is a story of friendship and of father-son relationships.

FIFTH CHINESE DAUGHTER, by Jade Snow Wong. Harper. The values Jade Snow Wong learned at the American school, which were very often in conflict with the values of her parents, influenced her decision to attend college and to become an artist.

THE LIGHT IN THE FOREST, by Conrad Richter. Knopf. After eleven years with an Indian Chief, John Butler, fifteen, returns home to his original family. This is a story of divided loyalties.

MAI PEN RAI MEANS NEVER MIND, by Carol Hollinger. Houghton. A woman who follows her husband to Thailand on government service writes a perceptive account of her new country, its customs, and its people.

MY LORD, WHAT A MORNING, by Marian Anderson. Viking. The great concert singer recalls both her struggles and her successes.

ONLY IN AMERICA, by Harry Golden. World. A newspaper editor has written a delightful collection of observations on American Jewish life.

A PROMISE IS A PROMISE, by Molly Cone. Houghton. A warm, sympathetic picture of a Jewish family and of Ruthy, who discovers that she doesn't want to be like everyone else.

THE SMALL WOMAN, by Alan Burgess. Dutton: The true story of Gladys Aylward, a woman with a consuming ambition to be a missionary in China.

WHEN THE LEGENDS DIE, by Hal Borland. Lippincott. This is a story of an Indian boy who finds it difficult to adjust to the white man's life.

TWO | Management in Family Living

Read one of the following books, or another of your choice, and describe the special resources this person used in order to develop his goals.

ABE LINCOLN GROWS UP, by Carl Sandburg. Harcourt. This shortened version of the original work begins with Lincoln's childhood in Kentucky and ends with his departure for New Salem, Illinois, to start life on his own.

ALBERT EINSTEIN, by Arthur Beckhard. Putnam. The biography of the great physicist, his life in Europe, and something of his scientific contributions.

THE BARRIOS OF MANTA, by Rhoda and Earl Brooks. New American Library. A young couple are sent to Ecuador on a Peace Corps assignment. They try to help people learn to solve problems caused by their environment. We see also how certain items can become valuable resources.

THE STORY OF HELEN KELLER, by Lorena Hickok. Grosset. A young woman, deaf and blind from infancy, is miraculously taught to communicate through the skillfulness of her great teacher.

A BOY TEN FEET TALL, by W. H. Canaway. Ballantine. Orphaned at the age of ten, Sammy sets out for Durban, a journey of five thousand miles through the heart of Africa.

THE CHORD OF STEEL, by Thomas B. Costain. Doubleday. The story of Alexander Graham Bell's great invention, the telephone, and the difficulties he encountered in getting a patent.

THE FAR JOURNEY, by Loula Grace Erdman. Dodd. A brave woman learns to meet the hardships of frontier life on a covered-wagon journey.

I AM FIFTEEN AND I DON'T WANT TO DIE, by Christine Arnothy. Dutton. The author recalls what it was like when her city of Budapest was occupied first by Germans and then by the Russians.

JENNIFER, by Zoa Sherbune. Morrow. The story of a girl with seemingly insurmountable problems and how she is finally able to cope with them.

THE LIFE AND TIMES OF FREDERICK DOUGLASS, adapted by Barbara Ritchie. Crowell. This shortened version of the original book tells of a slave who escaped from bondage before the Civil War, educated himself, and became one of the leaders of the abolition movement.

MARIA MONTESSORI, HER LIFE AND WORK, by E. M. Standing. New American Library. When her teaching methods proved successful with defective children, the famous woman educator used the same methods to teach normal children.

MRS. MIKE, by Benedict and Nancy Freedman. Coward-McCann. The story of a couple who establish a home close to the Arctic Circle. The book describes the adjustments and their interdependence upon neighbors in times of need.

ROOKIE QUARTERBACK, by Jackson Scholz. Morrow. The story of a high school drop-out who returns from the service and through his interest in football, resumes his high school education, finding a life goal.

UP FROM SLAVERY, by Booker T. Washington. Doubleday. This autobiography tells how Booker T. Washington educated himself and then went on to establish the Tuskegee Institute.

> *Read one of the following books, or another of your choice, and describe how the lives of family members were affected by the period of time in which they lived or by their social and economic background.*

ACT ONE, by Moss Hart. Random. The famous playwright recounts with considerable humor his growing-up years in New York City and his first experiences and final success in the theater.

ALICE ADAMS, by Booth Tarkington. Grosset. The story of Alice Adams is one of frustrated social ambitions and of disappointing attempts to keep up with people whose money and background seemed to place them above her.

AND NOW TOMORROW, by Rachel Rield. Macmillan. Emily was born into a prominent New England family that owned many mill factories. After Emily became deaf she reached out for new values and was able to understand the people who work for their daily bread.

ANYTHING CAN HAPPEN, by George and Helen Papashvily. Harper. An immigrant to this country finds many things happening to him but manages to retain his light-hearted philosophy.

DADDY WAS A NUMBER RUNNER, by Louise Meriwether. Prentice-Hall. A pre-adolescent black girl faces the daily hazards of life in the Harlem of the thirties.

THE DOLLMAKER, by Harriette Louisa Arnow. Macmillan. A Kentucky mother is transplanted with her family to Detroit. She is able to adjust to the new environment in spite of difficulties, including a non-cooperative family.

I ALWAYS WANTED TO BE SOMEBODY, by Althea Gibson and Ed Fitzgerald. Harper. The famous woman athlete tells how she grew from a defensive tomboy into an internationally-known tennis champion.

TO KILL A MOCKINGBIRD, by Lee Harper. Lippincott. A young girl sees the quiet life of her Alabama town disrupted when her father, Finch, an attorney, defends a black man unjustly accused of a crime.

KNOCK AT THE DOOR, EMMY, by Florence Crannel Means. Houghton. The story of a migrant family that travels the country working the crops and of Emmy, who aspires to a different way of life.

A LANTERN IN HER HAND, by Bess Streeter Aldrich. Appleton. Abbie could have married a doctor but she chose a farmer's son. Even though there were many hardships to overcome, their love and determination to make a successful life carried them through.

LET THE HURRICANE ROAR, by Rose Wilder Lane. McKay. The central characters, Caroline and Charles, live in a Dakota dugout, meeting the hardships of pioneer life with steadfastness.

MY ANTONIA, by Willa Cather. Houghton. A New York attorney describes his boyhood days in Nebraska and tells about his friendship with Antonia, a complex young Bohemian girl.

NECTAR IN A SIEVE, by Kamala Markandaya. John Day. A peasant woman in a primitive village in India cares for her family amidst poverty and disaster.

A TREE GROWS IN BROOKLYN, by Betty Smith. Harper. During the early years of this century, Francie Nolan, daughter of first generation immigrants, found out what life was like amidst the poverty in Brooklyn.

WE SHOOK THE FAMILY TREE, by Hildegarde Dolson. Random. The biography, charmingly told, of an adolescent girl's attempts to transform herself into a great beauty.

THE ROAD TO THE WHITE HOUSE, by Lorena Hickok. Chilton. A biography of the life of Franklin D. Roosevelt previous to his presidential years.

Read one of the books listed below, or another of your choice, and describe how decisions were made.

BEANY MALONE, by Lenora Mattingly Weber. Crowell. Sixteen-year-old Beany takes charge of the household while her father recuperates from a serious illness.

BELLES ON THEIR TOES, by Frank B. Gilbreth, Jr. and Ernestine G. Carey. Crowell. The mother from CHEAPER BY THE DOZEN becomes head of the family after the father dies, and sees all her children through college and into marriage.

CHEAPER BY THE DOZEN, by Frank B. Gilbreth, Jr. and Ernestine G. Carey. Crowell. A father who is an efficiency expert tries to use the principles of his profession to organize his family of twelve children.

THE EGG AND I, by Betty MacDonald. Lippincott. A woman is able to see herself and her life on a chicken farm with a sense of humor.

GRAPES OF WRATH, by John Steinbeck. Viking. In an effort to escape the Oklahoma dust bowl in the early thirties, the Joad family, numbering thirteen, migrated to the West Coast. The story is about their struggle for existence.

OF HUMAN BONDAGE, by W. Somerset Maugham. Doubleday. This story tells how Phillip, a deformed handicapped person with a club foot, is finally able to achieve a satisfying life and is able to develop confidence.

JAMIE, by Jack Bennett. Little, Brown. Jamie grows up on a South African farm under the firm discipline of his English father. His father is killed by a buffalo when Jamie is eleven years old. Jamie vows to kill the animal and the story tells how he carries out his vow.

MAMA'S BANK ACCOUNT, by Kathryn Forbes. Harcourt. The mother of this Norwegian carpenter's family is a wise and resourceful woman; her extraordinary sense of values make each episode in the story an object lesson in human relationships.

MR. AND MRS. BO JO JONES, by Ann Head. New American Library. The story of a teen-age marriage and the problems the couple face during their first year of married life.

PAPA'S WIFE, by Thyra Bjorn. Holt. At the age of sixteen, Maria goes to work as a maid in the home of Reverend Franzon, a bachelor. She falls in love with him immediately and makes up her mind to marry him. The delightful story tells how Maria was able to persuade Papa after she has made a decision.

PHOEBE, by Patricia Dizeno. McGraw-Hill. A story of a teenager who becomes pregnant and her search for maturity.

SHANE, by Jack Schaefer. Houghton. Shane, a drifter, stops at the homestead farm of Starrett. He stays long enough to help Starrett's fight against the man who is trying to force them out of the valley.

SOME MERRY-GO-ROUND MUSIC, by Mary Stolz. Harper. A New York secretary learns to face life with honesty.

Read one of the following books, or another of your choice, and describe what problems an individual or a family faced and how they attempted to solve their problems.

BIG DOC'S GIRL, by Mary Medearis. Lippincott. After their doctor father dies, Mary keeps the family together in the same community, serving the people through her music.

A CHOICE OF WEAPONS, by Gordon Parks. Harper. Now a well-known photographer for Life magazine, Gordon Parks tells a fascinating, if somewhat startling, story of what it was like for him growing up in a midwestern city.

FACE TO FACE, by Ved Mehta. Little, Brown. The author, totally blind since he was three years old, describes his growing-up in a Hindu family in India, followed by his years of education in the United States.

HOLD FAST TO YOUR DREAMS, by Catherine Blanton. Messner. Emmy Lou leaves Alabama to go to Arizona where she finds prejudice, too. She hopes to become a ballet dancer; the story presents the many problems she faces.

THE HUMAN COMEDY, by William Saroyan. Harcourt. On his job as a telegram messenger, fourteen-year-old Homer was in a good position to learn about human nature.

I NEVER PROMISED YOU A ROSE GARDEN, by Hannah Green. Holt. Deborah Blau, sixteen, is committed to a mental hospital as a severe schizophrenic. She fights her way back to sanity with the help of a psychiatrist.

JOY IN THE MORNING, by Betty Smith. Harper. A young college couple in the early nineteen-twenties is faced with many problems during their first two years of marriage.

THE LIGHT IN THE PIAZZA, by Elizabeth Spender. McGraw-Hill. A mother and her mentally retarded daughter are traveling through Italy when her daughter falls in love with a young Italian man who wants to marry her. The mother's problem is whether to allow her daughter to marry this man and find happiness or concede to the girl's retardation and prevent the marriage.

THE MIDDLE SISTER, by Lois Duncan. Dodd. Ruth, a middle sister who wants to become an individual, has mixed emotions and strong competition from her two talented sisters.

MY EYES HAVE A COLD NOSE, by Hector Chevigny. Yale. Blinded at the age of forty, Chevigny is able to continue his work as a radio writer with the help of his dog.

READY OR NOT, by Mary Stolz. Harper. Morgan faces early responsibility when she is left with the care of the household after her mother dies.

ROOM FOR ONE MORE, by Anna Perrott Rose. Houghton. A story of a couple who adopt three children with handicaps and raise them with their own family.

THE STORY OF THE TRAPP FAMILY SINGERS, by Maria Augusta Trapp. Lippincott. The governess who married the father of seven motherless children recounts the adventures and amusing incidents that occurred on the family's singing tours.

THE TREMBLING YEARS, by Elsie Barber. Macmillan. A young and attractive college girl who contracts polio but is finally able to overcome frustrations.

THE YEARLING, by Marjorie K. Rawlings. Scribner. When the fawn adopted by Jody Baxter destroys the family's meager crops, Jody has to make a sacrifice, and grows in the process.

THREE | Financial Information To Aid in Decision-Making

Read one of the following books, or another of your choice, and suggest some of the factors that have influenced our behavior as consumers.

THE AFFLUENT SOCIETY, by John Kenneth Galbraith. Houghton. The author criticizes the economic ideas and attitudes that have been responsible for our preoccupation with goods, our increasingly frantic effort to manufacture wants as rapidly as products, and our over-investment in things and our under-investment in people.

THE CONSUMER, edited by Gerald Leinwald. Washington Square Press. An informative and shocking disclosure of the marketing and selling practices that are commonplace in our society today.

THE DARKSIDE OF THE MARKETPLACE, by Senator Warren Magnuson and Jean Carper. Prentice-Hall. An investigation of the many areas in which consumers are taken advantage of: cosmetics, home improvements, packaging, credit, small loans, drugs, and mail frauds. Suggestions are made to help the consumer.

THE HIDDEN PERSUADERS, by Vance Packard. McKay. Motivational research has provided the accurate psychological information that has made possible the successful manipulation of our opinions, our votes, and our dollars.

THE JUNGLE, by Upton Sinclair. Doubleday. This book describes the terrible labor conditions in the stockyards in Chicago in the early years of this century.

MADISON AVENUE, USA, by Martin Mayer. Harper. A study of what really goes on in the advertising industry and the people who run it.

THE MEDICAL MESSIAHS, by James Young. Princeton University Press. Health quackery and home remedies are examined in the twentieth century against the broader background of science, government, sociology, and marketing.

THE SPENDERS, by Steuart Henderson Britt. McGraw. This book gives insight into consumer behavior and into product marketing and advertising, emphasizing the freedom of the consumer.

THE STATUS SEEKERS, by Vance Packard. Mckay. The author identifies the symbols of class that American families accumulate in order to attain status.

THE TASTEMAKERS, by Russell Lynes. Harper. The author gives an entertaining account of the people and pressures that have shaped American tastes in art, architecture, and interior decoration during the last century-and-a-quarter.

THE WASTE MAKERS, by Vance Packard. McKay. The author describes the American economic system as being based on the artificially-shortened lives of consumer products rather than on the relevant needs and desires of the consumer.

Read one of the following books, or another of your choice, and relate information that you think would be particularly useful to a prospective buyer.

BUYER BEWARE! by Fred Trump. Abingdon. The author reveals some of the common confidence games that are costing the American consumer millions of dollars a year, and tells how to avoid being defrauded and where to turn for help.

BUY NOW, PAY LATER, by Hillel Black. Morrow. Consumer credit, its several forms, and some of its abuses on the unsuspecting public are discussed; also covered is the growing use of teenage credit.

THE CRACK IN THE PICTURE WINDOW, by John Keats. Houghton. An amusing but disturbing view of the mass uniformity and corrupt practices connected with housing developments; and of the debt-ridden Americans living in them.

THE INSOLENT CHARIOTS, by John Keats. Lippincott. Everyone who drives a car will want to read this perceptive account of the drawbacks and objectionable features of today's cars.

NUTS AMONG THE BERRIES, by Ronald Deutsch. Ballantine. The author presents a fascinating exposé of America's food fads, with an introduction by Dr. Frederick J. Stare, noted nutritionist.

> *Read one of the following books, or another of your choice, and describe some of the ways in which money can be used to better advantage.*

HOW TO BUY STOCKS, by Louis Engel. Little, Brown. The author presents a readable, easy-to-understand, and comprehensive guide to planning an investment program.

HOW TO MAKE THE MOST OF YOUR MONEY, by Sidney Margolius. Meredith. A. helpful guide for families who are attempting to solve the complicated money problems that face them today.

MONEY: MAKE IT, SPEND IT, SAVE IT, by Pauline Arnold and Percival White. Holiday. This book provides the necessary information with which to make a workable plan for managing money.

A NEW AND DIFFERENT SUMMER, by Leonora Mattingly Weber. Crowell. In this story Katie Rose is called upon to manage the household for the summer while her mother is away. Because she wants things to look nice, she does not hesitate to buy the most attractive and interesting items at the store; but by the end of the summer she comes to appreciate her mother's frugal methods of budgeting.

STOP WASTING YOUR INSURANCE DOLLARS, by Dave Goodwin. Simon and Schuster. A guide to help the buyer think through his insurance needs.

UNDERSTANDING THE STOCK MARKET: A GUIDE FOR YOUNG INVESTORS, by Janet Low. Little, Brown. A book for teen-agers who are interested in the stock market. Discusses factors to consider before buying stock and how to read the stock market report in the newspaper.

Read one of the following books, or another of your choice on cars, and relate information on buying, owning, or driving a car that you think is particularly important for the beginning driver to know.

BOY GETS CAR, by Henry G. Felsen. Random. A boy grows in his thinking when his judgments about his car mature. In this novel the author reveals his deep understanding of a boy's feeling for his first car.

THE DAY OF THE DRAG RACE, by Philip Harkins. Morrow. A disorganized teenage boy, Oscar, learns the hard way that the future will not be built on hopes and dreams. Planning is essential for success.

FAST GREEN CAR, by W. E. Butterworth. Norton. The thing Tony wanted from college was the kind of education that would enable him to take over his father's trucking business. While he wasn't interested in sports cars at first, he found himself involved in them.

TO MY SON, THE TEEN-AGE DRIVER, by Henry G. Felsen. Dodd. The author gives some fatherly advice to the teenager on his responsibilities as a driver and on the dangers as well as the advantages of driving today; he also warns him not to let his car dominate his life to the exclusion of school and plans for his future.

THE SPEED MERCHANTS, by Will Cook. Duell. Skip Hudson, an automobile mechanic, is a test driver and not a racer. He is faced with many problems including a relationship with a potential juvenile delinquent.

A TEEN-AGER'S FIRST CAR, by Henry G. Felsen. Dodd. A teenager will find many good hints and sound information on all aspects of buying and owning a car.

WHEELS OF A FAST CAR, by W. E. Butterworth. Norton. Greg is arrested and his father takes away his keys and sends him to his uncle, who is a professional stock car racing driver. Here, Greg learns that there is more to good driving than just putting your foot down on the accelerator.

TEACHER REFERENCES

ONE | The Social and Economic Setting for Family Life

Bell, Carolyn Shaw, CONSUMER CHOICE IN THE AMERICAN ECONOMY. Random.

CONSUMERS ALL. THE YEARBOOK OF AGRICULTURE 1965, by the U.S. Department of Agriculture.

Galbraith, John K., THE AFFLUENT SOCIETY. Houghton (Mentor paperback).

Galbraith, John K., THE NEW INDUSTRIAL STATE. Houghton.

A GOOD LIFE FOR MORE PEOPLE. THE YEARBOOK OF AGRICULTURE 1971, by the U.S. Department of Agriculture.

de Grazia, Sebastian, OF TIME, WORK, AND LEISURE. Doubleday.

Hall, Edward, THE SILENT LANGUAGE. Fawcett Publication.

Harrington, Michael, THE OTHER AMERICA. Macmillan (Penguin paperback).

Jesus, Carolina Maria de, CHILD OF THE DARK. Dutton (New American Library paperback).

Katona, George, THE MASS CONSUMPTION SOCIETY. McGraw.

Katona, George, THE POWERFUL CONSUMER. McGraw.

Komarovsky, Mirra, BLUE COLLAR MARRIAGE. Random.

Lederer, William J. and Eugene Burdick, THE UGLY AMERICAN. Fawcett Publication.

Lee, Dorothy, FREEDOM AND CULTURE. Prentice.

Lewis, Oscar, FIVE FAMILIES: MEXICAN CASE STUDIES IN THE CULTURE OF POVERTY. Basic Books. (New American Library paperback).

Lewis, Oscar, LA VIDA. Random.

Linder, Staffan, THE HARRIED LEISURE CLASS. Columbia Press.

Magnuson, Warren G. and Jean Carper, THE DARK SIDE OF THE MARKETPLACE. Prentice.

May, Edgar, THE WASTED AMERICANS. Harper. (New American Library paperback).

Mayer, Martin, MADISON AVENUE, U.S.A. Harper. (Packer Books, Inc. paperback).

Miller, Herman P., RICH MAN, POOR MAN. Crowell. (New American Library paperback).

Rainwater, Lee, Richard P. Coleman, and Gerald Handel, WORKINGMAN'S WIFE. Oceana. (Macfadden paperback).

Raths, Louis E., Merrill Harmin, and Sidney B. Simon, VALUES AND TEACHING. Merrill.

Reisman, David, THE LONELY CROWD. Yale University Press.

Ruud, Josephine, TEACHING FOR CHANGED ATTITUDES AND VALUES. National Education Association.

Shostak, Arthur B. and William Gomberg, BLUE-COLLAR WORLD: STUDIES OF THE AMERICAN WORKER (ed. by D. Yoder). Prentice.

Shostak, Arthur B. and William Gomberg (eds.), NEW PERSPECTIVES ON POVERTY. Prentice.

Toffler, Alvin, FUTURE SHOCK. Random.

TWO | Management in Family Living

Goodyer, Margaret R. and Mildred C. Klahr, MANAGING FOR EFFECTIVE LIVING, 2nd ed. Wiley.

Gross, Irma H. and Elizabeth W. Crandall, MANAGEMENT FOR MODERN FAMILIES, 2nd ed. Appleton.

Nickell, Paulena and Jean Muir Dorsey, MANAGEMENT IN FAMILY LIVING, 4th ed. Wiley.

THREE | Financial Information to Aid in Decision-Making

Britton, Virginia, PERSONAL FINANCE. Van Nostrand-Reinhold.

Donaldson, Elvin F. and John K. Pfahl, PERSONAL FINANCE, 4th ed. Ronald.

Gordon, Leland and Stewart Lee, ECONOMICS FOR CONSUMERS, 6th ed. Van Nostrand-Reinhold.

Margolius, Sidney, HOW TO MAKE THE MOST OF YOUR MONEY. 2nd ed. Appleton.

Metz, Robert, TO SHAKE THE MONEY TREE. Putnam.

Nuccio, Sal, NEW YORK TIMES GUIDE TO PERSONAL FINANCE. Harper.

Phillips, E. Bryant and Sylvia Lane, PERSONAL FINANCE, 2nd ed. Wiley.

Smith, Carlton and Richard Pratt, TIME-LIFE BOOK OF FAMILY FINANCE. Time-Life Books.

Troelstrup, Arch W., THE CONSUMER IN AMERICAN SOCIETY, 4th ed. McGraw.

Unger, Maurice A. and Harold A. Wolf, PERSONAL FINANCE, 2nd ed. Allyn and Bacon.

West, David and Glenn Wood, PERSONAL FINANCIAL MANAGEMENT. Houghton.

MORE INFORMATION FOR STUDENTS

BASIC BUDGETING, T M 10. Coed/Forecast, A Division of Scholastic Magazines. Englewood Cliffs, New Jersey.

THE CONSUMER, edited by Gerald Leinwold. Washington Square Press.

CONSUMER HOUSING, by Pauline Garrett. Bennett.

THRESHOLDS TO ADULT LIVING, 2nd ed., by Hazel T. Craig. Bennett.

STEPS IN HOME LIVING, 2nd ed., by Florence M. Reiff. Bennett.

YOU ARE A CONSUMER OF CLOTHING, by Pauline G. Garrett and Edward J. Metzen. Ginn.

BEHIND EVERY FACE, by Arthur and Xenia Fane. Ginn.

THE CONSUMER AND HIS DOLLARS, by David Shoenfeld and Arthur Natella. Oceana.

CONSUMER BUYING GUIDE, by Better Business Bureau. Universal Publishing and Distributing Corporation.

CONSUMER ECONOMIC PROBLEMS, 7th ed., by W. Harmon Wilson and Elvin S. Eyster. Southwestern.

CONSUMER ECONOMICS, 3rd ed., by Fred T. Wilhelms, Ramon P. Heinerl, and Herbert M. Jelley. McGraw.

CONSUMERS ALL. THE YEARBOOK OF AGRICULTURE 1965, by the U.S. Department of Agriculture.

ECONOMICS FOR CONSUMERS, 6th ed., by Leland J. Gordon and S. M. Lee. Van Nostrand-Reinhold.

EXPLORING HOME AND FAMILY LIVING, by Henrietta Fleck and Louise Fernandez. Prentice.

FAMILY DEVELOPMENT, 3rd ed., by Evelyn Duvall. Lippincott.

THE FAMILY OF MAN, by Edward Steichen, Prologue by Carl Sandburg. Maco Company.

A GOOD LIFE FOR MORE PEOPLE. THE YEARBOOK OF AGRICULTURE 1971, by the U.S. Department of Agriculture.

THE HOME - ITS FURNISHINGS AND EQUIPMENT, by Ruth Morton, Hilda Guether, and Virginia Guthrie. McGraw-Hill, Webster Division.

HOME MANAGEMENT IS. . ., by Virginia Bratton. Ginn.

HOMES WITH CHARACTER, 3rd ed., by Hazel T. Craig. Heath.

HOW TO BUY A USED CAR, by Charles Jackson. Chilton.

INTRODUCTORY HOMEMAKING, by Aleene Cross. Lippincott.

MANAGEMENT FOR BETTER LIVING, 3rd ed., by Mary Catharine Starr. Heath.

PERSONAL FINANCE, by Virginia Bratton. Van Nostrand-Reinhold.

PERSONAL ADJUSTMENT, MARRIAGE, AND FAMILY LIVING, 4th ed., by Judson T. and Mary G. Landis. Prentice.

RELATIONSHIPS: A STUDY IN HUMAN BEHAVIOR, by Helen Westlake. Ginn.

TEEN HORIZONS AT HOME AND SCHOOL, by Dora S. Lewis, Anna K. Banks, and Marie Banks. Macmillan.

YOUNG TEENS AND MONEY, by Mary Beery. McGraw-Hill.

TEACHING MATERIALS

Case Studies

Feldman, Frances L., THE FAMILY IN A MONEY WORLD. Family Service Association.

CONSUMER AND HOMEMAKING EDUCATION: A CASE STUDY APPROACH, by Camille Bell and Berlie J. Fallon. Interstate Printers and Publishers, Inc.

THE SPENDER SYNDROME, by Brenda Dervin. University of Wisconsin.

FILMS AND FILMSTRIPS

Management Process

"The Exploited Generation." Guidance Associates, Harcourt, Brace and World. 35 mm. 28 min. Purchase: Guidance Associates, Harcourt, Brace and World. Includes discussion with teenagers of their spending habits and discusses ways of helping teenagers become more responsible consumers.

Consumer Filmstrip Services: 1) "Our Role as Consumers," 2) "Consumers in the Marketplace," 3) "Consumers in Action." Institute of Life Insurance. 35 mm. C. Purchase: Association Films. Designed to give a better understanding of wants and needs in relation to our role as consumers and to examine the external forces that contribute to wants and needs.

"Four Families." National Film Board of Canada. 16 mm. 60 min. B & W. Rental information at local library. Compares the child-rearing practices in four different countries—India, France, Japan, and Canada.

"Of Time, Work and Leisure." National Educational T.V., Inc. 16 mm. 29 min. B & W. Rental information at local library. Claims that man is best measured by his capacity for life when he is not working. Also shows there is a difference between free time and leisure.

"Phoebe—Story of Premarital Pregnancy." McGraw-Hill. 16 mm. 29 min. B & W. Rental information at local library. Deals with the mental and emotional reactions of a teenager who discovers she is pregnant.

"Roots of Happiness." Mental Health Film Board. 16 mm. 20 min. B & W. Rental information at local library. Centers around the role of the father in Puerto Rico helping his children have a satisfying life.

"Umpteen Ways of Shopping," from The Decision Making for Consumers Unit. J. C. Penney Company, Inc. 35 mm. C. Purchase: J. C. Penney Company, Inc. Shows how external forces contribute to individual and family wants and needs.

Money Management

"Consumer Education: Budgeting." Bailey Film Associates. 16 mm. 12 min. C. Rental information at local library. Discusses sound budget planning.

"Marriage and Money." Institute of Life Insurance. 35 mm. C. Purchase: Association Films. Uses the case study approach to show how a young couple can develop money management practices.

"Personal Financial Planning." National Consumer Finance Association. 16 mm. 11 min. B & W, C. Loan: Association Films. Designed to orient high school students to the economic problems of daily living. Teacher's Guide.

"Your Money and You." The Money Management Institute of Household Finance Corporation. 35 mm. 73 frames. C. Captions. Purchase: The Money Management Institute of Household Finance Corporation. This filmstrip outlines five steps for managing income in order to reach personal and family goals.

"Your Thrift Habits." Coronet. 16 mm. 11 min. B & W, C. Rental information at local library. Tony learns that thrift involves making choices as well as saving for short- and long-range goals and avoiding waste.

"Your World and Money." The Money Management Institute of Household Finance Corporation. 35 mm. 15–20 min. 58 frames. C. Purchase: The Money Management Institute of Household Finance Corporation. Encourages young people to practice good money habits.

Consumer Credit

"Consumer Education: Installment Buying." Bailey Film Associates. 16 mm. 13 min. C. Rental information at local library. Points out the principles of installment buying and the dangers to avoid.

"Consumer Education: Retail Credit Buying." Bailey Film Associates. 16 mm. 11 min. C. Rental information at local library. Points out the pitfalls of buying on credit.

"Consumers Want to Know." Consumers Union of U.S. 16 mm. 30 min. B & W. Loan: Consumers Union Film Department. Explains the function and the purpose of the Consumers Union.

"Be Credit Wise." The Money Management Institute of Household Finance Corporation. 35 mm. C. Purchase: The Money Management Institute of Household Finance Corporation. Dramatizes the credit experiences of three persons.

"Credit." Dunn and Bradstreet. 16 mm. 14 min. C. Loan: Modern Talking Picture Services. Explains how credit operates.

"Credit: A Consumer Resource Unit." J. C. Penney Company, Inc. 35 mm. Purchase: J. C. Penney Company, Inc. Identifies the different types of credit and presents the pros and cons for buying on credit.

Credit Education Package. (2 filmstrips: "The Cost of Credit" and "Credit in the U. S. Economy.") National Foundation for Consumer Credit, Inc. 35 mm. C. Purchase: National Foundation for Consumer Credit, Inc. Presents a basic approach to credit.

"Credit—Man's Confidence in Man." Dunn & Bradstreet. 16 mm. 14 min. C. Loan: Modern Talking Picture Service. Tells how the concept of credit developed; what role credit plays today in our economy; and how credit ratings are established.

"Every Seventh Family." 16 mm. 26 min. Loan: Modern Talking Picture Services, Inc. Explains consumer credit and the operations of a typical finance company.

"The Littlest Giant." National Consumer Finance Association. 16 mm. 14 min. C. Loan: Association Films. Cartoon showing how consumer credit functions and why it is important to the family, the home, and the nation.

"The Owl Who Gave a Hoot." Office of Economic Opportunity. 16 mm. 15 min. C. Loan: Modern Talking Picture Service. Describes the problems of consumers in low economic areas.

"A Penny Saved." CUNA International. 16 mm. 15 min. B & W. Loan: Association Films. Animated and live action. Tells how the credit union system aids family financial planning.

"'Til Debt Do Us Part." CUNA International. 16 mm. 15 min. B & W. Loan: Association Films. Purchase: CUNA International. Explains credit unions and their role in the nation's economy and points out the wisdom of sound money management.

"Truth in Lending." Federal Reserve System. 35 mm. 93 frames (with record). Loan; Nearest Federal Reserve Bank. Purchase: Public Services, Division of Administration, Federal Reserve System. Discusses the meaning of "finance charge" and "annual percentage rate" as used in the Truth in Lending Law.

"The Wise Use of Credit." National Consumer Finance Association. 16 mm. 11 min. C. Loan: Association Films. This film provides a basic understanding of consumer credit, introduces economic terms, types of credit, and guidelines for the wise use of credit. Teacher's Guide is provided.

"Your Money Matters." National Consumer Finance Association. 35 mm. C. Purchase: National Consumer Finance Association. Deals with financial decision-making before and after marriage.

"You Take the Credit." National Consumer Finance Association. 35 mm. C. Purchase: National Consumer Finance Association. Deals with the concept of credit.

Home Ownership

"At Home—2001." Union Carbide—CBS 21st Century. 16 mm. 30 min. C. Loan: Modern Talking Pictures Service. Shows the possibilities in housing for the 21st century.

"Homes Are For People." J. C. Penney Company, Inc. 35 mm. Purchase: J. C. Penney Company, Inc. Three filmstrips showing how psychological, sociological, and esthetic needs can be fulfilled in a home.

"A House is a Living Thing." Council of Better Business Bureaus. 16 mm. 14 min. C. Loan: Council of Better Business Bureaus. Explains how to buy a home.

"Patterns for Protection." Insurance Information Institute. 35 mm. 15 min. C. Sound. Purchase: Insurance Information Institute. A cartoon treatment of the property, persons, and perils involved in the homeowners policy and the factors affecting the cost of insuring a home.

"Revolution in Our Time." U.S. Savings and Loan League. 16 mm. 30 min. B & W. Loan: Modern Talking Pictures Service, Inc. Explains the role of home buying in the American economy with emphasis on saving and loans associations as financers.

"Year 1999 A.D." Ford Motor Company. 16 mm. 26 min. C. Loan: Ford Film Library. Explains the wonders of an almost controlled environment in the house of tomorrow.

Transportation

"Automobile Insurance." Insurance Information Institute. 35 mm. 18 min. Sound. Purchase: Insurance Information Institute. A cartoon treatment of bodily injury coverages; property damage coverages; and factors affecting automobile insurance rates and costs. Teacher's Guide.

"So You Want to Buy a Good Used Car?" Ford Motor Company. 16 mm. 15 min. C. Loan: Ford Film Library. Offers a useful formula for the used car buyer.

General Insurance

"Insurance—From the Farmer's Side of the Fence." National Association of Mutual Insurance Companies. 16 mm. 23 min. C. Loan: National Association of Mutual Insurance Companies.

Life Insurance

"Dollars and Sense." National Association of Life Underwriters. 16 mm. 14 min. C. Loan: National Association of Life Underwriters. Discusses the breakdown of life insurance needs.

"To Life With Love." Institute of Life Insurance. 16 mm. 14 min. C. Free loan: Association Films. A young couple discuss their ideas about security.

Social Security

"After the Applause." U.S. Department of Health, Education, and Welfare, Social Security Administration. 16 mm. 28 min. C. Loan: Local offices of the Social Security Administration. Explains retirement and disability benefits.

"The Social Security Story." U.S. Department of Health, Education, and Welfare, Social Security Administration. 16 mm. 14 min. C. Loan: Local offices of the Social Security Administration. Designed to show what happens to a person's Social Security record from the time it is established until application for benefits is made.

"You and Medicare." U.S. Department of Health, Education, and Welfare, Social Security Administration. 16 mm. 27 min. C. Loan: Local offices of the Social Security Administration. Shows how medicare helps to solve the financial problem created by unexpected illness.

Investment

"The Lady and the Stock Exchange." New York Stock Exchange. 16 mm. 27 min. C. Loan: Modern Talking Picture Service. Starring Janet Blair and Eddie Bracken, with Everett Sloane and Jim Backus; an American family learns about the risks and rewards of investing.

"What Makes Us Tick." New York Stock Exchange. 16 mm. 12 min. C. Loan: Modern Talking Picture Service. This cartoon film about the New York Stock Exchange explains stock transactions and how the investing public finances the growth of American business.

"Working Dollars." New York Stock Exchange. 16 mm. 15 min. C. Loan: Modern Talking Picture Service (cartoon form). Shows the use of money for investment dealings and the importance of dealing with a reliable broker.

"Your Share in Tomorrow." New York Stock Exchange. 16 mm. 27 min. C. Loan: Modern Talking Picture Service. Explains stock transactions and the purpose of brokers.

Banks and Savings Institutions

"Paying by Check." American Bankers Association. 16 mm. 14½ min. C. Explains check writing and handling a checking account through the experiences of a young man who purchases a sports car. Includes a 35 mm. filmstrip, teacher's guide, and student instructional aids.

"Your Town." American Bankers Association. 16 mm. 14½ min. C. A complete educational film package based on the services of a commercial bank and how they fit into community life. Includes a 35 mm. filmstrip, teacher's guide, and student instructional aids.

Consumer Information

"The Consumer Revolution." Chamber of Commerce of the United States. 35 mm. Purchase: Chamber of Commerce of the United States. Discusses consumer complaints in the marketplace.

"The Consumer Decides." J. C. Penney Company, Inc. 35 mm. C. Purchase: J. C. Penney Company, Inc. Relates consumer rights and responsibilities to consumer satisfaction with purchases.

"Managing Your Clothing Dollars." Money Management Institute of Household Finance Corporation. 35 mm. 63 frames. C. Purchase: Money Management Institute of Household Finance Corporation. Shows how to outfit the family attractively within budget limitations.

"The Role of Consumers." Joint Council of Economic Education. 35 mm. Purchase: Joint Council of Economic Education. Covers the importance and status of the consumer, and the role of an alert consumer.

"Spending Your Food Dollar." Money Management Institute of Household Finance Corporation. 35 mm. 73 frames. C. Captions. Purchase: Money Management Institute of Household Finance Corporation. Highlights the challenges and rewards of managing food dollars skillfully.

"Too Good to Be True." Council of Better Business Bureaus. 16 mm. 25 min. C. Loan: Local offices of Better Business Bureaus. Demonstrates bait and switch techniques.

"The United States Economy in Action." Joint Council of Economic Education. 35 mm. C. Loan: Joint Council of Economic Education. Defines consumer, considers the roles of production and consumption and discusses the problems of becoming an intelligent consumer.

"Your Money's Worth in Shopping." Money Management Institute of Household Finance Corporation. 35 mm. C. Purchase: Money Management Institute of Household Finance Corporation. Demonstrates how shopping wisely can help consumers in getting more for their money.

GAMES AND MULTI-MEDIA KITS

"Consumer: An Academic Game." Western Publishing Company, Inc. Purchase: Western Publishing Company, Inc. Provides the opportunity to gain experience in coping with the problems and economics of credit buying.

"Financing a New Partnership." J. C. Penney Company, Inc. Purchase: J. C. Penney Company, Inc. Designed to develop an awareness of costs involved in establishing a first home.

"The Home: An Environment for Human Growth." J. C. Penney Company, Inc. Purchase: J. C. Penney Company, Inc. A multi-media kit showing that homes are a result of man's attempt to fulfill basic needs.

"An Introduction to Value Clarification." J. C. Penney Company, Inc. Purchase: J. C. Penney Company, Inc. A multi-media kit designed to encourage thinking about value-laden choices and behavior in relation to them.

"Life Career: An Academic Game." Western Publishing Company, Inc. Purchase: Western Publishing Company, Inc. Designed to give practice in making career decisions and to discover how these earlier decisions will affect opportunities later in a person's life.

"Priorities, Decisions, Security: The Role of Life Insurance in a Young Life Style." Institute of Life Insurance. Purchase: Association Films. A multi-media kit that shows basic life insurance concepts and the role insurance plays in personal and family life.

"A Resource Kit for Teaching Consumer Education." Kit 1. Changing Times Education Service. Purchase: Changing Times Education Service. A teaching kit with five consumer concepts: Earning, Spending, Borrowing, Saving, and Budgeting.

"A Resource Kit for Teaching Consumer Education." Kit 2. Changing Times Education Service. Purchase: Changing Times Education Service. This kit covers three aspects of consumer education: Uses of advertising, ways to avoid gyps and frauds, and safeguards for shoppers.

LEARNING PACKETS

Home Economics Learning Packages (HELP). American Home Economics Association, 2010 Massachusetts Avenue N.W., Washington, D.C. 20036.

MISCELLANEOUS PUBLICATIONS

Teaching Topics. Education Division, Institute of Life Insurance, 277 Park Avenue, New York, New York 10017 (Several times a year). Free.

MMI Memo. Money Management Institute, Household Finance Corporation, Prudential Plaza, Chicago, Illinois 60601 (Several times a year). Free.

Finance Facts. National Consumer Finance Association, Educational Services Division, 701 Solar Building, 1000 Sixteenth Street, N.W., Washington, D.C. 20036. Free.

The Changing Times Teachers' Journal. Changing Times Education Service, 1729 H Street, N.W., Washington, D.C. 20006 (9 per year).

Kaleidoscope. Consumer Information Services, Department 703, Public Relations, 303 East Ohio Street, Chicago, Illinois 60611 (Semi-annual). Free.

A Department Store in the Classroom, by Sally R. Campbell. Sears, Roebuck, and Company, Consumer Information Services, Department 703, Public Relations, 303 East Ohio Street, Chicago, Illinois 606ll.

Consumer Education in an Age of Adaptation, by Sally Campbell. Sears, Roebuck, and Company, Consumer Information Services, Department 703, Public Relations, 303 East Ohio Street, Chicago, Illinois 60611.

Suggested Guidelines for Consumer Education, Grades K–12. Superintendent of Documents, Government Printing Office, Washington, D.C. 20402.

Consumer Education Bibliography. Superintendent of Documents, Government Printing Office, Washington, D.C. 20402.

Your Guide for Teaching Money Management. Money Management Institute of Household Finance Corporation, Prudential Plaza, Chicago, Illinois 60601.

Finance Facts Yearbook, published by the National Consumer Finance Association.

PAMPHLETS

A Date With Your Future. Institute of Life Insurance. Free.

Decade of Decision, by Jerome B. Cohen. Institute of Life Insurance. Free.

A Family Guide to Property and Liability Insurance. 4th edition. Insurance Information Institute. Free.

Money Management Series. Money Management Institute of Household Finance Corporation. A series of booklets on various topics aimed to give hints for effective shopping.

You and the Investment World. New York Stock Exchange. Free.

ADDRESSES FOR TEACHING MATERIALS

The American Bankers Association, Public Relations Committee, 815 Connecticut Avenue, N.W., Washington, D.C.

Association Films, 600 Grand Avenue, Ridgefield, New Jersey 07657.

Bailey–Film Associates, 2211 Michigan Avenue, Los Angeles, California 90404.

Chamber of Commerce of the United States, 1615 H Street, N.W., Washington, D.C. 20006.

Changing Times Education Service, 1729 H Street, N.W. Washington, D.C. 20006.

Consumers Union Film Department, Consumers Union of U.S., Inc., 256 Washington Street, Mount Vernon, New York 10550.

Coronet Instructional Films, 65 East South Water Street, Chicago, Illinois 60601.

Council of Better Business Bureaus, 845 Third Avenue, New York, N.Y. 10022.

Educational and Consumer Relations, J. C. Penney Company, Inc., 1301 Avenue of the Americas, New York, New York 10019.

Family Service Association, 44 East 23rd Street, New York, New York 10010.

Ford Motor Company, Film Library, The American Road, Dearborn, Michigan 48121.

Guidance Associates, Harcourt, Brace and World, Pleasantville, New York 10570.

Insurance Information Institute, 110 William Street, New York, N.Y.

Interstate Printers and Publishers, Inc., Danville, Illinois 61832.

Institute of Life Insurance, Educational Division, 277 Park Avenue, New York, New York 10017.

Joint Council on Economic Education, 1212 Avenue of the Americas, New York, New York 10036.

3M Company, Visual Products Division, Box 3100 A, St. Paul, Minnesota 55101.

McGraw-Hill Films, 330 West 42nd Street, New York, New York 10036.

Modern Talking Picture Services, Inc., 1212 Avenue of the Americas, New York, New York 10036.

The Money Management Institute of Household Finance Corporation, Prudential Plaza, Chicago, Illinois 60601.

National Association of Life Underwriters, 1922 F Street, N.W., Washington, D.C. 20006.

National Association of Mutual Insurance Companies, 2611 East 46th Street, Suite H, Indianapolis, Indiana 56205.

National Consumers Finance Association, 1000 – 16th Street, N.W., Washington, D.C. 20036.

National Film Board of Canada, 680 Fifth Avenue, Suite 819, New York, New York 10019.

National Foundation of Consumer Credit, Inc., Suite 510, 1819 H Street, N.W., Washington, D.C. 20006.

New York Stock Exchange, 11 Wall Street, New York, New York 10005.

Publication Services, Division of Administrative Services, Board of Governors of the Federal Reserve System, Washington, D.C. 20551.

University of Wisconsin, Center for Consumer Affairs, University Extension, 432 North Lake, Madison, Wisconsin 53706.

Western Publishing Company, Inc., School and Library Department, 850 Third Avenue, New York, New York 10022.

PERIODICALS

Changing Times. The Kiplinger Washington Editors, Inc., 1729 H Street, N.W., Washington, D.C. (Monthly).

Consumer Bulletin. Consumers' Research, Inc., Washington, New Jersey 07882 (Monthly).

Consumer Reports. Consumers Union of the United States, Inc., 256 Washington Street, Mount Vernon, New York 10550 (Monthly).

Everybody's Money. Credit Union National Association, Box 431, Madison, Wisconsin 52701 (Quarterly).

Forum. J. C. Penney Company, Inc., Educational and Consumer Relations, 1301 Avenue of the Americas, New York, New York 10019 (Twice a year).

Illinois Teacher. Illinois Teacher, 342 Education Building, University of Illinois, Urbana, Illinois 61801 (Six times a year).

Journal of Consumer Affairs. Council of Consumer Information, 15 Gwynn Hall, University of Missouri, Columbia, Missouri 65202 (Semi-annually).

Journal of Home Economics. American Home Economics Association, 2010 Massachusetts Avenue, N.W., Washington, D.C. 20036 (9 times a year).

Tips and Topics. College of Home Economics, P.O. Box 4170, Texas Technical College, Lubbock, Texas 79409 (Four issues a year).

U.S. Consumer. Consumer News, Inc., 601 National Press Building, Washington, D.C. 20004 (Bi-weekly).

Wall Street Journal. Dow Jones and Company, Inc., 44 Broad Street, New York, New York (Daily except Saturday and Sunday).

TRANSPARENCIES

Transparencies Directory of Concepts and Generalizations. Produced by 3M Color Transparencies. Available from 3M Company.

PHOTOGRAPH ACKNOWLEDGMENTS

Title page: H. Armstrong Roberts; 5: Museum of Science, Boston; 11: Christopher W. Morrow, Stock, Boston; 14: Max Tharpe; 17: Sharon L. Powers; 20: Elizabeth Bowen Hecker; 22: Peter Travers; 27: Dick Smith; 30: U.S. Department of Agriculture; 36, top: Elizabeth Bowen Hecker; 36, bottom: Rotkin, P. F. I.; 38: Eric L. Brown; 39: Patricia Hollander Gross, Stock, Boston; 42: Rita Freed, Nancy Palmer Photo Agency; 44: Ann Zane Shanks; 47: Ann Zane Shanks; 54: Culver Pictures, Inc.; 58: E. I. du Pont de Nemours & Co.; 59: U.S. Department of Agriculture; 61: Polyxane S. Cobb; 63: Dick Smith; 65: H. Armstrong Roberts; 74: Peter Travers; 77: Peter Travers; 79: Charles Gatewood; 80: Ronald Rosenstock; 83: Sharon L. Powers; 92: Mark Silber; 95: Rita Freed, Nancy Palmer Photo Agency; 96: Peter Travers; 99: Peter Travers; 104: Sharon L. Powers; 111: H. Armstrong Roberts; 122: Sharon L. Powers; 124: Sharon L. Powers; 127: Sharon L. Powers; 136: Ebony; 139: Sharon L. Powers; 140: Polyxane S. Cobb; 143: Bill Yoscary, Nancy Palmer Photo Agency; 148: Sharon L. Powers; 153: H. Armstrong Roberts; 155: Polyxane S. Cobb; 159: Ewing Galloway; 162: John Hancock Mutual Life Insurance Co.; 165: The Providence Journal; 167: Sharon L. Powers; 174: Wide World Photos; 181: Sharon L. Powers; 185: Dick Smith; 186: Sharon L. Powers; 189: Liberty Mutual Insurance Companies; 191: Alan D. Hewitt; 199: John Hancock Mutual Life Insurance Co.; 202: The Travelers Insurance Co.; 207: H. Armstrong Roberts; 209: H. Armstrong Roberts; 212: H. Armstrong Roberts; 213: Ebony; 222: Rita Freed, Nancy Palmer Photo Agency; 224: Eric L. Brown; 227: Polyxane S. Cobb; 229: Design Photographers International, Inc.; 232: Alfred Statler; 235: Rita Freed, Nancy Palmer Photo Agency; 240: State Street Bank, Boston; 245: Peace Corps; 248: Design Photographers International, Inc.; 250: Elizabeth Wilcox; 253: Elizabeth Wilcox.

INDEX